ANTI

ANTISEMITISM

The Oldest Hatred

John Mann

B L O O M S B U R Y

LONDON · OXFORD · NEW YORK · NEW DELHI · SYDNEY

Bloomsbury Continuum
An imprint of Bloomsbury Publishing Plc

50 Bedford Square
London
WC1B 3DP
UK

1385 Broadway
New York
NY 10018
USA

www.bloomsbury.com

Bloomsbury, Continuum and the Diana logo are trademarks
of Bloomsbury Publishing Plc

First published 2015

British Library Cataloguing-in-Publication Data
A catalogue record for this book is available from the British Library.

Library of Congress Cataloguing-in-Publication data has been applied for.

ISBN: PB: 978-1-4729-2075-1
ePDF: 978-1-4729-2077-5
ePub: 978-1-4729-2076-8

2 4 6 8 10 9 7 5 3 1

Printed and bound in Great Britain by CPI Group (UK) Ltd, Croydon CR0 4YY

To find out more about our authors and books visit www.bloomsbury.com.
Here you will find extracts, author interviews, details of forthcoming
events and the option to sign up for our newsletters.

TABLE OF CONTENTS

EXPLANATORY NOTE

I n drawing together the works of so many significant characters, it was considered useful and important to provide accompanying historical and contextual information. In addition to the speeches contained herein, a number of quotations were included in order to demonstrate the breadth of voices that have spoken out against antisemitism and racism. These quotations are, however, not connected to the speeches which precede or follow them. In addition, it should be noted that some of the speeches herein have been subjected to minor editing to remove some irrelevant historic references.

ACKNOWLEDGEMENTS

A number of people contributed to the research and publication of this book. I would primarily like to thank my daughter, Heather Mann, who was the researcher and played a key role throughout the drafting process. Thanks are also due to Danny Stone and Amy Wagner, who continue to be a great asset in the fight against antisemitism and racism, and to all my parliamentary team who work so hard to support my public life. I would also like to extend my gratitude to Stephen Rubin for his continuing interest and support and to Trevor Pears and the Pears Foundation, who made the publication of this book possible and who, through their work, continue to make a positive difference to our country and our world.

INTRODUCTION

As Chair of the All-Party Parliamentary Group Against Antisemitism since 2005, I have sought to combat anti-Jewish prejudice according to three underlying principles. First, that non-Jews should lead the fight against antisemitism, because the struggle against prejudice is not just the responsibility of its victims. Second, that any success we achieve in combating antisemitism should be used to fight all forms of racism and discrimination. Third, that parliament must set the national standard in these matters and do so across party political lines.

More broadly, we have sought to reshape the debate on antisemitism and to examine afresh some of red lines that have been eroded. I commissioned the All-Party Parliamentary Inquiries into Antisemitism which reported in 2006 and 2015 respectively. These processes provided unprecedented opportunities to evaluate the political landscape and to recommend improvements that would be of tangible benefit. The impact of the subsequent reports has been seen as considerable.

Working together with key stakeholder groups we have: inspired the establishment of a Whitehall Government Working Group on Antisemitism; secured improved recording and prosecuting of hate crimes; state funding for the security of Jewish schools; a school linking programme; collaborative British and Israeli academic exchange projects; the appointment of a UK Government Envoy for Post-Holocaust issues; and we have taken a lead in re-energizing international parliamentary efforts to combat antisemitism – devising global protocols for tackling online hate and inspiring similar inquiries in a number of other national parliaments. We also undertook our own secondary inquiry, which focused on the behaviour of politicians and political parties during elections.

The impact of our work has benefited not just the Jewish community but other victims of hate crime. We adhered to those principles, which have guided me, but there is a fourth key tenet that I perhaps overlooked, as for many of us it is a natural reaction to intolerance: speaking out.

I have been approached numerous times by Jewish young people and others, registering their concern that there are so few people willing to speak out and support them. Thankfully, our group is not alone in our anti-racist endeavours. There are household names, historical powerhouses and legendary leaders who have seen anti-Jewish hatred in their midst and addressed it. Their words have not been given due recognition. In bringing their works together for the first time, I hope more leaders will be inspired to speak out.

The importance of shining a light on antisemitism cannot be overstated. Would France, Hungary, Sweden and other European countries find themselves in the midst of a Jewish exodus from their countries if politicians were doing more to combat prejudice? The first section of the book aptly collates speeches for survival, given it is the continued existence of a people which is at stake.

Antisemitism, in its most developed form, does not just cause harm to Jews but to other minority communities, as Pastor Niemöller so eloquently explained. Jews will be first and the rest will follow. Uniquely as a form of racism, antisemitism, rather than casting its victims as lowly and inhuman, more often defines them as all-powerful. If McCarthyism has taught us anything, it is that irrational accusations of subversion and disloyalty know no bounds. Consequently, however, speaking out and acting against antisemitism benefits not just those suffering from anti-Jewish prejudice but rather all victims of hate crime. This idea is explored further in the second section of the book, which focuses on intersectionality.

Modern antisemitism has become all too frequent and is not as simple to deconstruct as classical antisemitism, given its common staging ground of the Middle East conflict. With this complexity has come a reluctance to recognize anti-Jewish prejudice for what it is, and so the third section of the book focuses on the links between anti-Zionism and antisemitism. Our group has worked to explain what the acceptable boundaries of discourse are, and we have asked parliamentarians to take the lead when problems occur in their own backyard. We ask them to speak out, rather than stay quiet.

Too often, civil leaders have taken the easy path: they have stayed silent. In the silence, antisemitism spreads.

In speaking out, combating silence, filling the void, the people in this book have inspired freedom: liberating minds from ignorance, prejudice, malice and lies. That is the raison d'être of our work and our resolve has not, nor will it ever, waver.

John Mann, Member of Parliament, United Kingdom

PART ONE

SURVIVAL

The history of Jewish persecution is as old as the written word, though the term 'antisemitism' was only conceived in the late nineteenth century as it reached the beginning of its most horrifying chapter. Throughout Christian history the hatred and prejudice against the Jewish people has often been blamed on the betrayal and crucifixion of Christ, but ethnic Jewish oppression began long before. The Torah chronicles ancient oppression, but non-biblical sources trace the earliest historically recorded instances back to third-century BC Alexandria in the writings of Manetho, an Egyptian priest and historian who mixed ethnic and religious differences in his hate-filled prejudice. The value and position of the holy land has led to many occupations and inevitable cultural and religious clashes between the Jewish people and their temporary overlords, whether polytheistic Egyptians, Greeks or Romans or the subsequent Christians and Islamists. The first focusing by Christians on the sin of deicide didn't occur till 167 AD, and as the centuries passed and Christianity became the dominant religion and supreme force, the hatred and prejudice spread throughout the medieval world. By the time of the Crusades and the Black Death the Jewish people had become a common enemy of the Christian world, to be blamed for all wrongs and used collectively or individually whenever a scapegoat was required. The advent of printing merely enabled the further spread of antisemitic sentiment and writings, though the fires of hatred and prejudice were long since lit.

In the history of antisemitism the 'Enlightenment' can be seen to be anything but. Though in many countries it brought brief respite from state-sanctioned oppression as civil liberties were extended to the Jewish population, anti-Jewish sentiment was still rife and the era sowed the seeds in false scientific developments for what grew into the racial antisemitism of the nineteenth and twentieth centuries. From the mid-1800s across mainland Europe, Jewish persecution grew increasingly sanctioned and increasingly violent and saw a wave of mass immigration to America as the Russian pogroms sought to completely eliminate the Jewish population through a combination of destruction, displacement and assimilation. As National Socialism rose in Germany, a policy of violent displacement was initially instilled, turning after 1938 to mass destruction.

He who allows oppression shares the crime.

DESIDERIUS ERASMUS (1466–1536), QUOTED IN
THE APOPHTHEGMES OF ERASMUS
(TRANS. NICHOLAS UDALL), LINCOLNSHIRE 1877

In all its myriad manifestations, the language of anti-Semitism through the ages is a dictionary of non-sequiturs and antonyms, a thesaurus of illogic and inconsistency.

PAUL JOHNSON, 'THE ANTI-SEMITIC DISEASE',
***COMMENTARY* MAGAZINE, JUNE 2005**

Charlie Chaplin

*B*y 1941, when The Great Dictator *was released, Chaplin had been one of the most famous men in the world for almost three decades. The Great Dictator was Chaplin's first significantly political work as well as being his first 'talkie' (he had continued to make silent films long after talkies became the established form of cinema in the 1930s).*

Chaplin plays the joint roles of a Jewish Barber and Adenoid Hynkel, a dictator explicitly based on Hitler. Following repeated persecution, internment and escape dressed as a soldier, the barber is eventually mistaken for Hynkel and taken to a rally to give a speech. Introduced by his number two, Garbitsch (a parody of Goebbels), who argues against free speech and for the subjugation of Jews, the barber gives his response, announcing a democracy and calling for our humanity to free us all.

The film was released to great acclaim, though arguments have been made that its overt politicization marked the beginning of the end for Chaplin's popularity. Chaplin himself said in his 1964 autobiography that he would never have made the film had he known the true monstrosity of the Nazis: 'Had I known of the actual horrors of the concentration camps, I could not have made The Great Dictator, *I could not have made fun of the homicidal insanity of the Nazis.'*

Speech from *The Great Dictator*

I'm sorry, but I don't want to be an emperor. That's not my business. I don't want to rule or conquer anyone. I should like to help everyone – if possible – Jew, Gentile – black man – white. We all want to help one another. Human beings are like that. We want to live by each other's happiness – not by each other's misery. We don't want to hate and despise one another. In this world there is room for everyone. And the good earth is rich and can provide for everyone. The way of life can be free and beautiful, but we have lost the way.

Greed has poisoned men's souls, has barricaded the world with hate, has goose-stepped us into misery and bloodshed. We have developed speed, but we have shut ourselves in. Machinery that gives abundance has left us in want. Our knowledge has made us cynical, our cleverness, hard and unkind. We think too much and feel too little. More than machinery we need humanity. More than cleverness we need kindness and gentleness. Without these qualities, life will be violent and all will be lost ...

The aeroplane and the radio have brought us closer together. The very nature of these inventions cries out for the goodness in men – cries out for universal brotherhood – for the unity of us all. Even now my voice is reaching millions throughout the world – millions of despairing men, women, and little children – victims of a system that makes men torture and imprison innocent people.

To those who can hear me, I say – do not despair. The misery that is now upon us is but the passing of greed – the bitterness of men who fear the way of human progress. The hate of men will pass, and dictators die, and the power they took from the people will return to the people. And so long as men die, liberty will never perish ...

Soldiers! Don't give yourselves to brutes – men who despise you – enslave you – who regiment your lives – tell you what to do – what to think and what to feel! Who drill you – diet you – treat you like cattle, use you as cannon fodder. Don't give yourselves to these unnatural men – machine men with machine minds and machine hearts! You are not machines! You are not cattle! You are men! You have the love of humanity in your hearts! You don't hate! Only the unloved hate – the unloved and the unnatural! Soldiers! Don't fight for slavery! Fight for liberty!

In the 17th Chapter of St Luke it is written: 'the Kingdom of God is within man' – not one man nor a group of men, but in all men! In you!

You, the people, have the power – the power to create machines. The power to create happiness! You, the people, have the power to make this life free and beautiful, to make this life a wonderful adventure.

Then – in the name of democracy – let us use that power – let us all unite. Let us fight for a new world – a decent world that will give men a chance to work – that will give youth a future and old age a security. By the promise of these things, brutes have risen to power. But they lie! They do not fulfil that promise. They never will!

Dictators free themselves but they enslave the people! Now let us fight to fulfil that promise! Let us fight to free the world – to do away with national barriers – to do away with greed, with hate and intolerance. Let us fight for a world of reason, a world where science and progress will lead to all men's happiness. Soldiers! In the name of democracy, let us all unite!

Albert Einstein

*E*instein *was born in Germany to secular Jewish parents in 1879. Awarded the Nobel Prize for Physics in 1921, he was visiting the US in 1933 when Hitler came to power and never returned to his homeland. Though calling himself an agnostic, he had a strong kinship with his fellow Jews and threw himself passionately – personally and publicly – into the refugee effort, giving dozens of speeches, participating in fundraisers and discreetly acting as guarantor to many escaping to America.*

He was also a public supporter of the Civil Rights movement. When the celebrated contralto Marian Anderson was refused a room in Princeton in 1937 when she came to give a concert, Einstein offered to put her up in his own home, and thereafter until his death she stayed with him whenever she was visiting Princeton. He was a member of the National Association for the Advancement of Colored People and in 1946 called racism America's 'worst disease', later saying: 'Race prejudice has unfortunately become an American tradition which is uncritically handed down from one generation to the next. The only remedies are enlightenment and education.'

In 1952, after the death of Israel's first president, Chaim Weizmann, Prime Minister David Ben-Gurion offered Einstein the largely ceremonial position. Einstein refused, claiming that he lacked 'both the natural aptitude and the experience to deal properly with people and to exercise official function'. He went on to say: 'I am the more distressed over these circumstances because my relationship with the Jewish people became my strongest human tie once I achieved complete clarity about our precarious position among the nations of the world.'

In 1938, when 'Why Do They Hate the Jews?' was published, there was a strong antisemitic current in American society. In Princeton, where Einstein taught and lived for his entire US career until his death in 1955, a poll among the incoming freshmen of 1938 declared Adolf Hitler 'the greatest living person', with Einstein coming second.

Why Do They Hate the Jews?

I should like to begin by telling you an ancient fable, with a few minor changes – a fable that will serve to throw into bold relief the mainsprings of political anti-Semitism.

The shepherd boy said to the horse: 'You are the noblest beast that treads the earth. You deserve to live in untroubled bliss; and indeed your happiness would be complete were it not for the treacherous stag. But he practised from youth to excel you in fleetness of foot. His faster pace allows him to reach the water holes before you do. He and his tribe drink up the water far and wide, while you and your foal are left to thirst. Stay with me! My wisdom and guidance shall deliver you and your kind from a dismal and ignominious state.'

Blinded by envy and hatred of the stag, the horse agreed. He yielded to the shepherd lad's bridle. He lost his freedom and became the shepherd's slave.

The horse in this fable represents a people, and the shepherd lad a class or clique aspiring to absolute rule over the people; the stag, on the other hand, represents the Jews.

I can hear you say: 'A most unlikely tale! No creature would be as foolish as the horse in your fable.' But let us give it a little more thought. The horse had been suffering the pangs of thirst, and his vanity was often pricked when he saw the nimble stag outrunning him. You, who have known no such pain and vexation, may find it difficult to understand that hatred and blindness should have driven the horse to act with such ill-advised, gullible haste. The horse, however, fell an easy victim to temptation because his earlier tribulations had prepared him for such a blunder. For there is much truth in the saying that it is easy to give just and wise counsel – to others! – but hard to act justly and wisely for oneself.

I say to you with full conviction: we all have often played the tragic role of the horse and we are in constant danger of yielding to temptation again.

The situation illustrated in this fable happens again and again in the life of individuals and nations. In brief, we may call it the process by which dislike and hatred of a given person or group are diverted to another person or group incapable of effective defence. But why did the role of the stag in the fable so often fall to the Jews? Why did the Jews so often happen to draw the hatred of the masses? Primarily because there are Jews among almost all nations and because they are everywhere too thinly scattered to defend themselves against violent attack.

A few examples from the recent past will prove the point: towards the end of the nineteenth century the Russian people were chafing under the tyranny of their government. Stupid blunders in foreign policy further strained their temper until it reached the breaking point. In this extremity the rulers of Russia sought to divert unrest by inciting the masses to hatred and violence toward the Jews. These tactics were repeated after the Russian government had drowned the dangerous revolution of 1905 in blood – and this manoeuvre may well have helped to keep the hated regime in power until near the end of the World War.

When the Germans had lost the World War hatched by their ruling class, immediate attempts were made to blame the Jews, first for instigating the war and then for losing it. In the course of time, success attended these efforts. The hatred engendered against the Jews not only protected the privileged classes, but enabled a small, unscrupulous and insolent group to place the German people in a state of complete bondage.

The crimes with which the Jews have been charged in the course of history – crimes which were to justify the atrocities perpetrated against them – have changed in rapid succession. They were supposed to have poisoned wells. They were said to have murdered children for ritual purposes. They were falsely charged with a systematic attempt at the economic domination and exploitation of all mankind. Pseudo-scientific books were written to brand them an inferior, dangerous race. They were reputed to foment wars and revolutions for their own selfish purposes. They were presented at once as dangerous innovators and as enemies of true progress. They were charged with falsifying the culture of nations by penetrating the national life under the guise of becoming assimilated. In the same breath they were accused of being so stubbornly inflexible that it was impossible for them to fit into any society.

Almost beyond imagination were the charges brought against them, charges known to their instigators to be untrue all the while, but which time and again influenced the masses. In times of unrest and turmoil the masses are inclined to hatred and cruelty, whereas in times of peace these traits of human nature emerge but stealthily.

Up to this point I have spoken only of violence and oppression against the Jews – not of anti-Semitism itself as a psychological and social phenomenon existing even in times and circumstances when no special action against the Jews is under way. In this sense, one may speak of latent anti-Semitism. What is its basis? I believe that in a certain sense one may actually regard it as a normal manifestation in the life of a people.

The members of any group existing in a nation are more closely bound to one another than they are to the remaining population. Hence a nation will never be free of friction while such groups continue to be distinguishable. In my belief, uniformity in a population would not be desirable, even if it were attainable. Common convictions and aims, similar interests, will in every society produce groups that, in a certain sense, act as units. There will always be friction between such groups – the same sort of aversion and rivalry that exists between individuals.

The need for such groupings is perhaps most easily seen in the field of politics, in the formation of political parties. Without parties the political interests of the citizens of any state are bound to languish. There would be no forum for the free exchange of opinions. The individual would be isolated and unable to assert his convictions. Political convictions, moreover, ripen and grow only through mutual stimulation and criticism offered by individuals of similar disposition and purpose; and politics is no different from any other field of our cultural existence. Thus it is recognized, for example, that in times of intense religious fervour different sects are likely to spring up whose rivalry stimulates religious life in general. It is well known, on the other hand, that centralization – that is, elimination of independent groups – leads to one-sidedness and barrenness in science and art because such centralization checks and even suppresses any rivalry of opinions and research trends.

Just What Is a Jew?

The formation of groups has an invigorating effect in all spheres of human striving, perhaps mostly due to the struggle between the convictions and aims represented by the different groups. The Jews, too, form such a group with a definite character of its own, and anti-Semitism is nothing but the antagonistic attitude produced in the non-Jews by the Jewish group. This is a normal social reaction. But for the political abuse resulting from it, it might never have been designated by a special name.

What are the characteristics of the Jewish group? What, in the first place, is a Jew? There are no quick answers to this question. The most obvious answer would be the following: a Jew is a person professing the Jewish faith. The superficial character of this answer is easily recognized by means of a simple parallel. Let us ask the question: what is a snail? An answer similar in kind to the one given above might be: a snail is an animal inhabiting a snail shell. This answer is not altogether incorrect; nor, to be sure, is it exhaustive; for the snail shell happens to be but one of the material products of the snail. Similarly, the Jewish faith is but one of the characteristic products of the Jewish community. It is, furthermore, known that a snail can shed its shell without thereby ceasing to be a snail. The Jew who abandons his faith (in the formal sense of the word) is in a similar position. He remains a Jew.

Difficulties of this kind appear whenever one seeks to explain the essential character of a group.

The bond that has united the Jews for thousands of years and that unites them today is, above all, the democratic ideal of social justice, coupled with the ideal of mutual aid and tolerance among all men. Even the most ancient religious scriptures of the Jews are steeped in these social ideals, which have powerfully affected Christianity and Mohammedanism[1] and have a benign influence upon the social structure of a great part of mankind. The introduction of a weekly day of rest should be remembered here – a profound blessing to all mankind. Personalities such as Moses, Spinoza and Karl Marx, dissimilar as they may be, all lived and sacrificed themselves for the ideal of social justice; and it was the tradition of their forefathers that led them on this thorny path. The unique accomplishments of the Jews in the field of philanthropy spring from the same source.

The second characteristic trait of Jewish tradition is the high regard in which it holds every form of intellectual aspiration and spiritual effort. I am convinced that this great respect for intellectual striving is solely responsible for the contributions that the Jews have made toward the progress of knowledge, in the broadest sense of the term. In view of their relatively small number and the considerable external obstacles constantly placed in their way on all sides, the extent of those contributions deserves the admiration of all sincere men. I am convinced that this is not due to any special wealth of endowment, but to the fact that the esteem in which intellectual accomplishment is held among the Jews creates an atmosphere particularly favourable to the development of any talents that may exist. At the same time a strong critical spirit prevents blind obeisance to any mortal authority.

I have confined myself here to these two traditional traits, which seem to me the most basic. These standards and ideals find expression in small things as in large. They are transmitted from parents to children; they colour conversation and judgement among friends; they fill the religious scriptures; and they give to the community life of the group its characteristic stamp. It is in these distinctive ideals that I see the essence of Jewish nature. That these ideals are but imperfectly realized in the group – in its actual everyday life – is only natural. However, if one seeks to give brief expression to the essential character of a group, the approach must always be by the way of the ideal.

Where Oppression Is a Stimulus

In the foregoing I have conceived of Judaism as a community of tradition. Both friend and foe, on the other hand, have often asserted that the Jews represent a race; that their characteristic behaviour is the result of innate qualities transmitted by *heredity* from one generation to the next. This opinion gains weight from the fact that the Jews for thousands of years have predominantly married within their own group. Such a custom may indeed *preserve* a homogeneous race – if it existed originally; it cannot *produce* uniformity of the race – if there was originally a racial intermixture. The Jews, however, are beyond doubt a mixed race, just as are all other groups of our civilization. Sincere anthropologists are agreed on this point; assertions to the contrary all belong to the field of political propaganda and must be rated accordingly.

Perhaps even more than on its own tradition, the Jewish group has thrived on oppression and on the antagonism it has forever met in the world. Here undoubtedly lies one of the main reasons for its continued existence through so many thousands of years.

The Jewish group, which we have briefly characterized in the foregoing, embraces about 16 million people – less than 1 per cent of mankind, or about half as many as the population of present-day Poland. Their significance as a political factor is negligible. They are scattered over almost the entire earth and are in no way organized as a whole – which means that they are incapable of concerted action of any kind.

Were anyone to form a picture of the Jews solely from the utterances of their enemies, he would have to reach the conclusion that they represent a world power. At first sight that seems downright absurd, and yet, in my view, there is a certain meaning behind it. The Jews as a group may be powerless, but the sum of the achievements of their individual members is everywhere considerable and telling, even though these achievements were made in the face of obstacles. The forces dormant in the individual are mobilized, and the individual himself is stimulated to self-sacrificing effort, by the spirit that is alive in the group.

Hence the hatred of the Jews by those who have reason to shun popular enlightenment. More than anything else in the world, they fear the influence of men of intellectual independence. I see in this the essential cause for the savage hatred of Jews raging in present-day Germany. To the Nazi group the Jews are not merely a means for turning the resentment of the people away from themselves, the oppressors; they see the Jews as a non-assimilable element that cannot be driven into uncritical acceptance of dogma, and that, therefore – as long as it exists at all – threatens their authority because of its insistence on popular enlightenment of the masses.

Proof that this conception goes to the heart of the matter is convincingly furnished by the solemn ceremony of the burning of the books staged by the Nazi regime shortly after its seizure of power. This act, senseless from a political point of view, can only be understood as a spontaneous emotional outburst. For that reason it seems to me more revealing than many acts of greater purpose and practical importance.

In the field of politics and social science there has grown up a justified distrust of generalizations pushed too far. When thought is too greatly dominated by such generalizations, misinterpretations of specific sequences of cause and effect readily occur, doing injustice to the actual multiplicity of events. Abandonment of generalization, on the other hand, means to relinquish understanding altogether. For that reason I believe one may and must risk generalization, as long as one remains aware of its uncertainty. It is in this spirit that I wish to present in all modesty my conception of anti-Semitism, considered from a general point of view.

In political life I see two opposed tendencies at work, locked in constant struggle with each other. The first, optimistic trend proceeds from the belief that the free unfolding of the productive forces of individuals and groups essentially leads to a satisfactory state of society. It recognizes the need for a central power, placed above groups and individuals, but concedes to such power only organizational and regulatory functions. The second, pessimistic trend assumes that free interplay of individuals and groups leads to the destruction of society; it thus seeks to base society exclusively upon authority, blind obedience and coercion. Actually this trend is pessimistic only to a limited extent: for it is optimistic in regard to those who are, and desire to be, the bearers of power and authority. The adherents of this second trend are the enemies of the free groups and of education for independent thought. They are, moreover, the carriers of political anti-Semitism.

Here in America all pay lip service to the first, optimistic, tendency. Nevertheless, the second group is strongly represented. It appears on the scene everywhere, though for the most part it hides its true nature. Its aim is political and spiritual dominion over the people by a minority, by the circuitous route of control over the means of production. Its proponents have already tried to utilize the weapon of anti-Semitism as well as of hostility to various other groups. They will repeat the attempt in times to come. So far all such tendencies have failed because of the people's sound political instinct.

And so it will remain in the future, if we cling to the rule: *Beware of flatterers, especially when they come preaching hatred.*

Abraham H. Foxman

braham Foxman was born in 1940 in what is now part of Belarus and emigrated with his parents to America in 1950. He joined the Anti-Defamation League in 1965 and in 1987 was the consensus choice for National Director. In February 2014 Foxman announced his plans to step down in 2015, fifty years after he joined the organization.

The Anti-Defamation League (ADL) was originally formed in 1913 in the USA by the Independent Order of B'nai B'rith, the oldest Jewish service organization, with the mission statement 'to stop, by appeals to reason and conscience and, if necessary, by appeals to law, the defamation of the Jewish people. Its ultimate purpose is to secure justice and fair treatment to all citizens alike and to put an end forever to unjust and unfair discrimination against and ridicule of any sect or body of citizens.'

It Cannot Be Business as Usual

Jerusalem, Israel, 16 December 2009

Ministers, your Excellencies, Ambassadors, Dear Friends.

There is something very depressing, ironic, sad, and exhilarating for a child survivor of the Shoah [the Holocaust], who was saved in

'Yerushalyim D'Lita', the 'Jerusalem of Lithuania' in Vilna, to be sharing a platform with the Foreign Minister of Lithuania, in the holy city of Jerusalem, the capital of the sovereign state of Israel, to address, again, and again, the subject of anti-Semitism. And so I find myself in a jumble of emotions at the very moment.

I know what brings us here, I know what motivates us to be here. I respect and appreciate the presence of so many good people who have come from across the globe, because they understand the importance and significance of standing against anti-Semitism.

And yet at the same time, I am very troubled. Troubled because in a sense this has become a ritual; this has become an undertaking where we come together almost once a year; we address and we analyse and we go home. Yes, we pass some resolutions; make some promises and declarations, but in fact so many of the wonderful words remain at the conference. Even the small commitments that were made in previous conference to do what? – to monitor, to report – that have not been implemented.

And so, this year has been probably the worst year of global anti-Semitism since the Second World War; the worst year since we have begun to monitor and report it. There has been no country, no city, no continent that was not witness to anti-Semitic manifestations, and we do not talk about thousands and thousands of Web sites, millions upon millions of hits to reinforce people's anti-Semitism.

This has been a year when the Jewish State has been vilified and defamed in ways none of us could have imagined. And yet we do not gather here in a sense of crisis, urgency and emergency. We gather again as we did in London in February this year to assess, to evaluate, to reinforce. We are in crisis. It has never, in our lifetime, or in most of our lifetimes, been more serious.

It is Hanukkah. Do you know there is a war against the menorah out there? Several years ago there was an issue in the United States that there was a war against Christmas. I have got news for you: menorahs are being desecrated in Austria, Moldova, in ten, twelve cities in the United States. And what do we do? We mark it down as a statistic. Another statistic of anti-Semitism.

Ten years ago when we witnessed an explosion of global anti-Semitism after we convinced the world to stop its denial, we met in crisis. And we did act together in a manner which began to stem the rise of this disease. So it was after the conferences in Vienna, in Berlin and in Brussels that countries began to take this disease more seriously and task forces were established, inter-ministerial meetings were convened and reporting processes and educational programmes put in place.

My dear friends, we are again in a crisis and it will not be enough to go from session to session and become more enlightened and better understand that which we will never understand, for it is against all reason, and morality and rationale. So maybe what we need to do is to bring back the spirit of Billings, Montana. For it is Hanukkah.

In 1993 in a small town in Midwest America, a menorah was desecrated. Rather than record it as another statistic in the annals of anti-Semitism, the town of Billings, Montana, 99.4 per cent non-Jewish, organized and stood up. The citizens were urged to stand up and put an image of the menorah published in the newspaper in their window for the next eight days. They did, and all the citizens of Billings, Montana became Jews and said 'No'. It is that spirit we need to rekindle in Jerusalem this week, a spirit in response to a crisis that we have not witnessed in a long time.

Finally, I apologize to the good people who are here, for it is almost like the rabbi complaining to those who came to synagogue, about those who did not come to synagogue. For you are the righteous, you are those who care. But I beg you, care a little more, when you go home, when you report to your countries. This cannot be business as usual.

R. L. Sheil

*T**he first recorded Jewish settlers in England arrived with William the Conqueror, but the following 200 years saw widespread and brutal oppression culminating in 1290 with their expulsion from England. From then until 1655, when Oliver Cromwell granted their readmittance, the only Jews living in England did so in secret.*

By the 1800s Jewish citizens were a vital part of British society, but they were still considerably restricted from holding office and public life. This restriction didn't just apply to Jews; it wasn't until 1829 that the Catholics were freed from all their civil disabilities by the Catholic Emancipation Bill, which gave great hope to Jewish campaigners for emancipation and equality. The bill was first presented in 1830 and it would occupy parliament for nigh on the next thirty years. Throughout the 1830s it was presented each year, eventually making it through the Commons in 1833 only to be continually rejected in the Lords. In 1840 the principal supporters and campaigners in both the Commons and Lords died, and though legal changes were made in the status of Jews, the barr on entering parliament still remained. The barrier was focused around the need to take a Christian oath, which Disraeli, born to Jewish parents but subsequently christened, had no issue with, and he became an MP in 1837. Things came to a head again in 1847, when Lionel de Rothschild was elected to serve as MP for the City of London but was legally unable to take his seat.

Richard Lailor Sheil was an Irish Catholic MP who was a prominent supporter of Catholic emancipation and was elected to parliament in 1830, the year after it became legal for him to stand. His experience of oppression for his Catholicism and as an Irishman made him a natural supporter of all who faced oppression. Sheil became ambassador to Tuscany in 1850 and died there in 1851, a full seven years before the Jewish Relief Act of 1858 finally allowed Jews to serve as MPs (though they were still restricted from directly advising Her Majesty) enabling Rothschild to take his seat. In 1890 all further restrictions on both Jews and Roman Catholics taking any position within the British Empire except that of monarch were removed.

On the Jewish Disabilities Bill

House of Commons, 7 February 1848

That men subject to all the duties should be deemed unworthy of the rights of Englishmen, appears to me to be a remarkable anomaly. The enjoyment of rights ought not to be dissociated from the liabilities to duties. A British subject ought in every regard to be considered a British citizen; and inasmuch as the professors of the most ancient religion in the world, which, as far as it goes, we not only admit to be true, but hold to be the foundation of our own, are bound to the performance of every duty which attaches to a British subject, to a full fruition of every right which belongs to a British citizen, they have, I think, an irrefragable title. A Jew born in England cannot transfer his allegiance from his Sovereign and his country; if he were to enter the service of a foreign power engaged in hostilities with England, and were taken in arms, he would be accounted a traitor.

Is a Jew an Englishman for no other purposes than those of condemnation? I am not aware of a single obligation to which other Englishmen are liable from which a Jew is exempt; and if his religion confers on him no sort of immunity, it ought not to affect him with any kind of disqualification. It has been said, in the course of these discussions, that a Jew is not subject to penalties, but to privations. But what is privation but a synonym for penalty? Privation of life, privation of liberty, privation of property, privation of country, privation of right, privation of privilege – these are degrees widely distant indeed, but still degrees in the graduated scale of persecution. The Parliamentary disability that affects the Jew has been designated in the course of these debates by the mollified expressions to which men who impart euphemism to severity are in the habit of resorting; but most assuredly an exclusion from the House of Commons ought, in the House of Commons itself, to be regarded as a most grievous detriment. With the dignity, and the greatness, and the power of this, the first assembly in the world, the hardship of exclusion is commensurate.

Some of the most prominent opponents of this measure are among the last by whom a seat in Parliament ought to be held in little account. On this branch of the case – the hardship of an exclusion from this House – I can speak as a witness as well as an advocate. I belong to that great and powerful community which was a few years ago subject to the same disqualification that affects the Jew; and I felt that disqualification to be most degrading. Of myself I will not speak, because I can speak of the most illustrious person by whom that community was adorned.

The Jew comes here with no other arguments than those which reason and truth supply; but reason and truth are of counsel with him; and in this assembly, which I believe to represent, not only the high intelligence, but the high-mindedness of England, reason will not long be baffled, and truth, in fulfilment of its great aphorism, will at last prevail. I will assume that the exclusion from this House is a great privation, and I proceed to consider whether it be not a great wrong. Nothing but necessity could afford its justification; and of this plea we should be taught, by a phrase which has almost grown proverbial, to beware.

The sophistications of intolerance are refuted by their inconsistencies. If a Jew can choose, wherefore should he not be chosen? If a Jew can vote for a Christian, why should not a Christian vote for a Jew? Again, the Jew is admissible to the highest municipal employment; a Jew can be High Sheriff – in other words, he can empanel the jury by which the first Christian Commoner in England may be tried for his life. But if necessity is to be pleaded as a justification for the exclusion of the Jew, it must be founded on some great peril which would arise from his admission. What is it you fear? What is the origin of this Hebrewphobia? Do you tremble for the Church? The Church has something perhaps to fear from eight millions of Catholics, and from three millions of Methodists, and more than a million of Scotch seceders. The Church may have something to fear from the assault of sectaries from without, and still more to fear from a sort of spurious Popery, and the machinations of mitred mutiny from within; but from the Synagogue – the neutral, impartial, apathetic and unproselytizing Synagogue – the Church has nothing to apprehend. But it is said that the House will become unchristianized. The Christianity of the Parliament depends on the Christianity of the country; and the Christianity of the country is fixed in the faith, and inseparably intertwined with the affections of the people. It is as stable as England herself, and as long as Parliament shall endure, while the Constitution shall stand, until the great mirror of the nation's mind shall have been shattered to pieces, the religious feelings of the country will be faithfully reflected here. This is a security far better than can be supplied by a test which presents a barrier to an honest Jew, but which a scornful sceptic can so readily and so disdainfully overleap.

Reference has been made in the course of these discussions to the author of *The Decline and Fall of the Roman Empire*. A name still more illustrious might have been cited. Was not the famous St John[1] – was not Bolingbroke, the fatally accomplished, the admiration of the admirable, to whom genius paid an almost idolatrous homage, and by whom a sort of fascination was exercised over all those who had the misfortune to approach him – was not the unhappy sceptic, by whom far more mischief to religion and morality must have been done than could be effected by half a hundred of the men by whom the Old Testament is exclusively received, a member of this House? Was he stopped by the test that arrests the Jew; or did he not trample upon it and ascend through this House to a sort of masterdom in England, and become the confidential and favourite adviser of his Sovereign? He was not only an avowed and ostentatious infidel, but he was swayed by a distempered and almost insane solicitude for the dissemination of his disastrous disbelief. Is it not then preposterous that a man by whom all revealed religion is repudiated, who doubts the immortality of the soul, doubts a future state of rewards and punishments, doubts in a super-intending Providence, believes in nothing, fears nothing, and hopes for nothing, without any incentive to virtue, and without any restraint upon depravity excepting such as a sense of conventional honour or the promptings of a natural goodness may have given him – is it not, I say, preposterous, and almost monstrous, that such a man, for whom a crown of deadly nightshade should be woven, should be enabled, by playing the imposture of a moment and uttering a valueless formula at the table of the House, to climb to the pinnacle of power; and that you should slap the doors of this House with indignity upon a conscientious man who adheres to the faith in which he was born and bred; who believes in the great facts that constitute the foundation of Christianity; who believes in the perpetual existence of the nobler portion of our being; who believes in future retribution and in recompense to come; who believes that the world is taken care of by its almighty and everlasting Author; who believes in the mercy of God, and practises humanity to man; who fulfils the ten great injunctions in which all morality is comprised; whose ear was never deaf to the supplications of the suffering; whose hand is as open as day to charity; and whose life presents an exemplification of the precepts of the Gospel far more faithful than that of many a man by whom, in the name of the Gospel, his dishonouring and unchristian disabilities are most wantonly, most injuriously, and most opprobriously maintained?

But where in the Scripture – in what chapter, in what text, in what single phrase – will you find an authority for resorting to the infliction of temporal penalty, or of temporal privation of any kind, as a means of propagating heavenly truth? You may find an authority, indeed, in the writings of jurists and of divines, and in the stern theology of those austere and haughty churchmen by whom the Pharisaical succession, far better than the Apostolical, is personally and demonstratively proved. But you will not find it in the New Testament; you will not find it in Matthew, nor in Mark, nor in Luke, nor in John, nor in the epistles of the meek and humble men to whom the teaching of all nations was given in charge; above all, you will not find it in anything that was ever said, or anything that was ever done, or anything that was ever suffered, by the Divine Author of the Christian religion, who spoke the Sermon on the Mountain, who said that the merciful should be blessed, and who, instead of ratifying the anathema which the people of Jerusalem had invoked upon themselves, prayed for forgiveness for those who knew not what they did, in consummating the Sacrifice that was offered up for the transgressions of the world. It was not by persecution, but despite of it – despite of imprisonment, and exile, and spoliation, and shame, and death, despite the dungeon, the wheel, the bed of steel, and the couch of fire – that the Christian religion made its irresistible and superhuman way. And is it not repugnant to common reason, as well as to the elementary principles of Christianity itself, to hold that it is to be maintained by means diametrically the reverse of those by which it was propagated and diffused? But, alas! for our frail and fragile nature, no sooner had the professors of Christianity become the co-partners of secular authority than the severities were resorted to which their persecuted predecessors had endured.

The Jew was selected as an object of special and peculiar infliction. The history of that most unhappy people is, for century after century, a trail of chains and a track of blood. Men of mercy occasionally arose to interpose in their behalf. St Bernard – the great St Bernard, the last of the Latin Fathers – with a most pathetic eloquence took their part. But the light that gleamed from the ancient turrets of the Abbey of Clairvaux was transitory and evanescent. New centuries of persecution followed; the Reformation did nothing for the Jew. The infallibility of Geneva was sterner than the infallibility of Rome. But all of us – Calvinists, Protestants, Catholics – all of us who have torn the seamless garment into pieces, have sinned most fearfully in this terrible regard. It is, however, some consolation to know that in Roman Catholic countries expiation of this guilt has commenced. In France and in Belgium all civil distinction between the Protestant and the Jew is at an end. To this Protestant country a great example will not have been vainly given. There did exist in England a vast mass of prejudice upon this question, which is, however, rapidly giving way. London, the point of Imperial centralization, has made a noble manifestation of its will. London has advisedly, deliberately, and with benevolence aforethought, selected the most prominent member of the Jewish community as its representative, and united him with the first Minister of the Crown. Is the Parliament prepared to fling back the Jew upon the people, in order that the people should fling back the Jew upon the Parliament? That will be a dismal game, in the deprecation of whose folly and whose evils the Christian and the statesman should concur.

But not only are the disabilities which it is the object of this measure to repeal at variance with genuine Christianity, but I do not hesitate to assert that they operate as impediments to the conversion of the Jews, and are productive of consequences directly the reverse of those for which they were originally designed. Those disabilities are not sufficiently onerous to be compulsory, but they are sufficiently vexatious to make conversion a synonym for apostasy, and to affix a stigma to an interested conformity with the religion of the State. We have relieved the Jew from the ponderous mass of fetters that bound him by the neck and by the feet; but the lines which we have left, apparently light, are strong enough to attach him to his creed, and make it a point of honour that he should not desert it.

There exists in this country a most laudable anxiety for the conversion of the Jews. Meetings are held, and money is largely subscribed for the purpose; but all these creditable endeavours will be ineffectual unless we make a restitution of his birthright to every Englishman who professes the Jewish religion. I know that there are those who think that there is no such thing as an English, or a French, or a Spanish Jew. A Jew is but a Jew; his nationality, it is said, is engrossed by the hand of recollection and of hope, and the house of Jacob must remain for ever in a state of isolation among the strange people by whom it is encompassed. In answer to these sophistries I appeal to human nature. It is not wonderful that when the Jew was oppressed, and pillaged, and branded in a captivity worse than Babylonian, he should have felt upon the banks of the Thames, or of the Seine, or the Danube, as his forefathers felt by the waters of the Euphrates, and that the psalm of exile should have found an echo in his heart. This is not strange; it would have been strange if it had been otherwise; but justice – even partial justice – has already operated a salutary change. In the same measure in which we have relaxed the laws against the Jews, that patriot instinct by which we are taught to love the land of our birth has been revived. British feeling has already taken root in the heart of the Jew, and for its perfect development nothing but perfect justice is required. To the fallacies of fanaticism give no heed. Emancipate the Jew – from the Statute-book of England be the last remnant of intolerance erased forever; abolish all civil discriminations between the Christian and the Jew, fill his whole heart with the consciousness of country. Do this, and we dare be sworn that he will think, and feel, and fear, and hope as you do; his sorrow and his exultation will be the same; at the tidings of English glory his heart will beat with a kindred palpitation, and whenever there shall be need, in the defence of his Sovereign and of his country, his best blood, at your bidding, will be poured out with the same heroic prodigality as your own.

Emile Zola

Zola, born in 1840, was a giant of the French literary scene and the most important proponent of literary naturalism. His involvement in the Dreyfus affair, which rocked turn-of-the-century French politics and society, also marked the beginning of the power of intellectuals in France to shape and inform public opinion.

In 1894 French Military Intelligence (the Section de renseignements or SR) found pieces of a letter which contained evidence that military secrets were being communicated to the German Embassy in Paris. France was extremely unstable, still suffering the effects of defeat in the Franco-Prussian War some twenty years before and a century of post-revolution instability. It was imperative that the culprit should be found. The authorities turned to Major Armand du Paty de Clam, who claimed an expertise in handwriting analysis and was put in charge of the investigation. A suitable suspect, Captain Dreyfus, a young French artillery officer of Jewish Alsatian descent, had already been identified, partly due to his Alsatian origins (Alsace was on the French–German border and had been annexed by Germany after *the Franco-Prussian War). Though his handwriting and that of the letter were noticeably different, du Paty de Clam wrote a memo suggesting the differences were negligible and subsequently arrested Dreyfus.*

The country was rife with antisemitism following the publication in 1886 of Eduard Drumont's Jewish France and his establishment of the virulently antisemitic newspaper La Libre Parole in 1892. The latter joined half a dozen other publications in blaming France's Jews for all social ills. With a huge profile and exhaustive and combative press coverage designed to whip public sentiment and force everyone to take sides, the trial was a sensation, but placed even more pressure on the need for a conviction. Held in a closed court, the trial yielded little evidence against Dreyfus till On intercepted note from the German military attaché to his Italian counterpart was produced. It referred to the 'Scoundrel D ...' and was used to presume Dreyfus' guilt because it used his initial. Dreyfus was duly found guilty of treason and sentenced to life imprisonment, in the penal colony of Devil's Island in French Guiana, based on little evidence.

Dreyfus' brother continued to work to clear his name, organizing a futile appeal and continuing to dig for evidence of the real spy's identity. In 1896, the SR had a new chief, Georges Picquart, who by chance uncovered irrefutable evidence that the real culprit was a debt-ridden officer, Ferdinand Walsin Esterhazy. Not wanting to admit a miscarriage of justice, the Army's General Staff suppressed the evidence and went so far as to fabricate counter-evidence and begin a campaign against Picquart. Picquart had confided in a friend who subsequently spoke to the Vice-President of the Senate, August Scherer-Kestner, who also happened to be Alsatian and began to take an interest in Dreyfus' innocence. Scherer-Kestner involved the highest levels of government for the first time. As evidence against Esterhazy was leaked to the pro-Dreyfus press, the army moved to hold a quick show trial, led by General Pellieux, which exonerated Esterhazy and instead saw Picquart denounced, disgraced and subsequently imprisoned.

On 13 January 1898, days after Esterhazy's acquittal, Zola wrote a blistering attack on the front page of the newspaper L'Aurore. Written as an open letter to the French President Félix Faure, it accused the French military of a cover-up and antisemitism. Zola's intention was that he be prosecuted for libel so that the evidence suppressed in the Esterhazy trial could be made public. Disgusted at the miscarriage of justice and the subsequent corruption used to cover it, Zola hoped that his fame as France's leading intellectual would change public opinion. He was indeed tried and convicted, in a farcical case that saw the courts cooperating with the military to suppress evidence.

Sentenced to a year in prison, Zola fled to England rather than be imprisoned. Though the trial internationally exposed France's wilful miscarriage of justice, politicians remained in denial about the Affair. Elections followed and the new Minister for War was convinced of Dreyfus' guilt but also wanted to see Esterhazy separately convicted. He therefore commanded a further investigation which only served to expose Esterhazy's collusion with the General Staff and the fabrication of evidence (the officer responsible confessed under duress and killed himself the next day). The scandal led to resignation by the Minister and several other senior figures, and the Affair, now four years on, was taking more and more political space, increasingly dividing the nation and reorganizing the French political landscape.

In 1899 President Faure died. The new President favoured a review and referred the original case to the Supreme Court. Following an exhaustive review the Court overturned Dreyfus' original conviction and the case was sent back to the Military Court for a retrial. Thousands of miles away, Dreyfus was unaware of much that had unfolded. He was returned to France in June 1899 – the same month Zola returned from his exile – but continued to be imprisoned. Tensions ran high at his retrial; one of his lawyers was shot, surviving but being forced from court at a crucial time. Zola assisted with the defence, but in spite of everything Dreyfus was once again found guilty of treason and sentenced to ten years. Dreyfus at once filed an appeal. Wary of any continuation of the Affair, the government offered him a pardon which he, exhausted by his ordeal, accepted, thereby tacitly admitting guilt. Many supporters were enraged by this final act but the public were as weary as Dreyfus of the events that had threatened to rip France apart. It wasn't until 1906 that Dreyfus was completely exonerated, the new government keen to draw a line under one of France's strangest and most traumatic periods.

Zola's early death in 1902 meant he never lived to see Dreyfus vindicated, though in a continued tying of their fates, Dreyfus was shot and injured in 1908 on the occasion of the transfer of Zola's ashes to the Pantheon. The subsequent trial of his would-be assassin, acquitted in another judicial misconduct, dredged up further antisemitic discontent. Dreyfus went on to serve his country as Lieutenant Colonel in the First World War and was finally promoted to the rank of Officier de la Légion d'Honneur in November 1918. He died in 1935, exactly twenty-nine years to the day after his official exoneration.

J'Accuse

'I ACCUSE … !'

Open Letter to the President of the French Republic
by Émile Zola
[Translation and notes © Shelley Temchin and Jean-Max Guieu,
Georgetown University, 2001]

Letter to Félix Faure

Mr President,

Would you allow me, grateful as I am for the kind reception you once extended to me, to show my concern about maintaining your well-deserved prestige and to point out that your star which, until now, has shone so brightly, risks being dimmed by the most shameful and indelible of stains.

Unscathed by the vilest slander, you have won over the hearts of all. You are radiant in the patriotic glory of our country's alliance with Russia,[1] you are about to preside over the solemn triumph of our World Fair,[2] the jewel that crowns this great century of Labour, Truth and Liberty. But what filth this wretched Dreyfus affair has cast on your name, or, might I say, your reign. A court martial, under orders, has just dared to acquit that character, Esterhazy, the supreme insult to all truth and all justice. And now the image of France is sullied by this filth, and History shall record that it was under your presidency that this crime against society was committed.

As they have dared, so shall I dare. Dare to tell the truth, as I have pledged to tell it, in full, since the normal channels of justice have failed to do so. My duty is to speak out, not to become an accomplice in this travesty. My nights would otherwise be haunted by the spectre of an innocent man, far away, suffering the most horrible of tortures for a crime he did not commit.

And it is to you, Mr President, that I shall proclaim this truth, with all the revulsion that an honest man can summon. Knowing your integrity, I am convinced that you do not know the truth. But to whom if not to you, the first magistrate of the country, shall I reveal the vile baseness of those who truly are guilty?

The truth, first of all, about the trial and conviction of Dreyfus.

At the root of it all is one evil man, Lt Colonel du Paty de Clam, who was at the time a mere Major. He *is* the entire Dreyfus case, and it can only be understood through an honest and thorough examination that reveals his actions and responsibilities. He appears to be the shadiest and most complex of creatures, spinning outlandish intrigues, stooping to the deceits of dime novels, complete with stolen documents, anonymous letters, meetings in deserted spots, mysterious women scurrying around at night, peddling damning evidence. He was the one who came up with the scheme of dictating the text of the *bordereau*[3] to Dreyfus; he was the one who had the idea of observing him in a mirror-lined room. And he was the one that Major Forzinetti caught carrying a shuttered lantern that he planned to throw open on the accused man while he slept, hoping that, jolted awake by the sudden flash of light, Dreyfus would blurt out his guilt.

I need say no more: let us seek and we shall find. I am stating simply that Major du Paty de Clam, as the officer of justice charged with the preliminary investigation of the Dreyfus case, is the first and the most grievous offender in the ghastly miscarriage of justice that has been committed.

The *bordereau* had already been for some time in the hands of Colonel Sandherr, Head of the Intelligence Office, who has since died of a paralytic stroke. Information was leaked, papers were disappearing, then as they continue to do to this day; and, as the search for the author of the *bordereau* progressed, little by little, an *a priori* assumption developed that it could only have come from an officer of the General Staff, and furthermore, an artillery officer. This interpretation, wrong on both counts, shows how superficially the *bordereau* was analysed, for a logical examination shows that it could only have come from an infantry officer.

So an internal search was conducted. Handwriting samples were compared, as if this were some family affair, a traitor to be sniffed out and expelled from within the War Office. And, although I have no desire to dwell on a story that is only partly known, Major du Paty de Clam entered on the scene at the first whiff of suspicion of Dreyfus. From that moment on, he was the one who 'invented' Dreyfus the traitor, the one who orchestrated the whole affair and made it his own. He boasted that he would confound him and make him confess all. Oh, yes, there was of course the Minister of War, General Mercier, a man of apparently mediocre intellect; and there were also the Chief of Staff, General de

Boisdeffre, who appears to have yielded to his own religious bigotry, and the Deputy Chief of Staff, General Gonse, whose conscience allowed for many accommodations. But, at bottom, it all started with Major du Paty de Clam, who led them on, hypnotized them, for, as an adept of spiritualism and the occult, he could converse with spirits. No one would ever believe the experiments to which he subjected the unfortunate Dreyfus, the traps he set for him, the wild investigations, the monstrous fantasies, the whole demented torture.

Ah, that first trial! What a nightmare it is for all who know it in its true details. Major du Paty de Clam had Dreyfus arrested and placed in solitary confinement. He ran to Mme Dreyfus, terrorized her, telling her that if she talked her husband would be ruined. Meanwhile, the unfortunate Dreyfus was tearing at his flesh and proclaiming his innocence. And this is how the case proceeded, like some fifteenth-century chronicle, shrouded in mystery, swamped in all manner of nasty twists and turns, all stemming from one trumped-up charge, that idiot *bordereau*. This was not only a bit of cheap trickery but also the most outrageous fraud imaginable, for almost all of these notorious secrets turned out in fact to be worthless. I dwell on this, because this is the germ of it all, whence the true crime would emerge, that horrifying miscarriage of justice that has blighted France. I would like to point out how this travesty was made possible, how it sprang out of the machinations of Major du Paty de Clam, how Generals Mercier, de Boisdeffre and Gonse became so ensnared in this falsehood that they would later feel compelled to impose it as holy and indisputable truth. Having set it all in motion merely by carelessness and lack of intelligence, they seem at worst to have given in to the religious bias of their milieu and the prejudices of their class. In the end, they allowed stupidity to prevail.

But now we see Dreyfus appearing before the court martial. Behind the closed doors, the utmost secrecy is demanded. Had a traitor opened the border to the enemy and driven the German Emperor straight to Notre-Dame, the measures of secrecy and silence could not have been more stringent. The public was astounded; rumours flew of the most horrible acts, the most monstrous deceptions, lies that were an affront to our history. The public, naturally, was taken in. No punishment could be too harsh. The people clamoured for the traitor to be publicly stripped of his rank and demanded to see him writhing with remorse on his rock of infamy. Could these things be true, these unspeakable acts, these deeds so dangerous that they must be carefully hidden behind closed doors to keep Europe from going up in flames? No! They were nothing but the demented fabrications of Major du Paty de Clam, a cover-up of the most preposterous fantasies imaginable. To be convinced of this one need only read carefully the accusation as it was presented before the court martial.

How flimsy it is! The fact that someone could have been convicted on this charge is the ultimate iniquity. I defy decent men to read it without a stir of indignation in their hearts and a cry of revulsion, at the thought of the undeserved punishment being meted out there on Devil's Island. He knew several languages. A crime! He carried no compromising papers. A crime! He would occasionally visit his birthplace. A crime! He was hard-working, and strove to be well informed. A crime! He did not become confused. A crime! He became confused. A crime! And how childish the language is, how groundless the accusation! We also heard talk of fourteen charges, but we found only one, the one about the *bordereau*, and we learn that even there the handwriting experts could not agree. One of them, M. Gobert, faced military pressure when he dared to come to a conclusion other than the desired one. We were told also that twenty-three officers had testified against Dreyfus. We still do not know what questions they were asked, but it is certain that not all of them implicated him. It should be noted, furthermore, that all of them came from the War Office. The whole case had been handled as an internal affair, among insiders. And we must not forget this: members of the General Staff had sought this trial to begin with and had passed judgement. And now they were passing judgement once again.

So all that remained of the case was the *bordereau*, on which the experts had not been able to agree. It is said that within the council chamber the judges were naturally leaning toward acquittal. It becomes clear why, at that point, as justification for the verdict, it became vitally important to turn up some damning evidence, a secret document that, like God, could not be shown, but which explained everything, and was invisible, unknowable and incontrovertible. I deny the existence of that document. With all my strength, I deny it! Some trivial note, maybe, about some easy women, wherein a certain D … was becoming too insistent, no doubt some demanding husband who felt he wasn't getting a good enough price for the use of his wife. But a document concerning national defence that could not be produced without sparking an immediate declaration of war tomorrow? No! No! It is a lie, all the more odious and cynical in that its perpetrators are getting off free without even admitting it. They stirred up all of France, they hid behind the understandable commotion they had set off, they sealed their lips while troubling our hearts and perverting our spirit. I know of no greater crime against the state.

These, Mr President, are the facts that explain how this miscarriage of justice came about; the evidence of Dreyfus' character, his affluence, the lack of motive and his continued affirmation of innocence combine to show that he is the victim of the lurid imagination of Major du Paty de Clam, the religious circles surrounding him, and the 'dirty Jew' obsession that is the scourge of our time.

And now we come to the Esterhazy case. Three years have passed, many consciences remain profoundly troubled, become anxious, investigate, and wind up convinced that Dreyfus is innocent.

I shall not chronicle these doubts and the subsequent conclusion reached by M. Scheurer-Kestner. But, while he was conducting his own investigation, major events were occurring at headquarters. Colonel Sandherr had died and Lt Colonel Picquart had succeeded him as Head of the Intelligence Office. It was in this capacity, in the exercise of his office, that Lt Colonel Picquart came into possession of a telegram addressed to Major Esterhazy by an agent of a foreign power. His express duty was to open an inquiry. What is certain is that he never once acted against the will of his superiors. He thus submitted his suspicions to his hierarchical senior officers, first General Gonse, then General de Boisdeffre, and finally General Billot, who had succeeded General Mercier as Minister of War. That famous much-discussed Picquart file was none other than the Billot file, by which I mean the file created by a subordinate for his minister, which can still probably be found at the War Office. The investigation lasted from May to September 1896, and what must be said loud and clear is that General Gonse was at that time convinced that Esterhazy was guilty and that Generals de Boisdeffre and Billot had no doubt that the handwriting on the famous bordereau was Esterhazy's. This was the definitive conclusion of Lt Colonel Picquart's investigation. But feelings were running high, for the conviction of Esterhazy would inevitably lead to a retrial of Dreyfus, an eventuality that the General Staff wanted at all cost to avoid.

This must have led to a brief moment of psychological anguish. Note that, so far, General Billot was in no way compromised. Newly appointed to his position, he had the authority to bring out the truth. He did not dare, no doubt in terror of public opinion, certainly for fear of implicating the whole General Staff, General de Boisdeffre and General Gonse, not to mention the subordinates. So he hesitated for a brief moment of struggle between his conscience and what he believed to be the interest of the military. Once that moment passed, it was already too late. He had committed himself and he was compromised. From that point on, his responsibility only grew, he took on the crimes of others, he became as guilty as they, if not more so, for he was in a position to bring about justice and did nothing. Can you understand this: for the last year General Billot, Generals Gonse and de Boisdeffre have known that Dreyfus is innocent, and they have kept this terrible knowledge to themselves? And these people sleep at night, and have wives and children they love!

Lt Colonel Picquart had carried out his duty as an honest man. He kept insisting to his superiors in the name of justice. He even begged them, telling them how impolitic it was to temporize in the face of the terrible storm that was brewing and that would break when the truth became known. This was the language that M. Scheurer-Kestner later used with General Billot as well, appealing to his patriotism to take charge of the case so that it would not degenerate into a public disaster. But no! The crime had been committed and the General Staff could no longer admit to it. And so Lt Colonel Picquart was sent away on official duty. He got sent further and further away until he landed in Tunisia, where they tried eventually to reward his courage with an assignment that would certainly have got him killed, in the very same area where the Marquis de Morès[4] had been killed. He was not in disgrace, indeed: General Gonse even maintained a friendly correspondence with him. It is just that there are certain secrets that are better left alone.

Meanwhile, in Paris, truth was marching on, inevitably, and we know how the long-awaited storm broke. M. Mathieu Dreyfus denounced Major Esterhazy as the real author of the *bordereau* just as M. Scheurer-Kestner was handing over to the Minister of Justice a request for the revision of the trial. This is where Major Esterhazy comes in. Witnesses say that he was at first in a panic, on the verge of suicide or running away. Then all of a sudden, emboldened, he amazed Paris by the violence of his attitude. Rescue had come, in the form of an anonymous letter warning of enemy actions, and a mysterious woman had even gone to the trouble one night of slipping him a paper, stolen from headquarters, that would save him. Here I cannot help seeing the handiwork of Lt Colonel du Paty de Clam, with the trademark fruits of his fertile imagination. His achievement, Dreyfus' conviction, was in danger, and he surely was determined to protect it. A retrial would mean that this whole extraordinary saga, so extravagant, so tragic, with its denouement on Devil's Island, would fall apart! This he could not allow to happen. From then on, it became a duel between Lt Colonel Picquart and Lt Colonel du Paty de Clam, one with his face visible, the other masked. The next step would take them both to the civil court. It came down, once again, to the General Staff protecting itself, not wanting to admit its crime, an abomination that has been growing by the minute.

In disbelief, people wondered who Commander Esterhazy's protectors were. First of all, behind the scenes, Lt Colonel du Paty de Clam was the one who had concocted the whole story, who kept it going, tipping his hand with his outrageous methods. Next General de Boisdeffre, then General Gonse, and finally General Billot himself were all pulled into the effort to get the Major acquitted, for acknowledging Dreyfus' innocence would make the War Office collapse under the weight of public contempt. And the astounding outcome of this appalling situation was that the one decent man involved, Lt Colonel Picquart, who alone had done his duty, was to become the victim, the one who got ridiculed and punished. O justice, what horrible despair grips our hearts? It was even claimed that he himself was the forger, that he had fabricated the letter-telegram in order to destroy Esterhazy. But, good God, why? To what end? Find me a motive. Was he, too, being paid off by the Jews? The best part of it is that Picquart was himself an anti-Semite. Yes! We have before us the ignoble spectacle of men who are sunken in debts and crimes being hailed as innocent, whereas the honour of a man whose life is spotless is being vilely attacked: a society that sinks to that level has fallen into decay.

The Esterhazy affair, thus, Mr President, comes down to this: a guilty man is being passed off as innocent. For almost two months we have been following this nasty business hour by hour. I am being brief, for this is but the abridged version of a story whose sordid pages will some day be written out in full. And so we have seen General de Pellieux, and then Major Ravary,[5] conduct an outrageous inquiry from which criminals emerge glorified and honest people sullied. And then a court martial was convened.

How could anyone expect a court martial to undo what another court martial had done?

I am not even talking about the way the judges were hand-picked. Doesn't the overriding idea of discipline, which is the lifeblood of these soldiers, itself undercut their capacity for fairness? Discipline means obedience. When the Minister of War, the commander in chief, proclaims, in public and to the acclamation of the nation's representatives, the absolute authority of a previous verdict, how can you expect a court martial to rule against him? It is a hierarchical impossibility. General Billot directed the judges in his preliminary remarks, and they proceeded to judgement as they would to battle, unquestioningly. The preconceived opinion they brought to the bench was obviously the following: 'Dreyfus was found guilty for the crime of treason by a court martial; he therefore is guilty and we, a court martial, cannot declare him innocent. On the other hand, we know that acknowledging Esterhazy's guilt would be tantamount to proclaiming Dreyfus innocent.' There was no way for them to escape this rationale.

So they rendered an iniquitous verdict that will forever weigh upon our courts martial and will henceforth cast a shadow of suspicion on all their decrees. The first court martial was perhaps unintelligent; the second one is inescapably criminal. Their excuse, I repeat, is that the supreme chief had spoken, declaring the previous judgement incontrovertible, holy and above mere mortals. How, then, could subordinates contradict it? We are told of the honour of the army; we are supposed to love and respect it. Ah, yes, of course, an army that would rise to the first threat, that would defend French soil, that army is the nation itself, and for that army we have nothing but devotion and respect. But this is not about that army, whose dignity we are seeking, in our cry for justice. What is at stake is the sword, the master that will one day, perhaps, be forced upon us. Bow and scrape before that sword, that god? No!

As I have shown, the Dreyfus case was a matter internal to the War Office: an officer of the General Staff, denounced by his co-officers of the General Staff, sentenced under pressure by the Chiefs of Staff. Once again, he could not be found innocent without the entire General Staff being guilty. And so, by all means imaginable, by press campaigns, by official communications, by influence, the War Office covered up for Esterhazy only to condemn Dreyfus once again. Ah, what a good sweeping out the government of this Republic should give to that Jesuit-lair, as General Billot himself calls it. Where is that truly strong, judiciously patriotic administration that will dare to clean house and start afresh? How many people I know who, faced with the possibility of war, tremble in anguish knowing to what hands we are entrusting our nation's defence! And what a nest of vile intrigues, gossip and destruction that sacred sanctuary that decides the nation's fate has become! We are horrified by the terrible light the Dreyfus affair has cast upon it all, this human sacrifice of an unfortunate man, a 'dirty Jew'. Ah, what a cesspool of folly and foolishness, what preposterous fantasies, what corrupt police tactics, what inquisitorial, tyrannical practices! What petty whims of a few higher-ups trampling the nation under their boots, ramming back down their throats the people's cries for truth and justice, with the travesty of state security as a pretext.

Indeed, it is a crime to have relied on the most squalid elements of the press, and to have entrusted Esterhazy's defence to the vermin of Paris, who are now gloating over the defeat of justice and plain truth. It is a crime that those people who wish to see a generous France take her place as leader of all the free and just nations are being accused of fomenting turmoil in the country, denounced by the very plotters who are conniving so shamelessly to foist this miscarriage of justice on the entire world. It is a crime to lie to the public, to twist public opinion to insane lengths in the service of the vilest death-dealing machinations. It is a crime to poison the minds of the meek and the humble, to stoke the passions of reaction and intolerance, by appealing to that odious anti-Semitism that, unchecked, will destroy the freedom-loving France of the Rights of Man. It is a crime to exploit patriotism in the service of hatred, and it is, finally, a crime to ensconce the sword as the modern god, whereas all science is toiling to achieve the coming era of truth and justice.

Truth and justice, so ardently longed for! How terrible it is to see them trampled, unrecognized and ignored! I can feel M. Scheurer-Kestner's soul withering and I believe that one day he will even feel sorry for having failed, when questioned by the Senate, to spill all and lay out the whole mess. A man of honour, as he had been all his life, he believed that the truth would speak for itself, especially since it appeared to him plain as day. Why stir up trouble, especially since the sun would soon shine? It is for this serene trust that he is now being so cruelly punished. The same goes for Lt Colonel Picquart, who, guided by the highest sentiment of dignity, did not wish to publish General Gonse's correspondence. These scruples are all the more honourable since he remained mindful of discipline, while his superiors were dragging his name through the mud and casting suspicion on him, in the most astounding and outrageous ways. There are two victims, two decent men, two simple hearts, who left their fates to God, while the devil was taking charge. Regarding Lt Col. Picquart, even this despicable deed was perpetrated: a French tribunal allowed the statement of the case to become a public indictment of one of the witnesses [Picquart], accusing him of all sorts of wrongdoing. It then chose to prosecute the case behind closed doors as soon as that witness was brought in to defend himself. I say this is yet another crime, and this crime will stir consciences everywhere. These military tribunals have, decidedly, a most singular idea of justice.

This is the plain truth, Mr President, and it is terrifying. It will leave an indelible stain on your presidency. I realize that you have no power over this case, that you are limited by the Constitution and your entourage. You have, nonetheless, your duty as a man, which you will recognize and fulfil. As for myself, I have not despaired in the least, of the triumph of right. I repeat with the most vehement conviction: truth is on the march, and nothing will stop it. Today is only the beginning, for it is only today that the positions have become clear: on one side, those who are guilty, who do not want the light to shine forth, on the other, those who seek justice and who will give their lives to attain it. I said it before and I repeat it now: when truth is buried underground, it grows and it builds up so much force that the day it explodes it blasts everything with it. We shall see whether we have been setting ourselves up for the most resounding of disasters, yet to come.

But this letter is long, Mr President, and it is time for me to conclude it.

I accuse Lt Col. du Paty de Clam of being the diabolical creator of this miscarriage of justice – unknowingly, I am willing to believe – and of defending this sorry deed, over the last three years, by all manner of bizarre and evil machinations.

I accuse General Mercier of complicity, at least by mental weakness, in one of the greatest inequities of the century.

I accuse General Billot of having held in his hands absolute proof of Dreyfus' innocence and concealing it, thereby making himself guilty of crimes against mankind and justice, as a political expedient and a way for the compromised General Staff to save face.

I accuse General de Boisdeffre and General Gonse of complicity in the same crime, the former, no doubt, out of religious prejudice, the latter perhaps out of that esprit de corps that has transformed the War Office into an unassailable holy ark.

I accuse General de Pellieux and Major Ravary of conducting a fraudulent inquiry, by which I mean a monstrously biased one, as attested by the latter in a report that is an imperishable monument to naïve insolence.

I accuse the three handwriting experts, Messrs Belhomme, Varinard and Couard, of having submitted reports that were deceitful and fraudulent, unless a medical examination finds them to be suffering from a disease that impairs their eyesight and judgement.

I accuse the offices of the War Office of having used the press, particularly L'Eclair and L'Echo de Paris,[6] to conduct an abominable campaign to mislead public opinion and cover up their own wrongdoing

Finally, I accuse the first court martial of violating the law by convicting the accused on the basis of evidence that was kept secret, and I accuse the second court martial of covering up this illegality, on orders, by committing the judicial crime of acquitting a guilty man with full knowledge of his guilt.

In making these accusations I am aware that I am making myself liable to articles 30 and 31 of the 29 July 1881 law on the press, making libel a punishable offence. I expose myself to that risk voluntarily.

As for the people I am accusing, I do not know them, I have never seen them, and I bear them neither ill will nor hatred. To me they are mere entities, agents of harm to society. The action I am taking is no more than a radical measure to hasten the explosion of truth and justice.

I have but one passion, the search for light, in the name of humanity which has suffered so much and is entitled to happiness. My fiery protest is simply the cry of my very soul.

Let them dare, then, to bring me before a court of law and investigate in the full light of day!

I am waiting.

With my deepest respect, Mr President

The Shield

T he Shield *was first published in 1916 by the short-lived Russian Society for the Study of Jewish Life, under the joint editorship of the author Maxim Gorky and two other eminent Russian writers of the era, Leonid Andreyev and Fyodor Sologub. The book consisted of essays as well as stories and poems by prominent non-Jewish Russian writers all considering the 'Jewish question'. It was translated and published in America in 1917 with an introduction by William English Walling, a wealthy American labour reformer and co-founder of the National Association for the Advancement of Colored People, who had visited Russia in 1905 and subsequently married a Russian–Jewish émigrée.*

In Walling's foreword, written the day after news of the February revolution – which saw the abdication of Tsar Nicholas II and the end of the Russian Empire – broke internationally, he looks at the position of the Jews in Russia in a broader light saying: 'It is useless for Americans to deceive themselves into thinking that the Russian Jewish question is either unimportant or incomprehensible from the point of view of our progress and democracy. Do we not have our Negro and Asiatic problems? Do not the English have their Irish and Indian questions?' In drawing these comparisons, he gave early birth to unity of understanding in the twentieth-century struggles of all oppressed peoples.

Maxim Gorky

G orky was born Alexei Maximovich Peshkov in 1868 in Nizhny Novgorod (which from 1932 to 1990 was renamed Gorky in his honour). After his father died when Gorky was five and his mother remarried, the boy was brought up by his grandmother, but ran away aged twelve. He moved to a small village and became a baker whilst receiving an education from the revolutionary group Land and Liberty. It was during this period that Gorky became a Marxist and his later political views began to take shape. In the 1880s Gorky witnessed a pogrom which he later wrote about and which shaped his views on racism, tolerance and antisemitism.

He became a journalist and writer and assumed the pseudonym Gorky, which literally means 'bitter'. Arrested on numerous occasions and publicly opposed to the tsarist regime, he befriended many revolutionaries, including Lenin, while simultaneously establishing his literary reputation. In 1906 Gorky toured Europe and America, giving an address to 5,000 in New York's Grand Central Palace, wherein he decried the Russian treatment of the Jews as 'one of the saddest and most shameful manifestations in the world'.

After settling in Capri, Gorky returned to Russia in 1913, but he fell out with the Bolsheviks over their oppression of freedom of speech. He left Russia again in 1921, partly on health grounds, but began to return regularly in the late Twenties and eventually settled there for good on Stalin's invitation *in 1932. As Stalinist oppression increased, Gorky fell out of favour. He was placed under house arrest in 1934 and died in 1936. His death remains shrouded in mystery following a confession of Gorky's murder by Genrikh Yagoda, former head of the NKVD, during his 1938 show trial.*

Russia and the Jews

From time to time – more often as time goes on! – circumstances force the Russian author to remind his compatriots of certain indisputable, elementary truths.

It is a very hard duty: – it is painfully awkward to speak to grown-up and literate people in this manner:

'Ladies and gentlemen! We must be humane; humaneness is not only beautiful, but also advantageous to us. We must be just; justice is the foundation of culture. We must make our own the ideas of law and civil liberty: the usefulness of such an assimilation is clearly demonstrated by the high degree of civilization reached by the Western countries, for instance, by England.

'We must develop in ourselves a moral tidiness, and an aversion to all the manifestations of the brute principle in man, such as the wolfish, degrading hatred for people of other races. The hatred of the Jew is a beastlike, brute phenomenon; we must combat it in the interests of the quicker growth of social sentiments and social culture.

'The Jews are human beings, just like others, and, like all human beings, the Jews must be free.

'A man who meets all the duties of a citizen, thereby deserves to be given all the rights of citizenship.

'Every human being has an inalienable right to apply his energy in all the branches of industry and all the departments of culture, and the broader the scope of his personal and social activities, the more does his country gain in power and beauty.'

There are a number of other equally elementary truths which should have long since sunk into the flesh and blood of Russian society, but which have not as yet done so.

I repeat – it is a hard thing to assume the rôle of a preacher of social proprieties and to keep reiterating to people: 'It is not good, it is unworthy of you to live such a dirty, careless, savage life – wash yourselves!'

And in spite of all your love for men, in spite of your pity for them, you are sometimes congealed in cold despair and you think with animosity: 'Where then is that celebrated, broad, beautiful Russian soul? So much was and is being said about it, but wherein does its breadth, might and beauty actively manifest itself? And is not our soul broad because it is amorphous? And it is probably owing to its amorphousness that we yield so readily to external pressure, which disfigures us so rapidly and radically.'

We are good-natured, as we ourselves express it. But when you look closer at our good-naturedness, you find that it shows a strange resemblance to Oriental indifference.

One of man's most grievous crimes is indifference, inattention to his neighbour's fate; this indifference is pre-eminently ours.

The situation of the Jews in Russia, which is a disgrace to Russian culture, is one of the results of our carelessness, of our indifference to the straight and just decrees of life.

In the interests of reason, justice, civilization, we must not tolerate that people without rights should live among us; we would never have tolerated it, if we had a strong sense of self-respect.

We have every reason to reckon the Jews among our friends; there are many things for which we must be grateful to them: they have done and are doing much good in those lines of endeavour in which the best Russian minds have been engaged. Nevertheless, without aversion or indignation, we bear a disgraceful stain on our consciousness, the stain of Jewish disabilities. There is in that stain the dirty poison of slanders and the tears and blood of numberless pogroms.

I am not able to speak of anti-Semitism in the manner it deserves. And this not because I have not the power or the right words. It is rather because I am hindered by something that I cannot overcome. I would find words biting, heavy, and pointed enough to fling them in the face of the man-haters, but for that purpose I must descend into a kind of filthy pit. I must put myself on a level with people whom I do not respect and for whom I have an organic aversion.

I am inclined to think that anti-Semitism is indisputable, just as leprosy and syphilis are, and that the world will be cured of this shameful disease only by culture, which sets us free, slowly but surely, from ailments and vices.

Of course, this does not relieve me of the duty to combat in every way the development of anti-Semitism and, according to my powers, to preserve people from getting infected by it. The Jew of today is dear to me, and I feel myself guilty before him, for I am one of those who tolerate the oppression of the Jewish nation, the great nation, which some of the most prominent Western thinkers consider, as a psychical type, higher and more beautiful than the Russian.

I think that the judgement of these thinkers is correct. To my mind, Jews are more European than the Russians are, because of their strongly developed feeling of respect for work and man, if not for any other reason. I admire the spiritual steadfastness of the Jewish nation, its manly idealisms, its unconquerable faith in the victory of good over evil, in the possibility of happiness on earth.

The Jews – mankind's old, strong leaven – have always exalted its spirit, bringing into the world restless, noble ideas, goading men to embark on a search for finer values.

All men are equal; the soil is no one's, it is God's; man has the right and the power to resist his fate, and we may stand up even against God – all this is written in the Jewish Bible, one of the world's best books. And the commandment of love for one's neighbour is also an ancient Jewish commandment, just as are all the rest, 'Thou shalt not kill' among them.

In 1885 the German-Jewish Union in Germany published *The Principles of the Jewish Moral Doctrine*. Here is one of these principles: 'Judaism teaches: "Love thy neighbour as thyself" and announces this commandment of love for all mankind to be the fundamental principle of Jewish religion. It therefore forbids all kinds of hostility, envy, ill-will and unkindly treatment of any one, without distinction of race, nationality and religion.'

These principles were ratified by 350 rabbis, and published just at the time of the anti-Jewish pogroms in Russia.

'Judaism teaches respect for the life, the health, the forces and the property of one's neighbour.'

I am a Russian. When, alone with myself, I calmly scrutinize my merits and demerits, it seems to me that I am intensely Russian. And I am deeply convinced that there is much that we Russians can and ought to learn from the Jews.

For instance, the seventh paragraph of *The Principles of the Jewish Moral Doctrine* says: 'Judaism commands us to respect work, to take part by either physical or mental labour in the communal work, to seek for life's goods in constant productive and creative work. Judaism, therefore, teaches us to take care of our powers and abilities, to perfect them and apply them actively. It therefore forbids all idle pleasure not based on labour, all idleness which hopes for the help of others.'

This is beautiful and wise, and this is just what we Russians lack. Oh, if we could educate our unusual powers and abilities, if we had the will to apply them actively in our chaotic, untidy existence, which is terribly blocked up with all kinds of idle clack and homespun philosophy, and which gets more and more saturated with silly arrogance and puerile bragging. Somewhere deep in the Russian soul – no matter whether it is the master's or the muzhik's[1] – there lives a petty and squalid demon of passive anarchism, who infects us with a careless and indifferent attitude toward work, society, people, and ourselves.

I believe that the morality of Judaism would assist us greatly in overcoming this demon – if only we have the will to combat him.

In my early youth I read – I have forgotten where – the words of the ancient Jewish sage – Hillel, if I remember rightly:

'If thou art not for thyself, who will be for thee? But if thou art for thyself alone – wherefore art thou?'

The inner meaning of these words impressed me with its profound wisdom, and I interpreted them for myself in this manner: I must actively take care of myself, that my life should be better, and I must not impose the care of myself on other people's shoulders; but if I am going to take care of myself alone, of nothing but my own personal life – it will be useless, ugly and meaningless.

This thought ate its way deep into my soul, and I say now with conviction: Hillel's wisdom served me as a strong staff on my road, which was neither even nor easy. It is hard to say with precision to what one owes the fact that one kept on his feet on the entangled paths of life, when tossed by the tempests of mental despair, but I repeat – Hillel's serene wisdom assisted me many a time.

I believe that Jewish wisdom is more all-human and universal than any other, and this not only because of its immemorial age, not only because it is the first-born, but also because of the powerful humaneness that saturates it, because of its high estimate of man.

'The true Shekinah – is man,'[2] says a Jewish text. This thought I dearly love, this I consider the highest wisdom, for I am convinced of this: that until we learn to admire man as the most beautiful and marvellous phenomenon on our planet, until then we shall not be set free from the abomination and lies that saturate our lives.

It is with this conviction that I have entered the world, and with this conviction I shall leave it, and in leaving it I will believe firmly that the time will come when the world will acknowledge that

'The holy of holies is man!'[3]

It is unbearably painful to see that human beings who have produced so much that is beautiful, wise and necessary for the world live among us oppressed by unfair laws, which in all ways restrain their right to life, work and freedom. It is necessary – for it is just and useful – to give the Jew equal rights with the Russians; it is imperative that we should do so not only out of respect to the people which has rendered and is constantly rendering yeoman service to humanity and our own nation, but also out of self-respect.

We must make haste with this plain, human reform, for the animosity against Jews is on the increase in our country, and if we do not make an attempt to arrest the growth of this blind hatred, it will prove pernicious to our cultural development. We must bear in mind that the Russian people have hitherto seen very little good, and therefore, believe all the evil things that man-haters whisper in their ears. The Russian peasant does not manifest any organic hatred for the Jew – on the contrary, he shows an exceptional attraction for Israel's religious thought, fascinating for its democratic spirit. As far as I can remember, the religious sects of 'judaizers' exist only in Russia and Hungary. In late years, the sects of 'Sabbathists' and 'The New Israel' have been developing rather rapidly in our country. In spite of this, when the Russian peasant hears of persecutions of Jews, he says with the indifference of an Oriental:

'No one sues or beats an innocent man.'

Who ought to know better than the Russian peasant that in 'Holy Russia' the innocent are too often tried and beaten? But his conception of right and wrong has been confused from time immemorial, the sense of injustice is undeveloped in his dark mind, dimmed by centuries of Tartardom, boyardom, and the horrors of serfdom.[4]

The village has a dislike for restless people, even when that restlessness is expressed in an aspiration for a better life. We Russians are intensely Oriental by nature, we love quiet and immobility, and a rebel, even if he be a Job, delights us in but an abstract way. Lost in the depth of a winter six months long, and wrapped in misty dreams, we love beautiful fairy-tales, but the desire for a beautiful life is undeveloped in us. And when on the plane of our lazy thought something new and disquieting makes its appearance, instead of accepting and sympathetically scanning it, we hasten to drive it into a dark corner of our mind and bury it there, lest it disturb us in our customary vegetative existence, amidst impotent hopes and grey dreams.

In addition to the people, there is also the 'populace', something standing outside of social classes and outside of culture, and united by the dark sense of hatred against everything surpassing its understanding and defenceless against brute force. I speak of the populace which thus defines itself in the words of Pushkin, our great poet, who himself suffered so cruelly from the aristocratic populace:

'We are insidious and shameless, Ungrateful, faint-hearted and wicked; At heart we are cold, sterile eunuchs, Traducers, born to slavery.'

It is mainly this populace that is the bearer of the brute principles, such as anti-Semitism.

The Jews are defenceless, and this is especially dangerous for them in the conditions of Russian life. Dostoevsky, who knew the Russian soul so well, pointed out repeatedly that defencelessness arouses in it a sensuous inclination to cruelty and crime. In late years there have appeared in Russia quite a few people who have been taught to think that they are the finest of the wheat, and that their enemy is the stranger, above all the Jew. For a long time these people were being persuaded that all the Jews are restless people, strikers and rioters. They were next informed that the Jews like to drink the blood of thievish boys. In our days they are being taught that the Polish Jews are spies and traitors.

If this preaching of hatred will not bring bloody and shameful fruits, it will be only because it will clash with our Russian indifference to life and will disappear in it; it will split against the Chinese wall behind which our still inexplicable nation is hidden.

But if this indifference be stirred up by the efforts of the hatred preachers, the Jews will loom up before the Russian nation as a race accused of all crimes.

And it is not for the first time that all the troubles of Russian life will be blamed on the Jew; time and again was he the scapegoat for our sins. Only recently he paid with his life and goods for the help he rendered us in our feverish struggle for freedom. I think no one has forgotten the fact that our 'emancipatory movements' [are] strangely wound up with anti-Jewish riots.

When the multiracial populace of Jerusalem demanded the death of the defenceless Jew, Christ, Pilate, believing Christ innocent, washed his hands, but allowed him to be put to death.

How then will honest Russian men and women act in Pilate's place? Their judgement is awaited.

M. Bernatzky

*O*ne of the writers of The Shield, *Mikhail Vladimirovich Bernatzky*
was born in 1878, and was a noted writer on economics, teaching
at Kiev University and at the Polytechnical Institute in Petrograd
(St Petersburg). Unlike many of his fellow essayists in The Shield, *he*
never came to international prominence, so comparatively little is known
about him.

In this tract, Bernatzky dismisses human rights and ethical arguments,
instead focusing only on the economic case for Jewish equality in Russia.
He not only sets out the conditions under which Russian Jews were living in
the early part of the twentieth century – the laws of the country effectively
limiting their entry into many forms of Russian society: 'limitations of
residence … forcing … a peculiar character of the Jewish occupations' –
but also sets out an economic case for equal rights of different racial groups
in Russian society. Bernatzky's argument, though limited, is ground-
breaking in the sense that much of this economic case set out a century
ago forms the basis of Western economic deliberations on subjects such as
multiculturalism and, critically, immigration today.

Bernatzky was acutely aware that by stifling the role that Jews played
in Russian society, the economic life of his country was put at risk. Today,
proponents of flexible immigration policies across the Western world
make a similar argument – that immigration can only enhance a nation's
prosperity and that cultural and racial factors must not be allowed to stand
in the way.

The Jews and Russian Economic Life

Much has been written about the insufferable situation of the Russian
Jews, these serfs of the twentieth century, chained to 'the Pale of
Settlement',[1] somewhat like the Roman *'glebae adscripti'.*[2] The tragic
history of late years and the epoch through which we are living can
disturb the inner composure of the most indifferent spectator of current
events. It is painful to touch upon many aching and essentially clear
questions, but life constantly and severely demands that they should be
brought before our minds, and life awaits an answer to them from the
thought and conscience of Russian society.

It is not our intention to discuss the necessity for the removal of Jewish disabilities from the humanitarian standpoint. However majestic may be those 'elementary principles of law and morality', which have been achieved by mankind on its long historic road and which are now the very basis of civilization, in the eyes of many they are still little more than fine words, stylistic embellishments of highbrow talk. Of course, the atmosphere of discrimination is equally pernicious for those who suffer and those who are privileged: did not serfdom corrupt the master as well as the slave? All this is eminently true. But there are arguments which, we regret to say, are more appealing and convincing. It is these arguments that we shall treat in the present paper.

The reader is well aware of the fact that in these days nothing has been discussed more vividly than the necessity of developing Russia's productive powers. The intimate connection between the general prosperity of our country and its economic progress has penetrated into the consciousness of people at large. It is the war, evidently, that has driven this truth home to us: namely that the ultimate success of the conflict depends not only on the activity of the armies, but also on the economic stability of the belligerent nations. The economic difficulties which are being experienced by Germany strengthen our faith in our final victory. More than a quarter of a century ago the Russian minister of finance, who took great pains to develop our industry, wrote in the explanatory memoir which accompanied the project of the state budget:

I believe it to be the duty I owe Your Imperial Majesty to express my firm, clear and profound conviction that economic prosperity of the people even when coupled with a somewhat imperfect military organization will be more useful in case of war than the most complete military preparedness combined with economic weakness. In the latter case, the people, however eager they may be to sacrifice both their life and property, can bring to the altar of the fatherland their life only, but they will be unable to furnish the necessary financial means for the State.

It is from this standpoint of economic interests that we shall approach the painful Jewish question. The time is long since past when it was possible to say with the Empress Elizabeth Petrovna: 'From Christ's enemies I desire no profit.'[3] It is precisely in this profit that both the Exchequer and the higher classes, and – what is most important – the people at large, are greatly interested. The basic productive force of a country is the living work of its population. The body politic of Russia contains about 6 million gifted and undoubtedly industrious Jews. The manner in which the forces of this people are applied will be treated further on. For the moment let us state this: it is to the interest of the Russian State to utilize economically this living Jewish energy as completely and rationally as possible. From this standpoint all the obstacles which are created for the Jews in the field of education are absolutely incomprehensible: it is as if our country, sorely lacking as it is not only in representatives of superior qualified labour, but actually in literate people, were striving to increase its ignorance and intellectual backwardness.

Of course, formal justification can be found for every act, and every evil-doer endeavours to convince himself of the justice of his evil deeds. So it is in this case, too: the intentional shutting-off of the Jewish masses from education is motivated by the desire to keep them from becoming superior to the Russian population, which, it is said, is intellectually inferior to the Jews. This argument is an outright insult flung in the face of the Russian people. It shows that the official guardians of the nation do not know its rich natural powers. But this argument cannot obscure the essential nature of Jewish disabilities as an intentional neglect of that productive power which is represented by a portion of the Russian subjects. Our economic organism does not get all the benefits to which it may rightfully lay claim.

Let us turn to those characteristic social and economic conditions under which the Jews exist in our country. Nearly all of them, upward of 5 million, live within the Pale of Settlement, which comprises fifteen governments and Poland, and only 6 per cent live outside of this territory. Within the Pale, Jews are not allowed to buy or take on lease real estate outside the towns and townlets, which circumstance makes it impossible for them to become farmers. This, in connection with the limitation of residence, has naturally resulted in a peculiar character of Jewish occupations. It is characteristic of the part the Jews play in Russia's economic life that nearly 73.08 per cent of them are forced to seek employment in the country's commerce and industry. Of the entire Jewish population throughout the Empire, only 2.4 per cent are engaged in agriculture, 4.7 per cent in liberal professions, 11.5 per cent in personal service (domestic service, etc.); the rest, minus the persons without any definite employment, are forced to seek means of livelihood in the field of commerce (31 per cent), industry (36.3 per cent), and transport (3 per cent). The same goes for the artificial congestion of the Jews in the cities: only 18 per cent live in the villages of the Pale of Settlement, while the rest – more than four-fifths – toil in the towns and townlets. Such a one-sided distribution of Jewish labour would not be a negative phenomenon if it were possible to spread it uniformly over the entire country. For, backward as Russia is industrially and commercially, the Jews would easily find a place in the fields of endeavour which suit them best and would greatly benefit the country by furthering the process of its industrialization. Under present circumstances they are crowded in one place and overburden the commerce and the industry of the Pale of Settlement ...

What has been said so far demonstrates clearly enough that the anti-Semitic economic policy is detrimental to the economic organism of Russia as a whole. The true interests of our country demand that Jewish labour and Jewish means should be given complete freedom of application. Russia will only gain from such a change of policy toward the Jews. Anti-Semitism, from the economic standpoint, is nothing but a tremendous waste of the country's productive powers.

Here is another aspect of the question. Whether the Jews as a race are to one's liking or not is a question of individual taste, the solution of which cannot be allowed to influence the sane economic policy of a state. This must be guided by objective data. As a matter of fact, the Jews constitute more than one third, 35 per cent, of the commercial class in Russia. If we believe our country's prosperity to be bound up with the process of its progressive industrialization, we must admit that the part the Jews play in Russia's commercial life is tremendous, that to a considerable degree they handle her entire commerce. All that hinders the untrammelled manifestation of the Jewish economic energies is harmful to Russia's economic organism ...

The Jewish people has grown to be a living part of Russia's economic organism, and the blows which are directed against the Jews affect in an equal, if not a greater, degree the mass of the aboriginal Russian population. We do not intend to discuss here the Zionistic dreams and aspirations of the Jews. One thing is clear to us, namely that a complete exodus of the Jews from Russia would be greatly detrimental to her economic development. The Western world understands this truth very well. Werner Sombart in his work *Die Zukunft der Juden* ('The Future of the Jews') reaches the following conclusion: 'If by a miracle all the Jews would decide tomorrow to emigrate to Palestine we (the Germans) would never allow them to. For it would mean a catastrophe in the field of economic relation, not to speak of other fields, such as we have never as yet experienced and which would probably cripple our economic organism for ever.'

But we, Russians, give little thought to such questions. As late as the year 1914 we did not hesitate to inaugurate new restrictive measures, which it took the great trial of this War to stop.

Whoever has our economic welfare at heart, whoever dreams about the mighty development of our country and of its real emancipation from foreign influence – inasmuch as this is generally possible – must understand that anti-Semitism is the worst foe of our economic prosperity, that, in short, the Jewish question is a Russian question. Full rights for the Jews, equal with those that the rest of the population of the Empire enjoy, are an indispensable condition for our peaceful cultural development. Only on that basis can we achieve the broad ideals which have come into prominence in this tragic struggle with German imperialism.

Edouard Herriot

*E*douard Herriot was a radical French politician who served three
times as Prime Minister, in 1924–5, 1926 and 1932, and held
numerous positions in government both before and after the war.
*From 1942 until 1945 he was exiled to Germany for opposing the Vichy
government, having been deposed by Marshal Pétain. In 1927 he was a
founding member of La Ligue Internationale Contre l'Antisémitisme. La
Ligue originated from the League Against Pogroms founded by the journalist
Bernard Lecarche in 1926 following the assassination in Paris of Symon
Petliura by Sholom Schwartzbard. Petliura was a Ukrainian general and
had been head of the Ukrainian government during the Russian Civil War.
After the formation of the Soviet Union Petliura fled to France. In 1919 the
Ukrainian state promised Jews full equality and autonomy, but Petliura
lost control of the army, which aggressively engaged in pogroms, killing as
many as 50,000 Jews including Schwartzbard's parents. Lecarche saw the
potential for a repeat of the endemic antisemitism of the Dreyfus affair
and the league was formed to lobby for Schwartzbard. The trial caused a
sensation, as Ukraine and the pogroms were essentially put on trial and
Schwartzbard acquitted.*

*In the aftermath the League evolved into La Ligue Internationale Contre
l'Antisémitisme (ultimately, after the Second World War, becoming La*

Ligue Internationale Contre le Racisme et l'Antisémitisme), with Einstein and Gorky also amongst its founding members.

April 1933 had seen the start of mass oppression of Germany's Jewish population with a series of orders banning Jews from certain professions, restricting education and announcing a census to identify all Jews and non-Aryans. It was also the first time individuals were identified as part of the Jewish race if only one of their grandparents was Jewish. Herriot was speaking out not just against German antisemitism but against the very real possibility of increasing legislation in France. In response to the mass exodus of Jewish doctors, France enacted the Armbruster Law, which limited the practice of medicine to French citizens and subjects who had been granted the diplome d'État *by France. Even the most renowned foreign doctors were directed to go through nine years of undergraduate and medical studies, as well as the last year of high school to obtain a baccalaureate, or be arrested for illegal practice of medicine.*

Contre l'Antisémitisme

Speech made in Lyon, 8 April 1933

Painful times give us the compensation and privilege of elevating our noble souls in order to bring them together before everything that spiritualizes and ennobles humanity. I feel the atmosphere of this meeting filled with the emotion and magnitude of the concerns and feelings that motivate it. It is a great joy and a great honour for me as Mayor of Lyon to see the elite representatives of the different religions and parties gathered around me.

I can only express here ideas drawn from philosophical education or historical culture, and my deep conviction is that we should respond to violence only with serenity and kindness. I will not speak any political words that might trouble the work of peace in which I have so often been involved.

It is not the first time the Jews have suffered in Germany. In the Middle Ages they were subjected to the worst oppression, and did not even the magnificent scholar Einstein himself protest against these latest manifestations? Moses, Mendelssohn, Kant, did they not protest before him? Remember Kant's sublime definition: 'Two things fill the mind with ever new and increasing admiration and awe (…): the starry heavens above me and the moral law within me'.

What the Jews are undergoing today is an offence to the moral law. Let us combine our efforts so that racial and class prejudices shall never again be revived. It is against them that all men of good will should be united.

I see all the deep forces of Pan-Germanism gathering once more, and to those forces I draw the attention of all those who have a pacifist and human conscience. If the spirit of men is profoundly troubled at this point, should we not fear the external manifestations of this distress?

I wish for a spirit of kindness to reign throughout France, a kindness that reflects our country's moderation, the character of its people, the harmonious rather than excessive proportions of its streams, rivers and forests. That spirit must have truly permeated our race in order that, from the eighteenth century onwards, we raised the most vigorous protest against these demonstrations of intolerance and barbarism.

Because we are human, because we are republicans, because we are French, we can, we must, raise the protest of justice against all forms of idiotic violence.

France's justice, fairness and goodness are brought together in Voltaire's *Treatise on Tolerance*, at the point when Calas is martyred;[1] in *The Spirit of the Laws* of our great philosopher Montesquieu, who, under the guardianship of the *ancien régime*, took a stand against the auto-da-fés in Portugal and the martyring of Jews; in the book by Abbé Grégoire, Christian according to the Gospel who, from the first years of his maturity, wrote a great work in defence of the Jews.[2] I have made this small book of familiar prayers in French and Latin one of the confidants in my life, a life that has so often been shaken by storms.

I want to pay homage to the greatest protector that you, the Jewish people, had among the French, who confronted all menaces with inflexible kindness and who was one of the most impressive factors of the young French Revolution. It was on 27 September 1791 that a decree of the Assembly removed every last exceptional measure against Israelites.

The constituent assembly revoked all the restrictions that the *ancien régime* placed upon Jews.

The future and indeed all eternity belong to justice. I recall the visits that I made before the war to a small museum in Alsace, in the shadow of Strasbourg cathedral, which even under German control housed mementos from French provinces. I often found Israelites meditating there.

One day I asked one of them: 'You like France, then?'

'We love it still,' he replied. 'France has always protected us. Even in the past, France treated us as it treated all its children.'

Let us recall the great teachings given to us by both human conscience and French conscience. Let us help those who suffer. Is tolerance not already a barbaric word? Must we tolerate the right of men to breathe, to live freely?

Do you love one another? Let us stay faithful to this sublime phrase which has united the elites from the Gospel to Beethoven's Ninth Symphony. Let us rush to the aid of the victims, whoever they may be, let us work with the same heart for this universal conscience which is no more than an aspiration, but one that we hope some day to make a reality.

Jean-Paul Sartre

*J*ean-Paul Sartre was one of the most prominent French writers and thinkers of the twentieth century and a leading existentialist. Born in 1905, he was drafted into the French army in his twenties and again in 1939, serving on both occasions as a meteorologist. He was captured by the Germans in 1940 and spent nine months as a prisoner of war before being released in 1941. In Vichy France he resumed teaching, being given a position replacing a Jewish teacher. Sartre dipped his toe in the resistance movement before throwing all his energy into writing, penning his earliest philosophical work. Shortly after the liberation of Paris in August 1944 he wrote Anti-Semite and Jew (under the more obviously controversial title Réflexions sur la question juive), an existential examination of four characters: the antisemite, the democrat, the authentic Jew, and the inauthentic Jew, and how each character both defines the others and is defined by them.*

The powerful first part, 'Portrait of the Antisemite' – an edited section of which is reproduced below – was published in December 1945, though the full text did not appear until 1946. The work gives a unique perspective from a unique point in history: attempting to take an existential view of the aetiology of hate by analysing antisemitic hate whilst the fires of the Shoah were still burning across Europe. Indeed one of the reasons for writing the book was Sartre's realization that in discussions about post-war

France the imminent return of French Jews deported by the Nazis was never mentioned. In 1944, in recently liberated France, Sartre perhaps did not know that so many were never to return (though rumours and evidence of the death camps had circulated amongst the Allies as early as 1942); by December 1945 the realities were apparent (the Nuremberg trials had begun in November), and by 1946 it was impossible to ignore. Even so, Sartre makes only brief mention.

The sociologist Patrick Baert in his recent work on the phenomenon of the public intellectual examines Sartre's position and motivation in a little more detail. He points to two reasons why Sartre stops short of condemnation or culpability, the first due to the political sensitivities of the day and the second due to Sartre's need and desire at this particular point in time to establish himself as a public intellectual:

> In short, whilst Sartre was one of the first to systematically analyse anti-Semitism and to bring it to the fore at this point in time, there is no doubt that he consciously or unconsciously curtailed his applied existentialism according to the political sensitivities of the day, stopping short of writing openly of the French treatment of the Jews and their involvement in their deportation to the concentration camps.
>
> More significantly, there is another omission in the text, one which concerns Sartre directly and which is intimately related to his silence about the French involvement. Whilst in other publications in this period Sartre positioned himself as an engaged writer and virulently condemned authors who did nothing to halt the injustice and atrocities of their time, it is worth qualifying this 'heroic' stance with two observations. Firstly, Sartre propagated this position precisely when the political context had become safer again and when taking a political stance had (at least for a while) become more of a symbolic act than one which made a 'real' difference. Secondly, at crucial points during the war he himself had not spoken out when it really mattered.

Anti-Semite and Jew

1944
Translated by George J. Becker

Never believe that anti-Semites are completely unaware of the absurdity of their replies. They know that their remarks are frivolous, open to challenge. But they are amusing themselves, for it is their adversary who is obliged to use words responsibly, since he believes in words. The anti-Semites have the right to play. They even like to play with discourse for, by giving ridiculous reasons, they discredit the seriousness of their interlocutors. They delight in acting in bad faith, since they seek not to persuade by sound argument but to intimidate and disconcert. If you press them too closely, they will abruptly fall silent, loftily indicating by some phrase that the time for argument is past. It is not that they are afraid of being convinced. They fear only to appear ridiculous or to prejudice by their embarrassment their hope of winning over some third person to their side.

If then, as we have been able to observe, the anti-Semite is impervious to reason and to experience, it is not because his conviction is strong. Rather his conviction is strong because he has chosen first of all to be impervious.

He has chosen also to be terrifying. People are afraid of irritating him. No one knows to what lengths the aberrations of his passion will carry him – but he knows, for this passion is not provoked by something external. He has it well in hand; it is obedient to his will: now he lets go the reins and now he pulls back on them. He is not afraid of himself, but he sees in the eyes of others a disquieting image – his own – and he makes his words and gestures conform to it. Having this external model, he is under no necessity to look for his personality within himself. He has chosen to find his being entirely outside himself, never to look within, to be nothing save the fear he inspires in others. What he flees even more than Reason is his intimate awareness of himself. But someone will object: What if he is like that only with regard to the Jews? What if he otherwise conducts himself with good sense? I reply that that is impossible. There is the case of a fishmonger who in 1942, annoyed by the competition of two Jewish fishmongers who were concealing their race, one fine day took pen in hand and denounced them. I have been assured that this fishmonger was in other respects a mild and jovial man, the best of sons. But I don't believe it. A man who finds it entirely natural to denounce other men cannot have our conception of humanity; he does not see even those whom he aids in the same light as we do. His generosity, his kindness are not like our kindness, our generosity. You cannot confine passion to one sphere …

For the anti-Semite, what makes the Jew is the presence in him of 'Jewishness', a Jewish principle analogous to phlogiston or the soporific virtue of opium. We must not be deceived: explanations on the basis of heredity and race came later; they are the slender scientific coating of this primitive conviction. Long before Mendel and Gobineau there was a horror of the Jew, and those who felt it could not explain it except by saying, like Montaigne of his friendship for La Boétie: 'Because he is he, because I am I.' Without the presence of this metaphysical essence, the activities ascribed to the Jew would be entirely incomprehensible. Indeed, how could we conceive of the obstinate folly of a rich Jewish merchant who, we are told, makes every effort to ruin his country, whereas if he were reasonable, he would desire the prosperity of the country in which he does business? How could we otherwise understand the evil internationalism of men whom their families, their affections, their habits, their interests, the nature and source of their fortunes should attach to the destiny of a particular country?

Facile talkers speak of a Jewish will to dominate the world. Here again, if we did not have the key, the manifestations of this will would certainly be unintelligible to us. We are told in almost the same breath that behind the Jew lurks international capitalism and the imperialism of the trusts and the munitions makers, and that he is the front man for piratical Bolshevism with a knife between its teeth. There is no embarrassment or hesitation about imputing responsibility for communism to Jewish bankers, whom it would horrify, or responsibility for capitalist imperialism to the wretched Jews who crowd the rue des Rosiers. But everything is made clear if we renounce any expectation from the Jew of a course of conduct that is reasonable and in conformity with his interests, if, instead, we discern in him a metaphysical principle that drives him *to do evil* under all circumstances, even though he thereby destroy himself. This principle, one may suspect, is magical. On the one hand, it is an essence, a substantial form, and the Jew, whatever he does, cannot modify it, any more than fire can keep itself from burning. On the other hand, it is necessary in order to be able to hate the Jew – for one does not hate natural phenomena like earthquakes and plagues of locusts – that it also have the virtue of freedom. Only the freedom in question is carefully limited: the Jew is free *to do evil*, not good; he has only as much free will as is necessary for him to take full responsibility for the crimes of which he is the author; he does not have enough to be able to achieve a reformation. Strange liberty, which instead of preceding and constituting the essence, remains subordinate to it, is only an irrational quality of it, and yet remains liberty.

There is only one creature, to my knowledge, who is thus totally free and yet chained to evil; that is the Spirit of Evil himself, Satan. Thus the Jew is assimilable to the spirit of evil. His will, unlike the Kantian will, is one which wills itself purely, gratuitously, and universally to be evil. It is *the* will to evil. Through him Evil arrives on the earth. All that is bad in society (crises, wars, famines, upheavals, revolts) is directly or indirectly imputable to him. The anti-Semite is afraid of discovering that the world is ill-contrived, for then it would be necessary for him to invent and modify, with the result that man would be found to be the master of his own destinies, burdened with an agonizing and infinite responsibility. Thus he localizes all the evil of the universe in the Jew. If nations war with each other, the conflict does not arise from the fact that the idea of nationality, in its present form, implies imperialism and the clash of interests. No, it is because the Jew is there, behind the governments, breathing discord. If there is a class struggle, it is not because the economic organization leaves something to be desired. It is because Jewish demagogues, hook-nosed agitators, have seduced the workers.

Anti-Semitism is thus seen to be at bottom a form of Manichaeism. It explains the course of the world by the struggle of the principle of Good with the principle of Evil. Between these two principles no reconciliation is conceivable; one of them must triumph and the other be annihilated. Look at Céline: his vision of the universe is catastrophic. The Jew is everywhere, the earth is lost, it is up to the Aryan not to compromise, never to make peace. Yet he must be on his guard: if he breathes, he has already lost his purity, for the very air that penetrates his bronchial tubes is contaminated. Does that not read like a diatribe by a Manichaean?

...

To be sure, not all the enemies of the Jew demand his death openly, but the measures they propose – all of which aim at his abasement, his humiliation, his banishment – are substitutes for that assassination which they meditate within themselves. They are symbolic murders. Only, the anti-Semite has his conscience on his side: he is a criminal in a good cause. It is not his fault, surely, if his mission is to extirpate Evil by doing Evil. The *real* France has delegated to him the powers of her High Court of Justice. No doubt he does not have occasion every day to make use of them, but we should not be misled on that account. These sudden fits of anger which seize him, these thundering diatribes which he hurls at the 'Yids', are so many capital executions. The anti-Semite has chosen to be a criminal, and a criminal *pure of heart*. Here again he flees responsibilities.

Though he censures his murderous instincts, he has found a means of sating them without admitting it to himself. He knows that he is wicked, but since he does Evil *for the sake of Good*, since a whole people waits for deliverance at his hands, he looks upon himself as a sanctified evil-doer. By a sort of inversion of all values, of which we find examples in certain religions – for example, in India, where there exists a sacred prostitution – the anti-Semite accords esteem, respect and enthusiasm to anger, hate, pillage, murder, to all the forms of violence. Drunk with evil, he feels in himself the lightness of heart and peace of mind which a good conscience and the satisfaction of a duty well done bring.

The portrait is complete. If some of those who readily assert that they detest the Jews do not recognize themselves in it, it is because in actual fact they do not detest the Jews. They don't love them either. While they would not do them the least harm, they would not raise their little fingers to protect them from violence. They are not anti-Semites. They are not anything; they are not *persons*. Since it is necessary to appear to be something, they make themselves into an echo, a murmur, and, without thinking of evil – without thinking of anything – they go about repeating learned formulas which give them the right of entry to certain drawing rooms. Thus they know the delights of being nothing but an empty noise, of having their heads filled with an enormous affirmation which they find all the more respectable because they have borrowed it. Anti-Semitism is only a justification for their existence. Their futility is such that they will eagerly abandon this justification for any other, provided that the latter be more 'distinguished'. For anti-Semitism is *distinguished*, as are all the manifestations of a collective and irrational soul which seek to create an occult and conservative France. It seems to all these featherbrains that by repeating with eager emulation the statement that the Jew is harmful to the country they are performing a rite of initiation which admits them to the fireside of social warmth and energy. In this sense anti-Semitism has kept something of the nature of human sacrifice.

It has, moreover, a considerable advantage for those people who are aware of their profound instability and are weary of it. It permits them to put on the externals of passion and, as has been fashionable since the Romantic movement, to confuse this with personality. These second-hand anti-Semites can provide themselves at little cost with an aggressive personality. One of my friends often used to tell me about an elderly cousin of his who came to dine with his family and about whom they said, with a certain air: 'Jules can't abide the English.' My friend doesn't recall that they ever said anything else about Cousin Jules. But that was enough. There was a tacit understanding between Jules and his family: they ostentatiously avoided talking about the English in front of him, and that precaution gave him a semblance of existence in the eyes of those about him at the same time that it provided them with the agreeable sensation of participating in a sacred ceremony. Then on occasion after careful deliberation, someone, as if by inadvertence, would throw out an allusion to Great Britain or her dominions. Cousin Jules, pretending to become very angry, would feel himself come to life for a moment, and everybody would be happy. Many people are anti-Semites in the way Cousin Jules was an Anglophobe, without, to be sure, realizing the true implications of their attitude. Pale reflections, reeds shaken by the wind, they certainly would not have invented anti-Semitism, if the conscious anti-Semite did not already exist. But it is they who with complete indifference assure the survival of anti-Semitism and carry it forward through the generations.

We are now in a position to understand the anti-Semite. He is a man who is afraid. Not of the Jews, to be sure, but of himself, of his own consciousness, of his liberty, of his instincts, of his responsibilities, of solitariness, of change, of society, and of the world – of everything except the Jews. He is a coward who does not want to admit his cowardice to himself; a murderer who represses and censures his tendency to murder without being able to hold it back, yet who dares to kill only in effigy or protected by the anonymity of the mob; a malcontent who dares not revolt from fear of the consequences of his rebellion. In espousing anti-Semitism, he does not simply adopt an opinion, he chooses himself as a person. He chooses the permanence and impenetrability of stone, the total irresponsibility of the warrior who obeys his leaders – and he has no leader. He chooses to acquire nothing, to deserve nothing; he assumes that everything is given him as his birthright – and he is not noble. He chooses finally a Good that is fixed once and for all, beyond question, out of reach; he dares not examine it for fear of being led to challenge it and having to seek it in another form. The Jew only serves him as a pretext; elsewhere his counterpart will make use of the Negro or the man of yellow skin. The existence of the Jew merely permits the anti-Semite to stifle his anxieties at their inception by persuading himself that his place in the world has been marked out in advance, that it awaits him, and that tradition gives him the right to occupy it. Anti-Semitism, in short, is fear of the human condition. The anti-Semite is a man who wishes to be pitiless stone, a furious torrent, a devastating thunderbolt – anything except a man.

Jean Pierre-Bloch

*J*ean Pierre-Bloch was a Jewish French politician and resistance
leader who succeeded Bertrand Lecache as President of LICA and
was instrumental in adding the fight against racism which changed
the name to LICRA in 1979. He was one of the few French politicians before
the war to oppose the Munich Agreement, fearing for the fate of the German
Jews. When war was declared he enlisted and was captured in 1940 before
escaping and joining the resistance. He was captured and escaped again
and this time joined de Gaulle in London, where he joined the Free French
government. Having been a member of LICA's executive committee since
1937, after the war he became president of the National Press Corporation,
formed by the French government to liquidate the property of newspapers
and advertising agencies that had collaborated with the Germans, before
succeeding Lecache in 1968, a position he held till 1992 and finally in an
honorary capacity till his death in 1999.

Discours au Centre de Documentation Juive Contemporaine

22 October 1951

It is with great pleasure that I accept your kind invitation to speak at the
Centre for Contemporary Jewish Documentation. I admire your work,

and I do not forget that the Centre lived through the sombre time of the occupation and that you, its President, Schneersohn, took this dangerous initiative whilst you were being hunted by the enemy.

You wish to oppose forgetting. You are right. We are criticized for speaking, for speaking too much. Silence is a form of forgetting.

In the past, Jewish thought, which was purely religious in essence, saw the abuses that Jews suffered in their diaspora as a curse from God, just like epidemics or earthquakes. The enemy itself, or its nature, or the motives for its actions, were of no interest to Jewish thought. Once a massacre had ended, we thought only of coming to the aid of the survivors, of burying the victims, of mourning their loss. The simple fact that in France, under occupation, Jewish people created an organization whose task was both to preserve unimpeachable documentary evidence of Nazi crimes and to study all facets of the nature, ideology and methods of action of the enemy, represents a new and significant aspect of Jewish attitudes in the face of danger.

To know one's enemy is of the greatest importance for whoever wishes to resist that enemy. Therein lies the deep significance which in 1943 we attributed to the opening of the Centre for Contemporary Jewish Documentation, and that is why I personally consider this to be a fighting institution rather than a purely scientific one.

Because, in fact, the Centre for Documentation does not merely collect documents, it makes use of the most precious ones. M. de Menthon, Member of Parliament for the Popular Republican Movement (MRP), my ex-colleague in the Provisional Government of the French Republic, has said that at the Nuremberg trials, where he chaired the French delegation, he was dependent in large part on documents from the Centre. He also affirms that if the Centre had not existed, the proceedings would not have had the same results.

The Centre possesses documents which prove the guilt of war criminals and their collaborators, and, it must be noted, if these documents were not present today it would be said that these people were not guilty. Personally, I must say that I would have liked to spend long hours in your offices in order to read and to devour everything, to reread all the admirable documents that you have collected.

The Centre does not work solely for France. The important material and documents it holds, and the eighteen works based on those documents that it has published, deal with German attitudes towards Jews in all the occupied countries. Thus the Centre has the great honour of having published a book which recounts the uprising in the Warsaw ghetto, where we recently celebrated a painful anniversary. It has been crucial, in the face of racists and anti-Semites, to show the world the reality of the struggle and heroism of the Jews, and to disprove the contemptible legend of the cowardly Jew.

I must say, however, how sad and distressing it is, five years after Liberation, to go from meeting to meeting, to talk to the public about the political causes of anti-Semitism and the means of combating it. Yes, for four years, during that at once painful and wonderful time when we fought alongside those men who were not our political allies and who did not share our philosophical convictions or our religious faith, but who, like us, thought of nothing else but the health of our homeland, the liberation of France, the restoration of freedoms, we did not think that upon emerging from this night we would have to repeat once more the words of Aristide Briand, to firmly grasp our pilgrim's staff, and to fight courageously against this leprosy called anti-Semitism.

We believed that once the storm had passed over France she would be more or less identical to how she had been before. It is a strange, deceptive sight that we see today, one that would lend itself well to bitter thoughts and could almost discourage us from action.

Each one of us said to himself: 'When the challenge has been overcome, I will live in a new country, with men who will be bound with me into new relationships, human relationships.' Yes, we thought that the day after Liberation we would find our old friends the same as they were before, as if nothing had happened.

As parents we all thought that perhaps our sons, our daughters, our children would never again hear a cry of 'Dirty Jew' at school or at college, that cry which struck us, which painfully marked us, and which although we had barely reached the age of reason made us fearfully ask our parents what that sinister war cry meant.

We must recognize now, in 1951, that we are still engaged in the struggle and the defence, because Hitler did win the war on that level: he knew very well that through racism he would corrupt the world.

Furthermore, in Germany, no one has renounced the legacy of hate which Hitler left in the last phrases of his testimony:

'I confer on the leaders of the nation and faithful Nazis the responsibility to scrupulously maintain racial laws and the implacable opposition against the global poisoner of all peoples, international Judaism.'

This sinister message from beyond the grave continues to infect minds in Germany. No one will be surprised to learn that at this time the action of the Centre for Jewish Documentation as a fighting institution is particularly important in the face of the impudent renaissance of Nazism.

The main characteristics of this renaissance are exposed in all the newspapers and are known by all. But certain traits, although not so well known, are no less significant to us. Let me cite an example. The Chancellery of the German Evangelical Church asked the Centre, in a letter dated 12 May 1951, to indicate the sources from which it calculated the exact number of Jewish victims of Nazi terror, since, the letter adds, 'a large part of German public opinion doubts the figure of six million, on the pretext of not knowing what data informed this estimate'. Likewise Bardèche, the French pro-Nazi writer, is, alas, no exception.

A further characteristic trait is the following. A German book, published this year in Stuttgart, is entitled *Mass Murders in World History*. The book's author is Gerhart Ludwig and with the meticulous precision of the Germans he examines the great massacres perpetrated over two thousand years, all with the evident aim of drowning out Hitler's massacres. Hitler's name is not even mentioned in the work. The massacres of Jews by the Nazis are admittedly not ignored, but they are cited in the same way as the attempted assassination of Hitler in a Munich restaurant in November 1939, of which there were but a few victims.

These facts say a lot about the underhand and methodical work that is taking place in Germany at the moment, if not to absolve Nazism of responsibility then at least to present it as a normal historical circumstance.

In order to react against such a spirit, of which we find traces not only in Germany but also, it must be said, elsewhere, there is no more effective means than the conservation in Jewish hands that are independent of all political pressure, whatever form that might take, and the presentation of those documents at the desired moment.

The Centre for Jewish Documentation is the only institution in Europe, if not in the world, which lends the Jewish cause such a service. For this reason, it is absolutely essential that this institution be supported. Its disappearance would constitute a great loss to Jewish action in practical and immediate terms as well as a loss to the moral prestige not only of Judaism but of all those who struggle for world liberation.

It is useful to recall that before the war the great Russian liberal historian and publicist Paul Milioukoff agreed to speak at the trial of the notorious *Protocols of the Elders of Zion*, which was taking place in Switzerland. He found himself short of documentation. So he said to his Jewish friends: 'How is it that the Jews, who give so much money to charity, have not found a way to create an institution which preserves the documentation of the persecutions of which they are the victims?' It is not necessary to pose such a question today, after everything that the Jews have endured under the swastika.

I speak before you this evening as a politician and as a socialist. I am obliged to note that, five years after Liberation, Xavier Vallat is free, busy contemplating the blue sky of the lovely Ardèche, and that Henri Béraud, who it would seem has been very ill, has left prison so that he should not have to feel the pain of dying behind bars. He is on parole, as one would say in legal jargon, and, for a reasonable sum; he is writing his *Rendez-Vous avec la Mort*, from which Brossolette, Péri and Médéric have not returned.[1] I see that all over France meetings are organized in favour of Charles Maurras, that great writer, since he is a great writer for a certain number of snobs, in favour of this man who, for political needs, and political games, has been one of the first to influence our navy, our army, and who has rotted our country more than anyone with his *Action Française*. And we are also forced to speak of Pétain. It is the French tradition to fall silent when a grave has only recently been filled. The French press have commented on the death of Philippe Pétain in moderation, but the old collaborators have tried to mark the ceremonies of his death with indecent demonstrations. Thus we too must speak of him.

There are those belonging to our religion who, in relation to this problem, avoid taking sides, the same people who, at the time of the Dreyfus affair, thought it was better not to get involved. Should I cite from memory the odious article by a certain Paul Lévy, in his newspaper *Aux Écoutes*, the reputation of which is already confirmed? As for us, we shoulder our responsibilities. Without Pétain, collaboration in France might not have been possible to the same extent. Without Pétain, there would have been no Laval. And Poliakov, in his book *Le Bréviaire de la Haine*, page 55, was able to declare with good reason:

The assistance Vichy gave to the Germans was essential, for it assured, through population census, the *numerus clausus*, and other preconditions, the isolation of Jews in the heart of the French population which was indispensable for the genocides, and it removed the occupier's concerns about police operations, carried out in the free zone, but also in the occupied zone, by the French police. Nothing will ever be able to clear the Vichy government of this deliberate complicity.

Without Pétain, there would never have been the roundups of elderly Israelites in Vichy. As far as I know the senile marshal did not protest in the least. Must we recall his disgusting response to the Chief Rabbi's protest? Let them not tell me that there was nothing he could do. That would be the proof that the Germans were the masters, and when a head of government wants to do something, he can, so long as he is free, set his moral strength against barbaric force.

Let us contrast with that the case of Christian X, who did everything he could to save the Jews of Denmark: 'An entirely natural action,' said the press attaché Helge Wamberg. 'Danish Jews are an integral part of the population.'

In spite of certain shameful Jews, we recall that Pétain and the Vichy government's assistance allowed racial legislation to be drawn up which, in its essence, went further than that of Berlin. To say that Pétain protected the Jews, as a weekly newspaper was blackmailed into saying, is to lie; it is to distort historical truth.

Anti-Semitism is a leprosy. Its roots are of distant origin, and they are in essence religious. A Christian, Nicolas Berdiaef, wrote in his *Christianisme Social* in April 1939: 'Religious anti-Semitism is the most serious form and the only one worth studying.'

Before anti-Semitism, there was an anti-Judaism which was pagan, Muslim, Christian, because if anti-Judaism belongs to all eras, anti-Semitism is a new term. It appeared relatively recently, in order to refer to a new ethos.

However, we must remember, Christianity is the daughter of Judaism. The Christian New Testament is built on the Jewish Old Testament. Based solely on this, Judaism should inspire respect. Must we remind Christians that Jesus was a Jew, that Saint Paul was a Jew, as were the Apostles? The Christians' holy book, the Bible, is the Jews' holy book translated into Latin. Rome inherited the Hebrew Bible. Who can deny that?

We understand perfectly well that such history may generate complexes, since it is usually possible to inherit only from someone who has died; otherwise it strangely resembles a theft. The Christian people, supposing that the relationship might be recognized, would in some way be the children of the Jewish people, and the church the daughter of the synagogue. This incontestable kinship should bring feelings of respect. It is true that this happened in the beginning, and we find traces even in the history of France. Many Christians attended Jewish temples before they attended the Roman church. But later the separation was brutal.

André Siegfried, like many other authors, recognized this formally:

'The West as we know it is the product of the Eastern Mediterranean, intellectually that of Greece, religiously that of Israel. Did not the Bible become our Book, out of preference over all others?'

Many Christians have at some time taken up the idea of the ritual crime of the Jews. In the Near East itself, this idea is deeply rooted in popular belief. And yet, in ancient times, it was not the Jews who were the recipients of that monstrous accusation but the first Christians. History is full of many testimonies to this hateful accusation. The facts have been clearly laid out in a recent work which merits careful reading, *Verus Israël* by Marcel Simon, and in the literature of the Middle Ages we find other accounts.

Minucius Felix, author of a dialogue entitled *Octavius*, at the beginning of the third century, produced the most striking document. Here is what he said about the Christians:

> The tale told of the initiation of recruits is as horrible as it is notorious. A very young boy, covered in flour so the novice may abuse without suspicion, is placed before the one who is to be initiated in the mysteries. Deceived by this floured mass that makes him think his blows are harmless, the neophyte kills the child by giving him invisible, hidden injuries. O sacrilege! They drink the blood of this child avidly; they squabble over his limbs and divide among themselves; they cement their alliance through this victim, through this complicity in the crime which they commit in mutual silence. (*Octavius*, IX, 6)

And how did the Christians defend themselves against these awful accusations? By invoking certain instructions of Jewish law to which most of them still submitted themselves, as the Council of Jerusalem had ordered (Acts 15: 29).

'We are so far from spilling human blood,' the Christian Octavius replied to Caelius, 'that we even abstain from the blood of the animals that we eat.'

It was the standard response to the standard accusation:

'How, an accused Christian said elsewhere, how could these people (the Christians) eat children, they who are forbidden even to eat the blood of animals without (special) reason?' (Eusebius, *Ecclesiastical History*, V, I, 26).

Let this not surprise us, the Christianity of the first centuries was Judaizing for a long time, more Judaizing and for longer than is commonly thought.

We have cited all the essential texts. They are suggestive. They clearly show that the accusation of the Jews of ritual crime has taken such a crude form that it was barely retained by the anti-Semites of the pagan world. It was against Christians that it took the form of infanticide and entered pagan public opinion, as Juster notes (*Les Juifs dans l'Empire Romain*, volume II, page 205), and it took certain Christians a curious lack of memory and centuries of forgetting to dare to use that monstrous accusation once more, against the Jews.

On a religious level, there is much to be done. Certain religious education books constantly appeal to the hatred of Jews. The curse of the death of Christ cannot lie upon the Jews for all eternity. This is not the place to show historically that it is false, and then, even if the Jews of Jerusalem did crucify Christ two thousand years ago, I do not see how my children or I myself are responsible.

Since the anti-Semites believe that the time has come to once again, glasses in hand, prepare for the eve of battle howling in the German fashion, and exchanging hateful words with the German masters of the French Stürmers and the German Gringoires[2], we take note, but let them not think that this will be as before; they will see that we are determined to defend ourselves.

Let us analyse their so-called doctrine. At the end of the seventeenth century and particularly at the beginning of the eighteenth century, so-called scholars, generally Germans, placing themselves on ethnic and national territory, denounced the Jews for the first time as foreigners of an inferior race, of suspect patriotism, as harmful parasites and conspirators lying in wait for any revolution. Throughout the history of the nineteenth century, we find the same key phrase with all anti-Semites everywhere: Jews are not men as others are.

This watchword comes from abroad. Deferral to foreigners is our constant recourse, the traditional recourse of factions and agitators. These are the Gauls who called Julius Cesar into Transalpine Gaul. The Bourguignons worked for the English kings. The Protestants turned to Britain, and members of the Catholic League to Spain. Finally, at the moment of revolution, the nobility asked for help from the German Emperor whilst noblemen from Brittany and the Vendée, despite their faith and their unshakable patriotism, did not hesitate to appeal to the English heretics. This nasty trait is the reverse side of a great French reality, which is none other than France's universal vocation.

Jews are foreigners: the theme of *Action Française* before the war, now taken up again by Nazi newspapers like *Rivarol*. Fine, let us accept their thesis. Jews are foreigners. Soon French Jews will officially have participated in two hundred years of French history. That is not much, but it is seventy years more than the Savoyards and the people of Nice, and it is at least as long as the Corsicans. It seems to me that not all their ancestors were French. Who would consider applying a worthless argument to them and calling them foreigners because, for example, they speak patois or because their great-grandfather was not French? What is true for them is true for the Israelites of France.

M. Isorni finished his electoral meetings with the cry of 'France for the French', and if Daniel Mayer or myself were to contradict this lawyer who has carved himself a Member of Parliament's seat from the body of an ex-Marshal of France, his friends would accuse us of being dirty wops. However, M. Isorni is a naturalized French citizen. It took a decree from Vichy to allow him to continue to represent cases at the Paris Bar. He has never even worn a French uniform. But oh yes, he is a model Frenchman. I apologize for talking about myself, but as far back as I can go, I find relatives and great-grandparents born in Paris, soldiers of Napoleon I, soldiers of 1870. Part of my family moved away from Alsace in 1870, they left everything behind so as not to become German. All around me, uncles and cousins are decorated with the Légion d'Honneur and the Croix de Guerre for the war of 1914–18. I myself fought in the war in 1939–40 and, at what was a very difficult time, I organized and prepared France's first arms drop by parachute. But as for me, I am a dirty wop and M. Isorni a great Frenchman. Strange. Strange. I wish I understood.

The properly anti-Semitic social classes pride themselves on their historical memory, and yet they forget that there have always been Jews in France. Under the Crusades, there were Jewish atrocities in France.

Therefore there were Jews in France. The Jews of Bordeaux, as Professor Malvesin's book shows, had citizenship rights in 1270, and certain individuals among them greatly honoured France.

During the occupation, the *Rivarol* of the time, *Je Suis Partout*, called Mendès-France 'Mendès-Egypt'. The author of this article was perhaps not even French, but he certainly did not know that, according to a notary act of 1685, which is to be found in the papers of the city of Bordeaux, the Mendès had the right to add 'France' to their name. But Mendès-France is also a wop, just as Montaigne was, that half-Jew from Bordeaux.

Anti-Semites heap contradictory criticisms on Jews, but as Péguy quite rightly said, anti-Semites do not know Jews at all, 'they speak about them, but they do not know them at all.'

He later added:

Well, think about it, it is not easy to be a Jew. You always aim contradictory criticisms at them. When the rich among them do not support others, when the rich among them are hard, you say: 'That's not surprising, they're Jews.' When the rich among them do support others you say: 'That's not surprising, they're Jews, they support their own.' Oh, my friend, wealthy Christians need only do the same. We do not prevent wealthy Christians from supporting others. No, it is not easy to be a Jew. When they remain impervious to the appeals of their brothers, to the cries of their wounded brothers around the world, you say: 'They are bad Jews.' And if they listen only to the cries coming from the Danube and the Dnieper, you say: 'They are betraying you, they are bad Frenchmen.' Thus, you pursue them, you continually heap contradictory criticisms upon them.

Alas, Péguy's writings are still terribly true today.

Anti-Semitism, whether political or religious, can be explained by a very plain psychological mechanism: among true Jews a particular trait can be identified, that is financial power, and it is applied to all Jews, rich or poor.

A banker is arrested. His name is Dupont. We would say that the banker Dupont has been arrested. If the banker is called Lévy, we would say that the Jewish banker Lévy has been arrested. I do not know if the hero of the Himalayas, [Maurice] Herzog, is Jewish, but I do know that if instead of a hero he had been a crook, an addition would have been made to his name: the Jew Herzog.

And nevertheless, every Christian has a Jewish friend. We all remember the words of Tristan Bernard who said: 'Every Christian has a perfect, honest, intelligent Jewish friend. Consequently, as there are thirty million Christians in France, there are many perfect, honest, intelligent Jews.'

When we speak of Tristan Bernard or Bergson, we do not add the word 'Jew' to their names. But when Stavisky was arrested, even though he wasn't Jewish, all the press wrote and repeated: the Jew Stavisky[3].

I remember another similar story. It was during the terrible years. An unfortunate coincidence meant that one day I found myself on a train with Philippe Henriot, a man for whom I held only contempt, and I was obliged to engage in conversation with him; I recalled this conversation in my memoirs *Mes Jours Heureux*. And as I was carrying secret papers in my case, I preferred to protect them throughout the journey. I told him that I had been reading *Gringoire*, and every time an article mentioned two politicians, Rosenfeld and Zyromsky, they wrote: 'the Jew Rosenfeld', 'the Jew Zyromsky', and that I knew for certain that neither one was Jewish. Philippe Henriot was very surprised. It was still at the beginning of the occupation. 'What you say is very interesting. From now on, when we refer to these two men in *Gringoire*, we will not use the word "Jew"'. The following week, I picked up *Gringoire*, and of course, there it was again, as usual, the word 'Jew' was placed squarely next to the names of Rosenfeld and Zyromsky.

Thus when a Jew commits a crime, all Jews are responsible, but if a Jew is a great artist, a great painter, we hesitate to recognize him. Moreover, when a politician holds certain opinions, for example when in Russia a man named Trotsky demonstrated a certain spirit of independence, there was renewed anti-Semitism because Trotsky was of Jewish origin.

I apologize for telling anecdotes at a conference which gives no grounds for laughter, but I believe that this anecdote about a Montmartre singer is entirely typical. A Jewish-looking man was attacked in the street by an individual, was beaten, and asked his aggressor: 'Why have you beaten me?' The reply came: 'Because your ancestors killed Christ.' 'But that was two thousand years ago.' 'That may be, but I've only just found out.' This encapsulates all the stupidity of anti-Semitism.

If Jews did not exist, they would have to be invented, said Göring. This is a fact, such are anti-Semitic tendencies. But we must recall that anti-Semitism is above all reactionary and Fascist. It is not because certain Jews will give their support to a right-wing league, one which does not flaunt itself openly, and which awaits the moment to show its true colours, that anything will change. We must fight openly against this leprosy which goes by the name of anti-Semitism, we must try to discover its causes and to combat them mercilessly.

Moreover, anti-Semitism is nothing but a pretext here. We could equally discriminate against Blacks or Asians. The entire history of the twentieth century makes this patently clear. Anti-Semitism is used to ends that have nothing to do with Jews. Jews play the role of the scapegoat, the cause of all wrongdoing. Sometimes, anti-Semitism is used in order to resolve social problems, whether in Russia, in Romania, in Poland, or in France during the Dreyfus affair.

In Russia, pogroms were organized by the Tsar's police. They constituted a useful diversion from the misery of the people and the growing revolt against the Tsar's authority. Jews were killed, popular anger was directed towards Jews, thus it was hoped that revolution would be avoided. The Tsar's police prepared and organized all the anti-Semitic literature and used arguments from the *Protocols of the Elders of Zion* to affirm the reality of a Jewish plot against society. A few weeks ago, in 1951, *Rivarol* did not hesitate to use and arrange the *Protocols* to suit their needs. In Hitler's speeches and in those of his party leaders, the authenticity of the *Protocols* is said to be as hard as iron. However, the circumstances and conditions of this falsification have long been known the world over.

According to the *Protocols*, secret representatives of the twelve tribes of Israel laid the plans for the Jewish plot at the Zionist congress in Bâle in 1897, in order to build Jewish hegemony on the ruins of the Christian world. In reality, the *Protocols* were written between 1890 and 1895 by Ratchowski and Nilus, agents of the Okhrana, the Russian secret police, who were residing in Paris, and they were published for the first time in Russia in a reactionary newspaper. These pseudo-protocols, utterly foreign to the Jewish spirit, are in fact plagiarized from a satirical pamphlet – a dialogue in hell between Machiavelli and Montesquieu, published in 1864 by a French lawyer and journalist, Maurice Joly, against Napoleon III – and from a novel entitled *Biarritz*, published between 1866 and 1870 by the German novelist Goetsche, under the pseudonym Sir John Redcliffe. The sources of the *Protocols* and the circumstances of their publication have been examined and irrefutably established, notably in a series of articles which appeared in the *Times* of London in 1921, following the discovery of Joly's book in Constantinople by Mr Kraf, a Russian émigré and correspondent of the *Times*. This confirmed previous declarations made in America by Princess Catherine Radziwill, and in the findings of the Berne tribunal of 14 May 1935, which declared that the *Protocols* constituted a fake, as well as an immoral publication, punishable by article 14 of the Berne law against obscene publications.

What is more, a wise Belgian Jesuit named Reverend Father Charles showed, similarly to Louvain[4], in a study reproduced in the *Nouvelle Revue Théologique* that the *Protocols of the Elders of Zion* are nothing more than a bizarre series of constructions without foundation, that at every moment they betray the incoherencies of their author and his ignorance of the most basic notions, and that no one could ever carry them out because they swarm with contradictions and visible insanities. The aim of the *Protocols* is to make Jews seem hateful by stirring up the thoughtless, blind passions of the masses against them. And the Reverend Father Charles writes: 'The evidence that they are false is so startling that even the fiercest opponents have been convinced. The desperate expedients to which they turned so as to not lay down this poisoned weapon that is the Protocols are based on no serious science whatsoever.'

The Reverend Father adds in his study written in 1943, which sadly has lost none of its relevance: 'We must put an end to this. The adversaries of the Jews have stated that to question the authenticity of the Protocols was completely futile because even if they were false, these Protocols remain true in that they perfectly depict Jewish ways of being and thinking.'

We see, by this anti-Semitic affirmation, that Péguy was right almost forty years ago. And it was through the use of the *Protocols of the Elders of Zion* that thousands and thousands of Jews were murdered in Russia, under the tyranny of the Tsars.

In Romania, when the middle classes judged that Jewish influence was extending too far and that Jews were becoming dangerous competitors, they adopted the slogan: 'Jews are the enemies of Christian society, they monopolize every space.'

Similarly in Poland, the fight against the Jews is full of contradictions. It was said that: 'Jews are friends of the Russians, we must kill them.' And when the Russians invaded Poland they said: 'Jews are friends of the Poles, we must kill them.'

Then in France we had the Dreyfus affair, a banal affair, one of those judicial errors of which there are sadly so many. But there, the captain accused of treason was a Jew. Politicians, writers, not all of whom are Jewish, were convinced of his innocence, and produced documents which proved that captain's innocence. Immediately, we heard the clamour of a Jewish union, composed of millions and millions, which came together to save the traitor. However, as Léon Blum, whose loss we keenly feel every day, wrote of the Dreyfus affair in his *Souvenirs sur l'Affaire*: 'The Jewish masses greeted the start of the revisionist campaign with great mistrust. The predominant feelings can be expressed in a formula like this: it is something the Jews should not get involved in. Above all they did not want to, in supporting a just cause, feed the fires of anti-Semitic passions.'

And yet, the anti-Semitic wave was unleashed. But this wave of anti-Semitism, our old folk recall, manifested as electoral brawls, fist fights, public meetings at which the words 'dirty Jew' were pronounced. Our grandparents could hardly imagine that these battles of anti-Semitism were nothing compared to what we were to endure between 1940 and 1944.

Under the Third Republic, there was always daily anti-Semitism. Which politician of Jewish origin, whether it was Léon Blum or Georges Mandel, did not hear the words 'dirty Jew' in a meeting? We did not fear contradictions. When Léon Blum was in power, Jews were still revolutionaries. When Georges Mandel became Minister of the Interior, all Jews wanted to work for capitalism and the war.

Those were magnificent moments, in 1914, when the sacred union silenced the anti-Semites, when Maurice Barrès called upon all the children of France, Catholic, Protestant and Jewish, to defend our motherland.

And then, long after that war, Hitler appeared, and preparations began in Munich. Hitler's work was carried out openly. Little by little, we saw supposedly French newspapers preparing, working public opinion, those newspapers that, during the occupation, placed themselves so readily at the service of the occupier. Today we unfortunately forget this too easily. Those newspapers received their orders from Berlin. Every day they repeated: the Jews want war to avenge their religious brothers who were massacred in Germany. But when mobilization came, the same newspapers, with *Je Suis Partout* at the helm, affirmed all of a sudden that the Jews had become pacifists, that they would not go to the front, they did not do their duty, that there was not a single Jew on the front line. The work was done bit by bit, it was thought that the slogan 'Go to war for Czechoslovakia' was outmoded, and a new slogan was made popular, which I remember having heard even in the corridors of the House, from parliamentarians who repeated: the war is for the Jews, it has nothing to do with France.

And I need not remind you this evening of the appalling drama which unfolded over four years, and which meant that, despite all the denial of anti-Semites, despite the ignoble discussion of these figures, 6 million Jews were exterminated in Europe between 1940 and 1944.

And still, today, anti-Semitism is not dead. On the contrary, it is beginning to hold its head high once more, and its political causes run deeper than ever, mixed with economic causes. Wright, the celebrated Black author, recently wrote that: 'There's no black problem in the United States, but a white problem.' I would similarly say that the fight against anti-Semitism is not a Jewish problem, it is the problem of all men of good will, and it is above all a Christian problem.

I know that this is a delicate issue, but I think that we must speak about it. The child who in their catechism has in a certain way learnt that the Jews crucified Christ is marked for the rest of his life, in the same way that the child who learnt that Joan of Arc was burnt in Rouen by the English will struggle to understand that the English are our friends. I would say however that the Rouen clergy is not struck with infamy because, centuries ago, a priest participated in the death of Joan of Arc.

Thus we must place the fight against anti-Semitism in the hands of the Catholic Church. There are courageous priests and bishops who battle against this problem, and I must say for my part that every time the Pope welcomes those who visit him in the name of Judeo-Christian friendship his words are full of hope. And we must remember the message of powerful reason and moving sensibility that was addressed to Rome at the Catholic Congress by the great writer Jacques Maritain, who was at that time French ambassador to the Vatican.

'The fight against anti-Semitism,' he said, 'is a fundamental obligation for our conscience, and a primordial duty of moral salubrity for what is left of our civilization.'

Jacques Maritain explored the problem of anti-Semitism above all from a Christian point of view, and with his Catholic faith, which he links, with infinite respect, to its origins. Does it not contain the elevated teachings of Moses and his prophets? He implores Christians to remember. How many more times, he frets, will many of them repudiate the teaching of Saint Paul, who teaches us that we were grafted onto the olive tree of Israel, and that we came to share its roots and its sap?

Pope Pius XI said that spiritually, we are Semites. More than being a problem of blood, or life, or of physical death for Jews, anti-Semitism is a problem of the spirit, of life or spiritual death for Christians, and I would add for all honest men. Never before had the duty of Christians been affirmed with such force. Let us pay tribute to Jacques Maritain who went as far as to say that: 'For as long as the world which calls itself Christian civilization does not cure itself of anti-Semitism, it will drag with it a sin which will be an impediment to its recovery.'

Nazism, with its anti-Christian as well as anti-Jewish excesses, has given us food for thought. We hope that Christians of good faith become numerous enough to bring about a complete reversal of the Church's political attitude in relation to the Synagogue.

We, as men infatuated with progress and freedom, must combat the relics of the Nazi racist spirit wherever they show themselves. Men of good will must form a chain with all those who are concerned with defending democracy and freedom. Jews must be at the front line of this struggle for their freedoms and the freedoms of others, they must be at the front line of the emancipation of their people anywhere in the world, and they must throw themselves into the struggle wherever men are persecuted because they are men.

It is precisely in such a struggle that the Centre for Contemporary Jewish Documentation has constituted a matchless arsenal. Thanks to the tens of thousands of authentic and unimpeachable German documents that are preserved in its archives we have the capacity to show, piece by piece, each cog of the most formidable and perfect extermination machine that racial hatred has ever set in motion. Is it necessary to underline the importance of such a contribution? It gives us the arms that are necessary in order to force racist propaganda to leave the vague and abstract domain it inhabits out of choice, and to confront it on the battleground of fact. With the Centre's documents in our hands, we are strong on this battlefield and it is easy for us to confound any attempt to minimize the extent of racist crimes or to prove the innocence of their perpetrators.

The document is an extraordinarily efficient weapon in our struggle. What can in fact be said when faced with a revelatory document duly signed by the executioner himself? Almost every document in the Centre's archives is a veritable confession on the part of the Nazis, a confession of their crimes, a confession of their criminal mentality par excellence.

I am thinking particularly of an official report, written by the 'expert' Wetzel, which exposes his ideas about the most rational way of exterminating – after the Jews and the Gypsies – the largest number of Slavs. This report, written at the order of a minister, officially presented to a State Government, thus far considered civilized and in the middle of the twentieth century, is startling proof that in the eyes of the Nazis the Jews were nothing more than the most defenceless prey, the easiest to seize but not the only one: their hatred extended much further; it aspired to destroy all of humanity.

The Wetzel report is only one document among thousands and thousands which the Centre has gathered, studied, classified and made immediately utilizable in the fight against racist Evil. I do not believe that it is an exaggeration in the slightest to say that the constitution of such an arsenal is an act of exceptional merit. It brings a new aspect to the struggle against anti-Semitism and racism, a struggle which already has a long history and which has had highs and lows, often tragically painful ones.

On a battlefield, a wounded man asked for a crucifix. The year was 1914. A chaplain went to find one, in the face of machine-gun fire, and was mortally wounded at the very moment he lifted the cross to the lips of the dying soldier. This chaplain was the great Rabbi Bloch of Lyon, of whom a poet wrote that he:

Falls and dies, sublime deist,
For a God that is not his own.

Thirty years later, a priest hid tens of Jewish children from the menace of deportation in his monastery near Lyon. He was later deported and would never return from Buchenwald.

Do these two images not prefigure the strongest reconciliation between Christianity and Israel?

Here is the basis of our Christian recognition of guilt in consideration of what happened. We did not recognize the Lord Christ when he came into our lives in the form of a suffering brother. I didn't recognize him when he was put in the camp as a Communist, nor did I recognize him, when he was murdered as an incurably ill person, nor did I recognize him, when he was gassed and burned as the poor victims of his own people. Here I became guilty in my very personal responsibility and I cannot excuse myself, neither before God, nor before humanity.

MARTIN NIEMÖLLER, *WAS WÜRDE JESUS DAZU SAGEN?*, 1980

Willy Brandt

W illy Brandt, a socialist politician, was Chancellor of West Germany from 1969 to 1974 and was awarded the Nobel Peace Prize in 1971 for his efforts to achieve reconciliation between West Germany and the Soviet bloc. A lifelong socialist, he was born in 1910 and fled from Germany to Norway in 1933 to escape Nazi persecution. During the war he escaped to neutral Sweden and became a Norwegian citizen, but he returned to Berlin in 1946, working for the Norwegian government before becoming a German citizen again in 1948. He was an active member of the Socialist Democratic Party for the rest of his life and as Mayor of West Berlin from 1957 to 1966 oversaw the city during one of its most tumultuous periods as the Berlin Wall was built. In 1961 John F. Kennedy saw Brandt as the best hope for Germany's future and invited him to visit him in the White House a month before the incumbent Chancellor was invited. Brandt didn't win the election and it would be another eight years till he took power, by which time West Germany had changed dramatically.

'Deutschland, Israel und die Juden' was delivered by Brandt six days after his meeting with Kennedy.

Later, as Chancellor, Brandt introduced the Neue Ostpolitik which achieved a degree of rapprochement with Eastern Germany and the Soviet Bloc. It was far from popular in West Germany but was the reason he was *awarded the Nobel Peace Prize. A seminal point came in December 1970 when Brandt, visiting Poland to sign the Treaty of Warsaw and finally and officially recognize Poland's borders, visited the Warsaw Ghetto to lay a wreath at the monument to the heroes of the uprising. Spontaneously and surprisingly, Brandt fell to his knees and remained there in silent commemoration for a short time, an unprecedented act by a German Chancellor. The act split German opinion, with a* Der Spiegel *poll finding that 48 per cent felt it was excessive, 41 per cent said it was appropriate and 11 per cent had no opinion. Nevertheless it is widely regarded as a key reason for his Nobel award.*

Germany, Israel and the Jews

OUR RESPONSIBILITY FOR THE PAST, MARCH 1961

It is not every day that a German is requested by his foreign Jewish friends to express his thoughts on the topic of 'Germany, Israel and the Jews'.

I would like to begin with the open profession that the relationship which exists today between Germany and the Jews is still nowhere near a state of relief and is also not in any condition to find itself in a state of harmony. Certainly, both sides have taken steps, and these I will address later on. However, no small acts of good will, reparations or restitutions can erase the horrendous crimes committed on millions of Jewish people in the name of the German people. These crimes will continue to burden the world in which we live for as long as it exists, and will only be wiped clean by the one who created us all.

This applies in general to the Nazi history as well. Nothing could be more improper than to attempt to blot out the years of the brown regime of terror, to deny its existence to a certain extent, and thereby to resume the cycle of German history which began in 1932. The history of Nazism exists, it must be borne. Our children and grandchildren must try to cope with this heritage. However, this does not mean that the shared burden becomes easier to bear by a constant referral to each individual's own responsibility or blame, his presence or his absence.

Spurred by outrage over the horrendous acts, the years following the war saw an organized attempt at the 'denazification' of millions of people, an attempt which failed, to a large extent, because those acts in question could never fully be grasped according to formal measurements. One could not, and one cannot, hope to progress by using generalizations. The German people are collectively neither good nor evil. They are not unalterable, and each individual's personal responsibility for what happened among the German people has – as we all know – little to do with their formal affiliation with this or that particular group. There were non-National Socialists who behaved worse during those dark years than other formal members of the Nazi party. There were judges of the Third Reich who attempted everything in their power to protect the victims of Nazi legislation who landed before their cabinet from prison and death. We should rather seek here to apply – and I am permitted to say this particularly before the Jewish people – the strict standards of the Ten Commandments. Against this standard, however, and in the most terrible ways possible, are not only hundreds, but thousands of people in violation.

The Unteachable are a Minority

But perhaps you are more likely to listen to the assessment of a man who abandoned his homeland as a young man in 1933, who was expatriated by Hitler, who was involved closely with both the Norwegian and German resistance movements, and who first returned to Germany when it had reached its lowest point – perhaps you are more likely to accept these statements than those coming from others who had either been forced or volunteered to take part in the wrongdoings that took place. In making your assessment, I must ask you, in the name of my people, to look as soberly and as justly as possible at the German situation. I would like to make my contribution by attempting to present to you an inventory of the internal situation of my people. I undertake to do this as a man who, unlike most others, has been able to travel throughout all parts of free Germany, who has got to know its people through countless conversations, and who, as the mayor of the German capital in the middle of the country, believes that he knows what this population looks like.

Of course, Germany can never be chemically wiped free of its 'Nazism' and from racial prejudices of any kind. The poison of Nazism penetrated too deeply into the national body to ever really be free of it. And of course, even today there are some unteachable individuals who claim that everything that happened was not really so bad, and of course one can still uncover anti-Semitic sentiment in Germany as well as, I fear, among many corners of the world. However, the problem of neo-Nazism should not be overestimated and thereby falsely evaluated.

Some of the most deplorable instances, such as those that were uncovered at the end of 1959 and in the first months of 1960, were in no way typical for the interior position of the German people or even of the youth. In a population of 50 million people – this based on the Federal Republic – there will always be aggressive factions of youth. But these swastika-bearing youths from Cologne or from other German cities are not symbolic of our youth. It would be a grave error to develop a prejudice against the entire adolescent generation of my country based on these terrible events.

Within the free part of Berlin, only a handful of youth among a population of 2.2 million people have been involved in right-wing extremist campaigns or organizations, and there is much to signal that their behaviour is more often due to adventurous urges or immaturity than to political identification. In a spontaneous and impressive demonstration held at the beginning of 1960, and without any preceding propaganda, 35,000 young Berliners took a stand opposite this handful to protest against anti-Semitism and chauvinism. This same thing has occurred in many other large cities.

The young generation of my country is sober and largely without illusions as well as – and I must include this, unfortunately – largely materialistic. There is little left of the romanticism of previous decades. Some may see this as the unfortunate manifestation of the lack of idealism, but this condition also contains an element of safety: these young people will certainly be much more cautious about following a brown-clad pied piper than their parents were. For example, when we play them records of Hitler's speeches, their reaction is usually a smile and complete incomprehension that such a significant portion of a relatively large population could appoint a maniac such as Hitler.

In the same way, the leading powers among the federal republic, I mean the men and women who consciously experienced the Nazi era and who are now in positions of political and cultural responsibility, are for the most part prepared to seriously confront the past and to be done with it. Of course not in small part due to a hapless law, there are still several officials in leading positions who would have been better off staying away from their current positions from a personal sense of shame. And of course, we are still facing personnel difficulties at our schools, at the universities and in our cultural establishments, which I do not wish to trivialize. But what I want to state with emphasis is this: Nazism no longer has a serious political home in Germany.

Our Honest Endeavour

Naturally, this is first of all only a negative finding, and it does not exclude the possibility that reactionary tendencies of one kind or another may still play a significant role in the future. It does not assume that anti-Semitism has disappeared. I rather believe that it has merely changed in character and that its foundation has worn thin. In any case, one cannot deny that for years now, earnest endeavours have been undertaken to enable an open and honest discussion about the relationship between Germany and the people of Jewish descent.

I would like to name a few examples to substantiate this. Together with other leading political powers, we participate in days of remembrance of our burdensome past, and every spring we observe a Week of Brotherhood, supported by the Society for Christian–Jewish Cooperation. We commemorate the destruction of the Warsaw Ghetto, most often combining this ceremony with a reference to the establishment of the state of Israel. We mark 20 July 1944 to honour the German resistance movement. We have committed 9 November to remember the frightful crime of the *Kristallnacht* in 1938. For years, our television, radio and press have presented an unvarnished portrayal of our past. An ongoing television series, lasting for several hours in the evening, has unsparingly confronted millions of Germans with the reality of these awful years of history. There are a multitude of films dealing with the fate of the Jews. We are pleased that these films are particularly attended by young people. The drama most often mentioned on the German stage in the last years has been *The Diary of Anne Frank*. This has actually led to a movement among the young generation as, year after year, young people have flocked to the mass grave in Bergen-Belsen which contains the remains of this Jewish girl.

We devote much of our attention in Berlin, as well as in other areas of free Germany, to political education, to civic instruction in our schools, and to the children of our officials. Above all, we encourage the political education of those who, as a function of their position, regularly engage with young people, in particular for teachers. For many older teachers, a political lesson nowadays often poses a confrontation with themselves. They were there, they participated – whether to a greater or lesser extent – in instructing young people with the ideologies of an unjust State during the Nazi era. And they are now faced with their students' uncomfortable questions, who are naturally interested in knowing about the personal stances that their teachers took during these years. Of even greater importance is that the new generation of teachers in our schools truly understand what happened, and that they recognize their responsibility, as instructors of these young people, to prepare them through their education to be more capable of resisting evil.

On this topic there are certainly not only success stories. There are also half-hearted measures and obvious inadequacies. But it has unmistakably been an honest endeavour throughout.

Pankow and the Jews

Let me pause here to make a particular remark about the situation in the other part of Germany, in the Soviet-occupied zone. Some people have felt compelled to involve themselves in the internal debates that I mentioned above, as well as with the Jewish populations in other countries, and in our relationship with the state of Israel. It would have been much better for these people to have remained silent.

By claiming to be the only real antifascists on German soil, the Communist Party propaganda machine, operated from East Berlin, have raised their voice and launched an exorbitant campaign against the German Federal Republic. They have unfortunately succeeded in garnering support in many parts of the world because their smokescreen of antifascist propaganda seeks to conceal their own sins. It is indeed a macabre fact and consequence of the nation's miserable division when people from both parts of the country accuse one another of Nazi tendencies before the eyes of the world. But we simply cannot tolerate the impression given to the rest of the world, that the Soviet zone, the so-called German Democratic Republic (GDR), is a hotbed of antifascism. This is not the case. There are men occupying highly influential and decisive positions among the East Berlin government who have given rise to the 'Thousand Year Reich'. The Soviet zone has persistently resisted restitutions of any kind from former Jewish residents living abroad today. It is therefore no coincidence that the number of Jewish citizens in the Soviet zone has decreased to 1,500, while the number in West-Berlin amounts to 27,000; 27,000 to 1,500 in a population ratio of 3:1.

Material Reparations

Let me now say some words about material reparations with a reminder of my comment at the beginning of the speech that none of what happened can in any way ever be repaired in the deepest sense of the word. The German Compensation Law, with a projected total liability of approximately 14 billion DM, has already settled some 52 per cent of the claims, accounting for almost 60 per cent of the entire sum of compensations. This is a remarkable feat, despite all of the law's shortcomings, and given the constant and necessary critique of the pace at which settlements have been reached. In its practical application, I am aware that the law has created considerable hardships, which the responsible committee of the German Bundestag is now working to address. It is my hope that these hardships will also be compensated. We will, admittedly, be unable to meet the original deadline set for the completion of compensations, 12 December 1961. This delay has arisen due to a number of practical difficulties related to the administrative processing of applications. The lion's share of reparation cases are located in Berlin, which is doing its best to process them as quickly and effectively as possible.

While the Reparation Act for Civil Service has been substantially settled, the Federal Law on Restitution still faces significant hurdles, not least due to the complex legal procedures involving international sources from beyond the German legal system.

If I may be permitted, I would also like to refer to a small, but not unimportant, form of relief that we have adopted in Berlin. The state of Berlin awards ongoing pensions or one-time allocations – depending on their current social situations – to non-Jewish citizens who offered protection and aid to persecuted Jews during the Nazi years. We do this to underscore the close relationships that existed between hundreds of Jews and non-Jews in Nazi Germany.

Israel and US

It is in this context that I would like to mention the Israel Agreement that the German Federal Republic has entered into in the course of making reparations, and that has transacted its material obligations of over 3 billion DM – this apart from agreements with Jewish organizations – very smoothly, from my point of view.

This brings me to the relationship of my own countrymen to that brave new state which has been forged by blood and tears in the ancient homeland of the Jewish people. It is with great pleasure that I am able to report that the younger generation of Germans in particular now view the State of Israel with an interest and a respect that few other countries have shown. The admiration for Israel's pioneering labour, for their determined self-assertion, but also for the realization that we occupy the same camp as Israel among international political debate – these are the factors that have raised our sympathies for the young nation; the fact that it is a particularly Jewish state does not play a key role.

Though it was limited to a brief visit last year, I was myself able to form a strong first impression of this state. The tremendous energy radiating from the state's unusual connection between modern development and the deep belief in the original unity of humankind has been one of the most powerful personal experiences I have had in the post-war years. Young Germans increasingly flock to this country. Some of them have volunteered themselves to undertake unpaid construction work in one of Israel's kibbutzes. This type of work is aptly referred to by young Germans as 'Action Reconciliation'. This is – and you will understand when I say this – just as invaluable as the payments that have been made to Israel.

Of course, my trip to Israel was misused by Soviet officials to incite the Arab states against Germany. If I may, I would briefly but emphatically respond by stating: my political colleagues and I are open for normal relationships with all countries who so desire and who accept without attaching unacceptable conditions. But I would like to emphasize that we – just as surely as in American politics – wish to promote a peaceful settlement among the peoples of the Middle East.

No Collective Guilt, But Collective Shame

Let me summarize my key points so far:

1. The adolescent and already partly grown-up generation offers a good foundation for human interaction and mutual understanding.
2. Leading powers amongst all parties in the German Federal Republic are now prepared to confront and deal with our past.

3. Anti-Semitism and chauvinism are no longer decisive forces in Germany.

4. We no longer need to start from ground zero, but have made strides in overcoming past prejudices.

The terrors of our past can neither be erased nor forgotten. However, if we continue only looking back, we risk losing the clarity of a future vision.

I must also ask for your understanding for a population of people in the post-war years who had to work hard in order simply to maintain a sparse existence. In 1945–6, the citizens of the German wasteland were not so much interested in their Nazi leaders and Nuremberg as they were in the question of how to obtain a few pounds of coal or potatoes.

In 1946, an American of German–Jewish descent made an enormous impression on me when he said: If a nation is to overcome hunger and begin rebuilding, its people must cease continuously hanging their heads and mumbling: we are guilty. It is precisely because the court of the victors did not pursue an internal self-cleansing in Germany that this much-quoted citation about the unresolved past of Germany could arise.

Our first Federal President, Professor Theodor Heuss, said that he did not believe in collective guilt. I agree with him accordingly, that there should rather be a sense of collective shame. Foreign observers have pointed out 1959 as the year in which the German Federal Republic began to deal meaningfully with its history. This same year gave rise to a series of court proceedings in which Nazi criminals were convicted. These proceedings aroused great public attention. They did not come about because of external pressure. They were not forced, and they began prior to the rise of neo-Nazism. This, and what has since arisen throughout the rest of the world, is not a sign that Nazism is making a comeback. Ruptured abscesses are the body's form of self-purification, and not a sign it has been newly poisoned.

The public debate throughout the last two years in my country has neither given rise to a revival nor to an increase in Nazi thought.

The Young German Democracy Requires Trust

No one can undo the past. This is a simple, and in this case, terrible truth. The past does not have a future. The present is the only opportunity for action.

This is about the reality of Germany today. This reality is called reparation, which no one has opposed. This reality is called legal security and belief in the law. I don't believe I have to convince you any longer that we Germans, and especially we Berliners, are determined to defend our democratic society and to sustain it in all of its vitality.

The land which I serve has evolved within the last sixteen years, despite the continued presence of criminals living undetected and hidden. No one can be sure how many such cases even exist. The fact that one of the worst may be discovered and brought to justice has just as much and just as little to do with the ongoing development of the Federal Republic of Germany as if he were never to be discovered.

And this is why, ladies and gentlemen, I may ask you to judge my country for what it is today, and not according to something which has only been a shadow since 1945 and which, if it does take shape again, is quick to resume a shadowy form once again.

I understand the problem of standing here as a German talking about reconciliation. But everything that Jewish religion and philosophy teaches is precisely about reconciliation, about justice, wisdom, and the love of humankind.

I have asked you to judge my country by its reality today. I must ask you to go a step further. Each of us is aware of how an unwarranted mistrust can maim and destroy. The German democracy requires trust. She deserves it because the innocent young generation should not be burdened with the sins and failings of their fathers. For the sake of these young people, I would like to ask for your oath, that you will help them to find a new beginning, so that the door may be opened for all those of good will to find their way in the family of free nations.

Translated by Becky L. Crook

Anatoly Shcharansky

*F*reedom For Soviet Jewry was the cause taken up by computer
scientist Anatoly (now Nathan) Shcharansky in the mid-1970s.
*The best-known 'refusenik' – denied permission to emigrate and
persecuted for having tried – was arrested in 1978, at the age of thirty,
and sentenced to thirteen years in prison and labour camp for 'treason,
espionage, and anti-Soviet agitation'. For eight years, his wife, Avital,
visited newspaper columnists and human-rights organizations and haunted
summit conferences to focus attention on his imprisonment and his cause
of free emigration. When he was freed, in what Soviet officials insisted was
an exchange of spies, the conclusion of his statement to the court on 14
July 1978 – as drawn from notes taken by his brother, Leonid – was widely
reprinted. Its drama is partly in the starkness of the choice he made to suffer
rather than to turn informer, partly in its rhetorical attitude: he addressed
his speech to the people in the courtroom and the world press present, and
at the end turned and expressed his contempt at the Soviet legal system with
a seven-word dismissal.*

Freedom for Soviet Jewry

In March and April, during interrogation, the chief investigators warned
me that in the position I have taken during investigation, and held to

here in court, I would be threatened with execution by a firing squad, or at least with fifteen years. If I agreed to cooperate with the investigation for the purpose of destroying the Jewish emigration movement, they promised me freedom and a quick reunion with my wife.

Five years ago, I submitted my application for exit to Israel. Now I am further than ever from my dream. It would seem to be cause for regret. But it is absolutely the other way around. I am happy. I am happy that I lived honourably, at peace with my conscience. I never compromised my soul, even under the threat of death.

I am happy that I helped people. I am proud that I knew and worked with such honourable, brave and courageous people as Sakharov, Orlov, Ginzburg, who are carrying on the traditions of the Russian intelligentsia. I am fortunate to have been witness to the process of the liberation of Jews of the USSR.

I hope that the absurd accusation against me and the entire Jewish emigration movement will not hinder the liberation of my people. My near ones and friends know how I wanted to exchange activity in the emigration movement for a life with my wife, Avital, in Israel.

For more than two thousand years the Jewish people, my people, have been dispersed. But wherever they are, wherever Jews are found, every year they have repeated: 'Next year in Jerusalem.' Now, when I am further than ever from my people, from Avital, facing many arduous years of imprisonment, I say, turning to my people, my Avital: 'Next year in Jerusalem.'

Now I turn to you, the court, who were required to confirm a predetermined sentence: to you I have nothing to say.

Elie Wiesel

*E*lie Wiesel was born in 1928 in Romania. His family were first placed in a ghetto before being transferred in May 1944 to Auschwitz-Birkenau. Separated from his mother and sisters, he worked in the hardest conditions for eight months alongside his father before being transferred to Buchenwald, where his father was severely beaten and finally sent to the crematoria just a few weeks before the Americans liberated the camp.

Wiesel became a journalist and after a decade finally wrote about his experience of the Shoah. When his book, Night, was first translated into English and published in America it sold just a few thousand copies, but gradually its power and its message spread and it has now sold millions of copies worldwide. Wiesel went on to write over forty books, both fiction and non-fiction, and in 1986 he was awarded the Nobel Peace Prize. The committee called him a 'messenger to mankind', stating that through his struggle to come to terms with 'his own personal experience of total humiliation and of the utter contempt for humanity shown in Hitler's death camps', as well as his 'practical work in the cause of peace', Wiesel had delivered a powerful message 'of peace, atonement and human dignity' to humanity. Wiesel continues to advocate human rights and an end to oppression in all its forms. He gave this speech

in the East Room of the White House on 12 April 1999, as part of the
Millennium Lecture series, hosted by President Bill Clinton and First
Lady Hillary Rodham Clinton.

The Perils of Indifference

12 April 1999

Fifty-four years ago to the day, a young Jewish boy from a small town
in the Carpathian Mountains woke up, not far from Goethe's beloved
Weimar, in a place of eternal infamy called Buchenwald. He was finally
free, but there was no joy in his heart. He thought there never would be
again.

Liberated a day earlier by American soldiers, he remembers their rage at
what they saw. And even if he lives to be a very old man, he will always be
grateful to them for that rage, and also for their compassion. Though he
did not understand their language, their eyes told him what he needed to
know – that they too would remember, and bear witness.

And now, I stand before you, Mr President – Commander-in-Chief of
the army that freed me, and tens of thousands of others – and I am filled
with a profound and abiding gratitude to the American people.

Gratitude is a word that I cherish. Gratitude is what defines the
humanity of the human being. And I am grateful to you, Hillary – or
Mrs Clinton – for what you said, and for what you are doing for children
in the world, for the homeless, for the victims of injustice, the victims of
destiny and society. And I thank all of you for being here.

We are on the threshold of a new century, a new millennium. What
will the legacy of this vanishing century be? How will it be remembered in
the new millennium? Surely it will be judged, and judged severely, in both
moral and metaphysical terms. These failures have cast a dark shadow
over humanity: two World Wars, countless civil wars, the senseless chain
of assassinations – Gandhi, the Kennedys, Martin Luther King, Sadat,
Rabin – bloodbaths in Cambodia and Nigeria, India and Pakistan, Ireland
and Rwanda, Eritrea and Ethiopia, Sarajevo and Kosovo; the inhumanity
in the gulag and the tragedy of Hiroshima. And, on a different level, of
course, Auschwitz and Treblinka. So much violence, so much indifference.

What is indifference? Etymologically, the word means 'no difference'.
A strange and unnatural state in which the lines blur between light

and darkness, dusk and dawn, crime and punishment, cruelty and compassion, good and evil.

What are its courses and inescapable consequences? Is it a philosophy? Is there a philosophy of indifference conceivable? Can one possibly view indifference as a virtue? Is it necessary at times to practise it simply to keep one's sanity, live normally, enjoy a fine meal and a glass of wine, as the world around us experiences harrowing upheavals?

Of course, indifference can be tempting – more than that, seductive. It is so much easier to look away from victims. It is so much easier to avoid such rude interruptions to our work, our dreams, our hopes. It is, after all, awkward, troublesome, to be involved in another person's pain and despair. Yet, for the person who is indifferent, his or her neighbour are of no consequence. And, therefore, their lives are meaningless. Their hidden or even visible anguish is of no interest. Indifference reduces the other to an abstraction.

Over there, behind the black gates of Auschwitz, the most tragic of all prisoners were the 'Muselmänner', as they were called. Wrapped in their torn blankets, they would sit or lie on the ground, staring vacantly into space, unaware of who or where they were, strangers to their surroundings. They no longer felt pain, hunger, thirst. They feared nothing. They felt nothing. They were dead and did not know it.

Rooted in our tradition, some of us felt that to be abandoned by humanity then was not the ultimate. We felt that to be abandoned by God was worse than to be punished by Him. Better an unjust God than an indifferent one. For us to be ignored by God was a harsher punishment than to be a victim of His anger. Man can live far from God – not outside God. God is wherever we are. Even in suffering? Even in suffering.

In a way, to be indifferent to that suffering is what makes the human being inhuman. Indifference, after all, is more dangerous than anger and hatred. Anger can at times be creative. One writes a great poem, a great symphony, one does something special for the sake of humanity because one is angry at the injustice that one witnesses. But indifference is never creative. Even hatred at times may elicit a response. You fight it. You denounce it. You disarm it. Indifference elicits no response. Indifference is not a response.

Indifference is not a beginning, it is an end. And, therefore, indifference is always the friend of the enemy, for it benefits the aggressor – never his victim, whose pain is magnified when he or she feels forgotten. The political prisoner in his cell, the hungry children, the homeless refugees – not to respond to their plight, not to relieve their solitude by offering them a spark of hope, is to exile them from human memory. And in denying their humanity we betray our own.

Indifference, then, is not only a sin, it is a punishment. And this is one of the most important lessons of this outgoing century's wide-ranging experiments in good and evil.

In the place that I come from, society was composed of three simple categories: the killers, the victims and the bystanders. During the darkest of times, inside the ghettoes and death camps – and I'm glad that Mrs Clinton mentioned that we are now commemorating that event, that period, that we are now in the Days of Remembrance – but then, we felt abandoned, forgotten. All of us did.

And our only miserable consolation was that we believed that Auschwitz and Treblinka were closely guarded secrets; that the leaders of the free world did not know what was going on behind those black gates and barbed wire; that they had no knowledge of the war against the Jews that Hitler's armies and their accomplices waged as part of the war against the Allies.

If they knew, we thought, surely those leaders would have moved heaven and earth to intervene. They would have spoken out with great outrage and conviction. They would have bombed the railways leading to Birkenau, just the railways, just once.

And now we knew, we learned, we discovered that the Pentagon knew, the State Department knew. And the illustrious occupant of the White House then, who was a great leader – and I say it with some anguish and pain, because, today is exactly fifty-four years marking his death – Franklin Delano Roosevelt died on April the 12th, 1945, so he is very much present to me and to us.

No doubt, he was a great leader. He mobilized the American people and the world, going into battle, bringing hundreds and thousands of valiant and brave soldiers in America to fight fascism, to fight dictatorship, to fight Hitler. And so many of the young people fell in battle. And, nevertheless, his image in Jewish history – I must say it – his image in Jewish history is flawed.

The depressing tale of the *St Louis* is a case in point. Sixty years ago, its human cargo – maybe 1,000 Jews – was turned back to Nazi Germany. And that happened after the Kristallnacht, after the first state-sponsored pogrom, with hundreds of Jewish shops destroyed, synagogues burned, thousands of people put in concentration camps. And that ship, which was already on the shores of the United States, was sent back.

I don't understand. Roosevelt was a good man, with a heart. He understood those who needed help. Why didn't he allow these refugees to disembark? A thousand people – in America, a great country, the greatest democracy, the most generous of all new nations in modern history. What happened? I don't understand. Why the indifference, on the highest level, to the suffering of the victims?

But then, there were human beings who were sensitive to our tragedy. Those non-Jews, those Christians, that we called the 'Righteous Gentiles,' whose selfless acts of heroism saved the honour of their faith. Why were they so few? Why was there a greater effort to save SS murderers after the war than to save their victims during the war?

Why did some of America's largest corporations continue to do business with Hitler's Germany until 1942? It has been suggested, and it was documented, that the Wehrmacht could not have conducted its invasion of France without oil obtained from American sources. How is one to explain their indifference?

And yet, my friends, good things have also happened in this traumatic century: the defeat of Nazism, the collapse of communism, the rebirth of Israel on its ancestral soil, the demise of apartheid, Israel's peace treaty with Egypt, the peace accord in Ireland. And let us remember the meeting, filled with drama and emotion, between Rabin and Arafat that you, Mr President, convened in this very place. I was here and I will never forget it.

And then, of course, the joint decision of the United States and NATO to intervene in Kosovo and save those victims, those refugees, those who were uprooted by a man who I believe that, because of his crimes, should be charged with crimes against humanity. But this time, the world was not silent. This time, we do respond. This time, we intervene.

Does it mean that we have learned from the past? Does it mean that society has changed? Has the human being become less indifferent and more human? Have we really learned from our experiences? Are we less insensitive to the plight of victims of ethnic cleansing and other forms of injustices in places near and far? Is today's justified intervention in Kosovo, led by you, Mr President, a lasting warning that never again will the deportation, the terrorization of children and their parents be allowed anywhere in the world? Will it discourage other dictators in other lands to do the same?

What about the children? Oh, we see them on television, we read about them in the papers, and we do so with a broken heart. Their fate is always the most tragic, inevitably. When adults wage war, children perish. We see their faces, their eyes. Do we hear their pleas? Do we feel their pain, their agony? Every minute one of them dies of disease, violence, famine. Some of them – so many of them – could be saved.

And so, once again, I think of the young Jewish boy from the Carpathian Mountains. He has accompanied the old man I have become throughout these years of quest and struggle. And together we walk towards the new millennium, carried by profound fear and extraordinary hope.

Jan Karski

J an Karski was born Jan Kozielewski in 1914 in Łódź, a Roman
Catholic raised in a majority Jewish neighbourhood. Before the war
he joined the diplomatic service, taking up a number of postings
overseas, and he joined the army at the outbreak of war. He was captured by
the Red Army but managed to conceal his true rank of 2nd Lieutenant and
was handed over to the Germans during an exchange of POWs – his fellow
officers were massacred by the Soviets at Katyn. He escaped and found his
way to Warsaw, where he became a member of the resistance and began to
go on courier missions taking dispatches from the Polish underground to the
Polish Government in Exile, first in Paris then in London. In 1940 he was
captured by the Gestapo and brutally tortured, leading to a suicide attempt
before he escaped from hospital. In 1942 Karski was selected to visit the
Polish prime minister and inform him about the Nazi atrocities in Poland,
including the fate of the Jews. Smuggled into the Warsaw Ghetto and a
concentration camp, Karski reported to the Polish, British and American
governments – some of his experience of what happened is laid out in this
speech.

After the war Karski settled in America and became a professor at
Georgetown. Over the years details of his attempts to publicize and stop the
Holocaust became known and he was widely honoured by Poland, Israel

and America and was nominated for the Nobel Peace Prize. Till his death in 2000 he remained one of the most eloquent speakers on Jewish–Gentile relations and the horrors and degradations of antisemitism.

In November 1990 the Anti-Defamation League and the Arch-Diocese of Washington jointly honoured Karski at the Washington Hebrew Congregation's temple (synagogue) with tributes given by the Polish and Israeli ambassadors, the Archbishop of Washington and the Director of the ADL.

Response to the Tribute of the Anti-Defamation League of B'nai B'rith and the Archdiocese of Washington

28 November 1990

A few years ago, John Paul II let himself be invited by the Rabbi of the leading synagogue in Rome to participate in joint prayers. There the Pope addressed the Hebrew congregation, concluding:

You are our older brethren.

We are all children of Abraham.

Today we have gathered in this temple – the spiritual source of us all. What a gathering! A Cardinal and a Rabbi; Christians and Jews; ambassador of Israel and ambassador of Poland. In the audience I see some Poles – all of them prominent and worthy. I am infinitely proud that I became a cause – or better, a pretext – for this inspiring event.

Our meeting is also significant because in some countries – this blessed country included – anti-Semitism is raising its ugly head. This – after the Holocaust. After the Second Vatican Council.

My personal observation shows that for many people, anti-Semitism is not much more than realization of their own inferiority, insecurity or jealousy. Because so many Jews attained prominence. Because Jews value so much hard work and education. Because they are so enterprising. Because they help each other. Because they contribute generously to their own causes. Because they know how to adapt themselves to the social environment in which they live. Because throughout history they had made such tremendous contributions in sciences, literature, medicine, philosophy, economy. Because – as some believe – they are so powerful.

Well, as to the alleged power, the Jews were unable to prevent or to stop the Holocaust. As to the rest, it took them centuries to learn and to become what they are – centuries of enslavement, expulsions, inquisitions, pogroms, discrimination; not only did they learn, but they also preserved their spiritual identity. We all should learn from them.

The Jews being a minority in every country, they always sought cooperation and friendship of others, so they do today.

But how to recognize a true friend? What are the criteria?

I have no right or intention to speak for the Jews. I am a Pole and a Catholic. So I speak for myself.

The Jews, all Jews, live with an open wound – the memory of the Holocaust. They expect – and they have a right to expect – that people of good will recognize the uniqueness of the Jewish Holocaust.

We Poles, we knew what suffering, persecution, death mean: some three million ethnic Poles perished in the last war. My nation passed through a gehenna, martyrdom, crucifixion, annihilation of the national elite. The Soviet Union lost some twenty million people All nations under the Nazi domination had victims. Millions of them. But *all* Jews were victims. If a Nazi official saw a local child on the streets of Warsaw or Belgrade or Athens, he would pass the child indifferently. The child was to grow into a slave of the master race. If he saw a Jewish child, he would dispatch the child for destruction, as a vermin of humanity. That the Jews chose to call the Holocaust. Let no nation, no government, no church appropriate this sacred, this cursed term. Holocaust is Jewish.

The Jews prayed or fought for centuries to recover their promised land. Now they have it and will not be pushed out. But they are surrounded by an ocean of hatred and enmity. So they seek and fight for the security of Israel. For me friendship or good will towards the Jews requires at least [friendship] for or better support of Israel. Never again.

Many people profess good will towards the Jews. For me it is not enough. Those who are sincere and honest should join ranks with the Jews openly and loudly, combating anti-Semitism, racism, chauvinism, intolerance and bigotry.

So much for my views.

Now I want to tell you a story which lies deeply in my heart. From those who will consider it inappropriate, I ask forgiveness.

In the summer of 1942, the leaders of the so-called Polish underground state decided to send me secretly to London with a variety of messages. By the end of September 1942, on recommendation of the nominal head of the Underground Resistance, I met two Jewish leaders: one representing the Zionists and the other the Socialist Bund. They also entrusted me with their own information, messages and demands to be passed to their representatives in London, to the Polish government-in-exile and to those allied leaders whom I would be able to reach.

The essence of their information and demands was as follows:

> Hitler and his henchmen decided to exterminate all Jews. The Jewish masses do not realize it yet. Both of them, however, know it. The Jews are totally helpless. They cannot rely on the Polish Underground. They can save some individuals but they cannot stop the extermination. They are persecuted themselves. Only the powerful Allied governments can effectively help.

Both Jews specified several ways of help, the most important being a public and formal Allied declaration that stopping extermination of the Jews would become a part of the Allied war strategy.

Both Jews were in utter despair. In utter despair they asked me to pass a special message to their representatives in London. After forty-eight years, I remember that terrible message:

> Tell them to stop sending us messages that they are doing everything they can. It is not enough. Let them go to the Allies' offices and ask for action. Until commitment is made, let them stand in front of the offices. Let them refuse food and water. Let them die in view of the whole world. We are dying here. Perhaps that will shake the conscience of humanity.

I reached London in early November 1942 and began reporting. The most memorable was my meeting with the Bund representative, Shmuel Zygelboym.

He seemed depressed, nervous, suspicious and – towards me – less than courteous. When I finished my report, he burst out: 'You didn't tell me anything I don't know. I know more than you told me. I am doing everything I can.'

Then I spelled out the special message, as instructed. He jumped and started to run from wall to wall shouting: 'The world is mad. Do you think that they will let me die on a street? They will send two policemen, arrest me, send me to some psychiatric clinic. They will not let me die on a street.'

And running and jumping, he repeated over and over again: 'The world is mad. The world is mad.'

Then a few months later, in April 1943, the Jews of the Warsaw ghetto declared a war against the Third Reich. With primitive weapons they held out for three weeks. Then in the middle of May 1943, the enemy burned the entire ghetto and all who were inside. Nothing but smouldering ruins remained.

Then, Shmuel Zygelboym took his life in London. He left a letter that he decided to die as a protest against the passivity of the Allies towards the fate of the Jews. Hoping that his death would save some lives of the remaining Jews.

We all know that taking one's own life violates the Judaic-Christian tradition and teaching. But my conscience tells me that a distinction should be made: one takes his life because he cannot handle any longer his *personal* misfortune, bankruptcy of his life, or because he wants to escape from the responsibility of his acts, or because he suffers a nervous breakdown. Zygelboym took his life out of compassion for the suffering of his people, hoping that his death would help or save those he loved.

I know of many awards after the names of the great. Noble personalities, respectfully and humbly I submit that such an award should bear the name 'Shmuel Zygelboym'. Thank you.

Michael Douglas

*M*ichael Douglas *is an award-winning actor/producer with over forty years' experience in theatre, film and television. He is the recipient of two Academy Awards, one for producing the classic* One Flew Over the Cuckoo's Nest *and the other as Best Actor for his role in* Wall Street. *He began his acting career in the successful TV series* Streets of San Francisco *and amongst his film appearances are* Fatal Attraction, Romancing the Stone, The China Syndrome, Falling Down, Basic Instinct, The American President, Traffic *and* Behind the Candelabra, *for which he won the Emmy Award, Golden Globe Award and Screen Actors Guild award for Best Actor for his portrayal of the legendary entertainer Liberace.*

In 1998 Michael Douglas was made a United Nations Messenger of Peace. His concentration on nuclear proliferation and the reduction of small arms continues today. He is also involved in the Motion Picture & Television Fund; the University of California at Santa Barbara; the Ploughshares Fund; the Nuclear Threat Initiative and the Eugene O'Neill Theatre amongst other philanthropic causes. In 2015 he received the 2015 Genesis Prize, which honours 'exceptional people whose values and achievements will inspire the next generation of Jews'.

Op-ed, Michael Douglas finds Judaism and faces anti-Semitism

Los Angeles Times, 14 March 2015

Last summer our family went to Southern Europe on holiday. During our stay at a hotel, our son Dylan went to the swimming pool. A short time later he came running back to the room, upset. A man at the pool had started hurling insults at him.

My first instinct was to ask: 'Were you misbehaving?'

'No,' Dylan told me through his tears.

I stared at him. And suddenly I had an awful realization of what might have caused the man's outrage: Dylan was wearing a Star of David.

After calming him down, I went to the pool and asked the attendants to point out the man who had yelled at him. We talked. It was not a pleasant discussion. Afterward, I sat down with my son and said: 'Dylan, you just had your first taste of anti-Semitism.'

My father, Kirk Douglas, born Issur Danielovitch, is Jewish. My mother, Diana, is not. I had no formal religious upbringing from either of them, and the two kids I have with Catherine Zeta-Jones are like me, growing up with one parent who is Jewish and one who is not.

Several years ago Dylan, through his friends, developed a deep connection to Judaism, and when he started going to Hebrew school and studying for his bar mitzvah, I began to reconnect with the religion of my father.

While some Jews believe that not having a Jewish mother makes me not Jewish, I have learned the hard way that those who hate do not make such fine distinctions.

Dylan's experience reminded me of my first encounter with anti-Semitism, in high school. A friend saw someone Jewish walk by, and with no provocation he confidently told me: 'Michael, all Jews cheat in business.'

'What are you talking about?' I said.

'Michael, come on,' he replied. 'Everyone knows that.'

With little knowledge of what it meant to be a Jew, I found myself passionately defending the Jewish people. Now, half a century later, I have to defend my son. Anti-Semitism, I've seen, is like a disease that goes dormant, flaring up with the next political trigger.

In my opinion there are three reasons anti-Semitism is appearing now with renewed vigilance.

The first is that historically, it always grows more virulent whenever and wherever the economy is bad. In a time when income disparity is growing, when hundreds of millions of people live in abject poverty, some find Jews to be a convenient scapegoat rather than looking at the real source of their problems.

If we confront anti-Semitism ... if we combat it individually and as a society, and use whatever platform we have to denounce it, we can stop the spread of this madness.

A second root cause of anti-Semitism derives from an irrational and misplaced hatred of Israel. Far too many people see Israel as an apartheid state and blame the people of an entire religion for what, in truth, are internal national-policy decisions. Does anyone really believe that the innocent victims in that kosher shop in Paris and at that bar mitzvah in Denmark had anything to do with Israeli–Palestinian policies or the building of settlements 2,000 miles away?

The third reason is simple demographics. Europe is now home to 25 million to 30 million Muslims, twice the world's entire Jewish population. Within any religious community that large, there will always be an extremist fringe, people who are radicalized and driven with hatred, while rejecting what all religions need to preach – respect, tolerance and love. We're now seeing the amplified effects of that small, radicalized element. With the Internet, its virus of hatred can now speed from nation to nation, helping fuel Europe's new epidemic of anti-Semitism. It is time for each of us to speak up against this hate.

Speaking up is the responsibility of our political leaders. French Prime Minister Manuel Valls has made it clear that anti-Semitism violates the morals and spirit of France and that violent anti-Semitic acts are a crime against all French people that must be confronted, combated and stopped. He challenged his nation to tell the world: without its Jews, France would no longer be France.

Speaking up is the responsibility of our religious leaders, and Pope Francis has used his powerful voice to make his position and that of the Catholic Church clear, saying: 'It's a contradiction that a Christian is anti-Semitic. His roots are Jewish. Let anti-Semitism be banished from the heart and life of every man and every woman.'

In New York, Cardinal Timothy M. Dolan is well known for building a bridge to the Jewish community. His words and actions and the pope's are evidence of the reconciliation between two major religions, an inspiring example of how a past full of persecution and embedded hostility can be overcome.

It's also the responsibility of regular citizens to take action. In Oslo, members of the Muslim community joined their fellow Norwegians to form a ring of peace at a local synagogue. Such actions give me hope – they send a message that together, we can stand up to hatred of the Jewish people.

So that is our challenge in 2015, and all of us must take it up. Because if we confront anti-Semitism whenever we see it, if we combat it individually and as a society, and use whatever platform we have to denounce it, we can stop the spread of this madness.

My son is strong. He is fortunate to live in a country where anti-Semitism is rare. But now he too has learned of the dangers that he as a Jew must face. It's a lesson that I wish I didn't have to teach him, a lesson I hope he will never have to teach his children.

PART II

INTERSECTIONALITY

Intersectionality is the study of how groups exposed to different kinds of oppression relate to one another and frequently overlap. The theory holds that the classical conceptualizations of oppression within society, such as racism, sexism, homophobia and belief-based bigotry, including nationalism, do not act independently of one another; instead, these forms of oppression interrelate, creating a system of oppression that reflects the 'intersection' of multiple forms of discrimination.

Thus we see the varying experiences of differently oppressed groups, whether separated by time, nationality or prejudice, intersect with one another in a deep understanding of each other's struggles. There is a long history, particularly in America and South Africa, of close relationships between the Jewish and Black communities and activists born out of a shared oppression, but there have also been extreme tensions born out of petty prejudice and jealousy.

Since the start of the Civil Rights movement in the 1950s the American-Jewish community was extremely active in support of African-American rights, but at another level there have also been internecine struggles as the most oppressed struggle with and against one another for individual and specific rights, freedoms and advantages.

George Washington

To the Hebrew Congregation in Newport
Rhode Island.

Gentlemen.

While I receive, with much satisfaction, your Address replete with expressions of affection and esteem; I rejoice in the opportunity of assuring you, that I shall always retain a grateful remembrance of the cordial welcome I experienced in my visit to Newport, from all classes of Citizens.

The reflection on the days of difficulty and danger which are past is rendered the more sweet, from a consciousness that they are succeeded by days of uncommon prosperity and security. If we have wisdom to make the best use of the advantages with which we are now favored, we cannot fail, under the just administration of a good Government, to become a great and a happy people.

The Citizens of the United States of America have a right to applaud themselves for having given to mankind examples of an enlarged and liberal policy: a policy worthy of imitation. All possess alike liberty of conscience and immunities of citizenship. It is now no more that toleration is spoken of, as if it was by the indulgence of one class of people, that another enjoyed the exercise of their inherent natural rights. For happily the

*I*n 1790 Washington visited Rhode Island for the first time, along with Jefferson and other founding fathers. Though the other States had ratified the Constitution, Rhode Island had demurred till May 1790 (when the Bill of Rights was ratified and able to be incorporated), so Washington had avoided them on his New England tour the previous autumn. The government's role in religion had been a particular sticking point around ratification. Though the country was built on Christian principles, many immigrants had fled religious persecution in Europe and were wary of a government prohibiting freedom of religion.

Washington was met by representatives from many of the State's religious groups, including the Hebrew Congregation, who all gave addresses. Heretofore Jews were not allowed to vote or become naturalized citizens, although their status as merchants and economic contributors protected them from overt discrimination. As a result the Jewish statement, made by Moses Seixas, one of the officials of Yeshuat Israel, the first Jewish congregation in Newport, was one of great joy at the potential they saw in being freed from oppression by the protection of the First Amendment:

> Deprived as we heretofore have been of the invaluable rights of free Citizens, we now (with a deep sense of gratitude to the Almighty disposer of all events) behold a Government, erected by the Majesty of the People – a Government, which to bigotry gives no sanction, to persecution no assistance – but generously affording to All liberty of conscience, and immunities of Citizenship: deeming every one, of whatever Nation, tongue, or language, equal parts of the great governmental Machine.

A few days later, the President wrote to the citizen groups which he'd met. First amongst his responses was his letter to the Hebrew Congregation, laying out the new government's position towards those whose religious beliefs were perceived as different. In it he echoed Seixas' statements about bigotry and persecution directly, statements which were to become the bedrock of American religious freedom to this day.

Letter to the Hebrew Congregation in Newport, Rhode Island

18 August 1790

Gentlemen.

While I receive, with much satisfaction, your Address replete with expressions of affection and esteem; I rejoice in the opportunity of assuring you, that I shall always retain a grateful remembrance of the cordial welcome I experienced in my visit to Newport, from all classes of Citizens.

The reflection on the days of difficulty and danger which are past is rendered the more sweet, from a consciousness that they are succeeded by days of uncommon prosperity and security. If we have wisdom to make the best use of the advantages with which we are now favoured, we cannot fail, under the just administration of a good Government, to become a great and a happy people.

The Citizens of the United States of America have a right to applaud themselves for having given to mankind examples of an enlarged and liberal policy: a policy worthy of imitation. All possess alike liberty of conscience and immunities of citizenship. It is now no more that toleration is spoken of, as if it was by the indulgence of one class of people, that another enjoyed the exercise of their inherent natural rights. For happily the Government of the United States, which gives to bigotry no sanction, to persecution no assistance, requires only that they who live under its protection should demean themselves as good citizens, in giving it on all occasions their effectual support.

It would be inconsistent with the frankness of my character not to avow that I am pleased with your favourable opinion of my Administration, and fervent wishes for my felicity. May the Children of the Stock of Abraham, who dwell in this land, continue to merit and enjoy the good will of the other Inhabitants; while every one shall sit in safety under his own vine and figtree, and there shall be none to make him afraid. May the father of all mercies scatter light and not darkness in our paths, and make us all in our several vocations useful here, and in his own due time and way everlastingly happy.

G Washington

We are all bound up together in one great bundle of humanity, and society cannot trample on the weakest and feeblest of its members without receiving the curse in its own soul.

**FRANCES ELLEN WATKINS HARPER,
'WE ARE ALL BOUND UP TOGETHER', ADDRESS TO
THE ELEVENTH NATIONAL WOMEN'S RIGHTS
CONVENTION MAY 1866**

Jesse Jackson

Since the 1960s, Reverend Jesse Jackson has been a prominent member of the American Civil Rights movement, working first, as a young man, with Martin Luther King Jr and latterly as one of the movement's leaders. In 1984 he sought the Democratic nomination for President, ultimately coming third in the primaries. In this speech he sets out his vision for 'The Rainbow Coalition' – a coalition of racial minorities as well as all those hurt by Reagan's policies – which he founded upon losing the primary and still continues to this day.

Part of the background to Jackson's speech was the controversy in 1984 surrounding antisemitic comments he'd made. Referring off the record to a reporter to Jews as 'hymies' and New York as 'Hymietown', Jackson issued firm and consistent denials when his comment was subsequently published. To make the situation worse, his long-time friend and supporter and leader of the Nation of Islam, Louis Farrakhan, stepped in to defend him. Farrakhan had once described Hitler as a 'great man' (though he did acknowledge he was wicked too) and appearing at a Chicago rally with Jackson proclaimed: 'If you harm this brother, I warn you in the name of Allah this will be the last one you harm. Leave this servant of God alone.'

With a simple, and simply offensive, off-guard comment threatening not only Jackson's presidential bid but also African-American–Jewish relations across the country, Jackson appeared at a New Hampshire synagogue to admit his responsibility and apologize.

In this speech, delivered just two weeks after Time *magazine stated: 'By failing to repudiate Farrakhan and his inflammatory rhetoric, Jackson continues to raise questions about his claim to be a conciliator and peacemaker', Jackson directly summons the spirit of intersectionality which had seen the nation rocked and communities joined by the Mississippi lynching of two Jewish civil rights activists alongside an African-American, as well as the vital support and understanding the two communities should share. Jackson stood again in 1988 and tried seriously to heal the wounds he'd opened with America's Jewish community, but his refusal to disavow Farrakhan and his support for Palestine meant the suspicions about his antisemitism never went away.*

As Rabbi Robert J. Marx, founder of the Jewish Council on Urban Affairs in Chicago, said in a 1987 New York Times *article on Jackson: 'Everyone wants to say Jesse is an anti-Semite or is not an anti-Semite, but he's more complex. He is a humanitarian. When Jews are attacked, he will rise to their defence. But his blind spot is his perception of Jewish power. He has a problem with thinking Jews have more power than they have. I'll be at a meeting of 30 people, at which I'm the only rabbi present, and Jesse will say, "We've got to form a coalition – isn't that right, Rabbi Marx?" In other words, he'll turn to me, single me out, as if there is some superhuman power the Jewish community has.'*

Jackson continues to be a prominent, if still at times controversial, Civil Rights leader to this day, whose passionate desire and drive to end oppression at every level cannot be denied, and has been a powerful force for change in the last forty years.

Address to the Democratic National Convention

San Francisco, 17 July 1984

Our flag is red, white and blue, but our nation is a rainbow – red, yellow, brown, black and white – and we're all precious in God's sight.

America is not like a blanket – one piece of unbroken cloth, the same colour, the same texture, the same size. America is more like a quilt: many patches, many pieces, many colours, many sizes, all woven and held together by a common thread. The white, the Hispanic, the black, the Arab, the Jew, the woman, the native American, the small farmer, the businessperson, the environmentalist, the peace activist, the young, the old, the lesbian, the gay, and the disabled make up the American quilt.

Even in our fractured state, all of us count and fit somewhere. We have proven that we can survive without each other. But we have not proven that we can win and make progress without each other. We must come together.

From Fannie Lou Hamer[1] in Atlantic City in 1964 to the Rainbow Coalition in San Francisco today; from the Atlantic to the Pacific, we have experienced pain but progress, as we ended American apartheid laws. We got public accommodations. We secured voting rights. We obtained open housing, as young people got the right to vote. We lost Malcolm, Martin, Medgar, Bobby, John, and Viola.[2] The team that got us here must be expanded, not abandoned.

Twenty years ago, tears welled up in our eyes as the bodies of Schwerner, Goodman and Chaney[3] were dredged from the depths of a river in Mississippi. Twenty years later, our communities, black and Jewish, are in anguish, anger and pain. Feelings have been hurt on both sides. There is a crisis in communications. Confusion is in the air. But we cannot afford to lose our way. We may agree to agree; or agree to disagree on issues; we must bring back civility to these tensions.

We are co-partners in a long and rich religious history – the Judeo-Christian traditions. Many blacks and Jews have a shared passion for social justice at home and peace abroad. We must seek a revival of the spirit, inspired by a new vision and new possibilities. We must return to higher ground. We are bound by Moses and Jesus, but also connected with Islam and Mohammed. These three great religions, Judaism, Christianity and Islam, were all born in the revered and holy city of Jerusalem.

We are bound by Dr Martin Luther King Jr and Rabbi Abraham Heschel, crying out from their graves for us to reach common ground. We are bound by shared blood and shared sacrifices. We are much too intelligent, much too bound by our Judeo-Christian heritage, much too victimized by racism, sexism, militarism and anti-Semitism, much too threatened as historical scapegoats to go on divided one from another. We must turn from finger-pointing to clasped hands. We must share our burdens and our joys with each other once again. We must turn to each other and not on each other and choose higher ground.

Twenty years later, we cannot be satisfied by just restoring the old coalition. Old wineskins must make room for new wine. We must heal and expand. The Rainbow Coalition is making room for Arab Americans. They, too, know the pain and hurt of racial and religious rejection. They must not continue to be made pariahs. The Rainbow Coalition is making room for Hispanic Americans who this very night are living under the threat of the Simpson-Mazzoli bill;[4] and farm workers from Ohio who are fighting the Campbell Soup Company with a boycott to achieve legitimate workers' rights.

The Rainbow is making room for the Native American, the most exploited people of all, a people with the greatest moral claim amongst us. We support them as they seek the restoration of their ancient land and claim amongst us. We support them as they seek the restoration of land and water rights, as they seek to preserve their ancestral homeland and the beauty of a land that was once all theirs. They can never receive a fair share for all they have given us. They must finally have a fair chance to develop their great resources and to preserve their people and their culture.

The Rainbow Coalition includes Asian Americans, now being killed in our streets – scapegoats for the failures of corporate, industrial, and economic policies.

The Rainbow is making room for the young Americans ...

The Rainbow includes disabled veterans. The colour scheme fits in the Rainbow. The disabled have their handicap revealed and their genius concealed; while the able-bodied have their genius revealed and their disability concealed. But ultimately, we must judge people by their values and their contribution. Don't leave anybody out. I would rather have Roosevelt in a wheelchair than Reagan on a horse.

The Rainbow is making room for small farmers....

... In 1984, my heart is made to feel glad because I know there is a way out – justice. The requirement for rebuilding America is justice. The linchpin of progressive politics in our nation will not come from the North; they, in fact, will come from the South. That is why I argue over and over again. We look from Virginia around to Texas, there's only one black Congressperson out of 115. Nineteen years later, we're locked out of the Congress, the Senate and the Governor's mansion. What does this large black vote mean? Why do I fight to win second primaries and fight gerrymandering and annexation and at-large [elections]? Why do we fight over that? Because I tell you, you cannot hold someone in the ditch unless you linger there with them. Unless you linger there.

If you want a change in this nation, you enforce that Voting Rights Act. We'll get twelve to twenty Black, Hispanics, female and progressive congresspersons from the South. We can save the cotton, but we've got to fight the boll weevils. We've got to make a judgement. We've got to make a judgement.

It is not enough to hope ERA will pass. How can we pass ERA? If Blacks vote in great numbers, progressive Whites win. It's the only way progressive Whites win. If Blacks vote in great numbers, Hispanics win. When Blacks, Hispanics and progressive Whites vote, women win. When women win, children win. When women and children win, workers win. We must all come up together. We must come up together.

… I have a message for our youth. I challenge them to put hope in their brains and not dope in their veins. I told them that like Jesus, I, too, was born in the slum. But just because you're born in the slum does not mean the slum is born in you, and you can rise above it if your mind is made up. I told them in every slum there are two sides. When I see a broken window – that's the slummy side. Train some youth to become a glazier – that's the sunny side. When I see a missing brick – that's the slummy side. Let that child in the union and become a brick mason and build – that's the sunny side. When I see a missing door – that's the slummy side. Train some youth to become a carpenter – that's the sunny side. And when I see the vulgar words and hieroglyphics of destitution on the walls – that's the slummy side. Train some youth to become a painter, an artist – that's the sunny side.

We leave this place looking for the sunny side because there's a brighter side somewhere. I'm more convinced than ever that we can win. We will vault up the rough side of the mountain. We can win. I just want young America to do me one favour, just one favour. Exercise the right to dream. You must face reality – that which is. But then dream of a reality that ought to be – that must be. Live beyond the pain of reality with the dream of a bright tomorrow. Use hope and imagination as weapons of survival and progress. Use love to motivate you and obligate you to serve the human family.

Young America, dream. Choose the human race over the nuclear race. Bury the weapons and don't burn the people. Dream – dream of a new value system. Teachers who teach for life and not just for a living; teach because they can't help it. Dream of lawyers more concerned about justice than a judgeship. Dream of doctors more concerned about public health than personal wealth. Dream of preachers and priests who will prophesy and not just profiteer. Preach and dream!

Our time has come. Our time has come. Suffering breeds character. Character breeds faith. In the end, faith will not disappoint. Our time has come. Our faith, hope, and dreams will prevail. Our time has come. Weeping has endured for nights, but now joy cometh in the morning. Our time has come. No grave can hold our body down. Our time has come. No lie can live for ever. Our time has come. We must leave racial battleground and come to economic common ground and moral higher ground. America, our time has come. We come from disgrace to amazing grace. Our time has come. Give me your tired, give me your poor, your huddled masses who yearn to breathe free and come November, there will be a change because our time has come.

Thank you and God bless you.

John F. Kennedy

P ost-war America was both a time of almost unprecedented social change and improvement and a hotbed of tensions and issues. During the Second World War the effects of the New Deal and wartime labour saw wages more than double and the 1950s was a hugely prosperous decade that saw substantial advances in many areas. This new prosperity saw huge cultural, social and attitude changes, heavily influenced by the post-war freedom and the gradual shift away from America's traditional inward facing as well as the increasing paranoia about Communism and the Cold War. In 1955 Rosa Parks's refusal to give up her seat in a coloured section of a bus to a white passenger sparked new impetus in the Civil Rights movement that would boil through society till, in the eyes of the law at least, all men and women were equal.

Prior to 1960 all Presidential candidates had been male WASPs (White, Anglo-Saxon Protestants) who could trace their American ancestry back to the early settlers. Kennedy's great-grandparents had all emigrated from Ireland to Boston in the 1840s to escape the potato famine and much was made of his Catholicism by opponents who feared that he would favour Catholic interests and compromise the separation of Church and State by an allegiance to the Vatican. Kennedy's victory and brief presidency *changed the way Americans viewed the office of president, and in 1964 the first Jewish candidate for a major party stood as the Republican nominee against Kennedy's Vice-President, Lyndon Johnson.*

As well as seeing a recasting of social and cultural attitudes, the 1960s also saw a change in public rhetoric with the wide-scale adoption of television altering and expanding the audience for many political speeches – what would once be delivered to a limited audience and disseminated via newspapers more widely was now broadcast straight from the orator's lips.

The Kind of America in which I Believe

12 September 1960

While the so-called religious issue is necessarily and properly the chief topic here tonight, I want to emphasize from the outset that we have far more critical issues to face in the 1960 election:

- the spread of Communist influence, until it now festers ninety miles off the coast of Florida;
- the humiliating treatment of our president and vice president by those who no longer respect our power;
- the hungry children I saw in West Virginia; the old people who cannot pay their doctor bills;
- the families forced to give up their farms; an America with too many slums, with too few schools, and too late to the moon and outer space.

These are the real issues which should decide this campaign. And they are not religious issues – for war and hunger and ignorance and despair know no religious barriers.

But because I am a Catholic, and no Catholic has ever been elected president, the real issues in this campaign have been obscured – perhaps deliberately, in some quarters less responsible than this.

So it is apparently necessary for me to state once again not what kind of church I believe in – for that should be important only to me – but what kind of America I believe in.

I believe in an America ...

- where the separation of church and state is absolute, where no Catholic prelate would tell the president (should he be Catholic) how to act, and no Protestant minister would tell his parishioners for whom to vote;

- where no church or church school is granted any public funds or political preference;

- and where no man is denied public office merely because his religion differs from the president who might appoint him or the people who might elect him.

I believe in an America ...

- that is officially neither Catholic, Protestant nor Jewish; where no public official either requests or accepts instructions on public policy from the Pope, the National Council of Churches or any other ecclesiastical source;

- where no religious body seeks to impose its will directly or indirectly upon the general populace or the public acts of its officials; and

- where religious liberty is so indivisible that an act against one church is treated as an act against all.

For while this year it may be a Catholic against whom the finger of suspicion is pointed, in other years it has been, and may someday be again, a Jew – or a Quaker or a Unitarian or a Baptist.

It was Virginia's harassment of Baptist preachers, for example, that helped lead to Jefferson's statute of religious freedom.

Today I may be the victim, but tomorrow it may be you – until the whole fabric of our harmonious society is ripped at a time of great national peril.

Finally, I believe in an America where ...

- religious intolerance will someday end; where all men and all churches are treated as equal;

- where every man has the same right to attend or not attend the church of his choice;

- where there is no Catholic vote, no anti-Catholic vote, no bloc voting of any kind; and

- where Catholics, Protestants and Jews, at both the lay and pastoral level, will refrain from those attitudes of disdain and division which have so often marred their works in the past, and promote instead the American ideal of brotherhood.

That is the kind of America in which I believe. And it represents the kind of presidency in which I believe – a great office that must neither be humbled by making it the instrument of any one religious group, nor tarnished by arbitrarily withholding its occupancy from the members of any one religious group.

I believe in a president whose religious views are his own private affair, neither imposed by him upon the nation, or imposed by the nation upon him as a condition to holding that office.

I would not look with favour upon a president working to subvert the First Amendment's guarantees of religious liberty. Nor would our system of checks and balances permit him to do so.

And neither do I look with favour upon those who would work to subvert Article VI of the Constitution by requiring a religious test – even by indirection – for it. If they disagree with that safeguard, they should be out openly working to repeal it.

A Chief Executive Responsible to All Groups

I want a chief executive whose public acts are responsible to all groups and obligated to none; who can attend any ceremony, service or dinner his office may appropriately require of him; and whose fulfilment of his presidential oath is not limited or conditioned by any religious oath, ritual or obligation.

This is the kind of America I believe in, and this is the kind I fought for in the South Pacific, and the kind my brother died for in Europe. No one suggested then that we may have a 'divided loyalty', that we did 'not believe in liberty', or that we belonged to a disloyal group that threatened the 'freedoms for which our forefathers died'.

And in fact, this is the kind of America for which our forefathers died ...

- when they fled here to escape religious test oaths that denied office to members of less favoured churches;
- when they fought for the Constitution, the Bill of Rights and the Virginia Statute of Religious Freedom; and

- when they fought at the shrine I visited today, the Alamo. For side by side with Bowie and Crockett died McCafferty and Bailey and Carey. But no one knows whether they were Catholic or not, for there was no religious test at the Alamo.

I ask you tonight to follow in that tradition, to judge me …

- on the basis of my record of fourteen years in Congress,
- on my declared stands against an ambassador to the Vatican, against unconstitutional aid to parochial schools, and against any boycott of the public schools (which I have attended myself) …

instead of judging me on the basis of these pamphlets and publications we all have seen that carefully select quotations out of context from the statements of Catholic church leaders, usually in other countries, frequently in other centuries, and always omitting, of course, the statement of the American Bishops in 1948, which strongly endorsed church–state separation, and which more nearly reflects the views of almost every American Catholic.

I do not consider these other quotations binding upon my public acts. Why should you?

Opposed to a Country Controlled by Any Religious Group

But let me say, with respect to other countries, that I am wholly opposed to the state being used by any religious group, Catholic or Protestant, to compel, prohibit, or persecute the free exercise of any other religion.

And I hope that you and I condemn with equal fervour those nations which deny their presidency to Protestants, and those which deny it to Catholics. And rather than cite the misdeeds of those who differ, I would cite the record of the Catholic Church in such nations as Ireland and France, and the independence of such statesmen as Adenauer and De Gaulle.

But let me stress again that these are my views. For contrary to common newspaper usage, I am not the Catholic candidate for president.

I am the Democratic Party's candidate for president, who happens also to be a Catholic. I do not speak for my church on public matters, and the church does not speak for me. Whatever issue may come before me as president – on birth control, divorce, censorship, gambling or any other subject – I will make my decision in accordance with these views, in accordance with what my conscience tells me to be the national interest, and without regard to outside religious pressures or dictates.

And no power or threat of punishment could cause me to decide otherwise.

But if the time should ever come – and I do not concede any conflict to be even remotely possible – when my office would require me to either violate my conscience or violate the national interest, then I would resign the office; and I hope any conscientious public servant would do the same.

But I do not intend to apologize for these views to my critics of either Catholic or Protestant faith, nor do I intend to disavow either my views or my church in order to win this election.

If I should lose on the real issues, I shall return to my seat in the Senate, satisfied that I had tried my best and was fairly judged.

But if this election is decided on the basis that forty million Americans lost their chance of being president on the day they were baptized, then it is the whole nation that will be the loser – in the eyes of Catholics and non-Catholics around the world, in the eyes of history, and in the eyes of our own people.

But if, on the other hand, I should win the election, then I shall devote every effort of mind and spirit to fulfilling the oath of the presidency – practically identical, I might add, to the oath I have taken for fourteen years in the Congress.

For without reservation, I can 'solemnly swear that I will faithfully execute the office of president of the United States, and will to the best of my ability preserve, protect, and defend the Constitution, so help me God'.

At the real heart of battle for equality is a deep-seated belief in the democratic process. Equality depends not on the force of arms or tear gas but upon the force of moral right; not on recourse to violence but on respect for law and order.

LYNDON JOHNSON: SPECIAL MESSAGE TO THE CONGRESS: 'THE AMERICAN PROMISE', 15 MARCH 1965

Joachim Prinz

Joachim Prinz was born in a small town in Germany in 1901, his family the one Jewish family in their community. When he was in his teens, they moved to a larger town and Prinz became more interested in his Jewish heritage, eventually deciding to become a rabbi against his father's wishes. A natural orator, by his mid-twenties he was already a sought-after preacher, having settled in Berlin with his young family. Even before Hitler seized power in 1933 Prinz spoke out against National Socialism, urging people to leave long before the danger of remaining became real. By the mid-Thirties he was preaching in Berlin's largest synagogue and serving the entire community, as well as being frequently arrested and harassed by the Gestapo. In 1937, perhaps because of his prominence and popularity, he was expelled and travelled with his pregnant wife and children to America, where the sponsorship of Rabbi Stephen Wise gave him citizenship and a lecture tour, though much of what he said fell on disbelieving ears.

He eventually settled in Newark as the spiritual leader of Temple B'nai Abraham and, after the war, became highly active in American and International Jewish organizations, holding numerous positions and travelling all over the world, including movingly returning to his destroyed synagogue in Berlin in 1946.

Seeing the plight of African-Americans and other minority groups in the context of his own experience of oppression under the Nazis, he became closely involved in the Civil Rights movement. As President of the American Jewish Congress he represented the Jewish community at the March on Washington and this speech was delivered from the foot of the Lincoln memorial immediately before Dr King delivered his 'I have a dream' speech.

I speak to you as an American Jew

August 1963

As Americans we share the profound concern of millions of people about the shame and disgrace of inequality and injustice which make a mockery of the great American idea.

As Jews we bring to this great demonstration, in which thousands of us proudly participate, a twofold experience – one of the spirit and one of our history.

In the realm of the spirit, our fathers taught us thousands of years ago that when God created man, he created him as everybody's neighbour. Neighbour is not a geographic term. It is a moral concept. It means our collective responsibility for the preservation of man's dignity and integrity.

From our Jewish historic experience of three and a half thousand years we say:

Our ancient history began with slavery and the yearning for freedom. During the Middle Ages my people lived for a thousand years in the ghettos of Europe. Our modern history begins with a proclamation of emancipation.

It is for these reasons that it is not merely sympathy and compassion for the black people of America that motivates us. It is above all and beyond all such sympathies and emotions a sense of complete identification and solidarity born of our own painful historic experience.

When I was the rabbi of the Jewish community in Berlin under the Hitler regime, I learned many things. The most important thing that I learned under those tragic circumstances was that bigotry and hatred are not the most urgent problem. The most urgent, the most disgraceful, the most shameful and the most tragic problem is silence.

A great people which had created a great civilization had become a nation of silent onlookers. They remained silent in the face of hate, in the face of brutality and in the face of mass murder.

America must not become a nation of onlookers. America must not remain silent. Not merely black America, but all of America. It must speak up and act, from the President down to the humblest of us, and not for the sake of the Negro, not for the sake of the black community, but for the sake of the image, the idea and the aspiration of America itself.

Our children, yours and mine in every school across the land, each morning pledge allegiance to the flag of the United States and to the republic for which it stands. They, the children, speak fervently and innocently of this land as the land of 'liberty and justice for all'.

The time, I believe, has come to work together – for it is not enough to hope together, and it is not enough to pray together – to work together that this children's oath, pronounced every morning from Maine to California, from North to South, may become. a glorious, unshakeable reality in a morally renewed and united America.

Albie Sachs

T here were Jews amongst the first colonists of the Cape, and by the time of independence there were considerable numbers, though they suffered considerably from antisemitic discrimination prior to the Second World War. The Nationalist government of 1948 apologized to the Jewish community for its previous antisemitism, and apartheid saw the Jews included in the category of Whites and given equal rights. In the vast majority, though, South African Jews opposed apartheid and many became radical activists (though Mandela's defence team in the Rivonia trial contained a Jewish attorney, the attorney-general who prosecuted him was also Jewish).

Albie Sachs was born in South Africa in 1935 into a family of Lithuanian descent. His father had been exiled from South Africa in the early Thirties owing to his communist activity but subsequently returned, more active than ever, and eventually left South Africa for good in 1953. Albie trained as a lawyer, attended the Congress of the People where the Freedom Charter was adopted and was called to the bar the following year. For his work in the freedom movement he was arrested and imprisoned, including five months in solitary confinement before he went into exile, first in England then in Mozambique, where he continued to work for the ANC. In 1988 he lost an eye and arm and *narrowly escaped death in a car bombing organized by South African security officials. Following the end of apartheid he returned to South Africa and was made a judge on the Constitutional Court of South Africa by Nelson Mandela.*

Voices on Anti-Semitism

9 October 2008[1]

For me, the anti-apartheid struggle was a form of combating racism, which had manifested itself in anti-Semitism, reaching ghastly proportions through the genocide. But it was all part and parcel of a similar form of inhumanity of human beings to other human beings.

I was born into the struggle. I just didn't stand a chance.

My dad was often in the newspapers. Solly Sachs arrested. Solly Sachs tells the government something or another.

My mom worked for Moses Katani, who was then the general secretary of the Communist Party of South Africa and a very prominent member of the ANC, African National Congress. And I can still remember as a child my mom saying: 'Tidy up, tidy up, Uncle Moses is coming.'

And it meant the first contact that I had as a child with an African personality was not somebody coming as a servant, but, if you like, she was the servant, but in a very dignified and very affectionate way.

So that was the kind of world I grew up in.

And World War Two just dominated everything. Stories of battles, and particularly as a young boy growing up, the idea of heroism, of courage, was overwhelming.

And then my parents both being very, very active in relation to, not that kind of physical combat and that kind of courage, but to idealism, transforming South Africa – rights for workers, for poor people, anti-racism.

The democratic struggle in South Africa for rights for everybody, for non-racialism, was linked with the struggle against Nazism and the ideology of Nazism. The National Party that had been in power since 1948, effectively only whites having the vote, parliament being for whites only, everything was white, white, white, white, white all the way through. And the leaders of the National Party, many had been interred during World War Two because they'd supported Hitler. They saw Nazism – not only did they support the racial ideology of it – but as a way of getting at the British.

So the Jewish dimension was a very important part of the background, the context. It was why my parents had fled from Lithuania, but more than that, the ideals they carried with them, their responsiveness to the idea of a world based on justice, rights for everybody.

In my own case, most of the work I did was defending people charged under racist statutes. It was fulfilling work, but in many ways terrible work because the laws were totally unjust. Everything was weighted against people struggling for their rights.

Eventually, I couldn't leave the area of Cape Town. I couldn't go into what were called 'black areas'. And finally I was detained under what was called 'The 90-day Law' – detention without trial. And then two years later, detained a second time.

I never got over that. I never got over that. I found, when I was blown up afterwards, years later, the attack on my body was far less lasting than the attack on my mind. And I function more comfortably and easier without an arm than I was able to function after the sleep deprivation and solitary confinement.

Eventually in 1966, it was impossible for me to carry on practising as a lawyer, and I decided I just couldn't function in South Africa any more.

At the beginning of 1990, the ANC was unbanned. Nelson Mandela was released. Serious negotiations started. I could go back to South Africa.

And my major ambition then was to contribute towards a new constitution for South Africa. And we just worked around the clock on just getting it right. We had a new democratic parliament. The parliament chose Nelson Mandela as president, and I was one of the eleven judges put onto the Constitutional Court.

It's been quite wonderful work, defending the constitution that we all helped to write. And you don't submerge or lose your identity. You bring that into the new South Africa. So, I'm pretty optimistic. No guarantees in life or politics, but I'm pretty optimistic that we are on the right road.

Nelson Mandela

Whilst Dr Joachim Prinz and Dr Martin Luther King Jr were speaking for freedom in America at the March to Washington, Nelson Mandela was awaiting the Rivonia trial that would see him imprisoned for the next twenty-five years. Speaking at his trial Mandela said: 'This is the struggle of the African people, inspired by their own suffering and experience. It is a struggle for the right to live. I have cherished the ideal of a democratic and free society, in which all persons live together in harmony and with equal opportunity. It is an ideal which I hope to live for and achieve. But, if needs be, my Lord, it is an ideal for which I am prepared to die.'

Thirty years after King's 'I have a dream' speech and twenty-five years after his assassination, Mandela and South African President F. W. de Klerk shared the Nobel Peace Prize 'for their work for the peaceful termination of the apartheid regime, and for laying the foundations for a new democratic South Africa'. In his acceptance speech Mandela drew a clear line between the struggle for Civil Rights in the US and the struggle against apartheid in South Africa, demonstrating the intersectionality that links the fight for freedom across time and nations.

Throughout his Presidency he praised the role that religious organizations took in opposing apartheid and reinforced the value of intersectionality when considering the century of oppression and struggle.

On Being Awarded an Honorary Doctorate by Ben-Gurion University of the Negev

Friday, 19 September 1997

Although I have on a number of occasions had the privilege of receiving honorary academic degrees, because of my position, each award is unique in its meaning. And it is always a humbling experience.

Such occasions, in both the giving and the receiving, affirm shared aspirations and hopes. They pledge a common commitment to the values that define particular institutions, peoples or struggles.

In Ben-Gurion University of the Negev we have a centre of excellence which represents the best in the traditions of the Jewish people: a sense of mission; internationalism; inventiveness. It is an institution that gives inspiration through its chosen mission, summed up in the words of the prophecy: 'The desert shall rejoice and blossom as the rose.'

This bold confidence in the capacity of humans to transform barren and hostile conditions into their opposite is bearing welcome fruit across the world through the university's support for development programmes in countries challenged by arid conditions.

South Africa's reconstruction and development programme is high on the list of the beneficiaries of Ben-Gurion University's expertise, thanks to the efforts of the University's South African Associates. In this they are carrying on a long tradition of contribution to our national life by South African Jewry.

Ladies and gentlemen,

Although you are bestowing an honorary Doctorate on me, I do know that it is not any personal achievement that is being given recognition. Rather it is the triumph of the whole South African nation. They have turned apartheid's desert of division and conflict into a society where all can work together to make the people of our rainbow nation blossom.

I humbly accept the award on their behalf, in the fervent hope that what we have achieved will serve as a symbol of peace and reconciliation, and of hope, wherever communities and societies are in the grip of conflict.

South Africa does not believe it can solve the problems of others. But we do believe that our own humble experience has shown that negotiated solutions can be found even to conflicts that have come to seem intractable and that such solutions emerge when those who have been divided reach out to find the common ground.

That experience confirmed for us that in situations of conflict such actions are the special responsibility of leaders; and that when they act in this way they lessen tensions and create the conditions for the good men and women who exist amongst all people, communities and parties to work together in the interests of all.

That is why amongst our fondest memories is the meeting, so filled with promise for the Middle East, of President Ezer Weizmann and then-Chairman Yasser Arafat, during the inauguration of South Africa's first democratic government in 1994.

That was why the tragic assassination of Prime Minister Yitzhak Rabin was at once so shocking and yet still unable to extinguish the hope which had been engendered by the peace process.

And that was why we were so honoured last year to receive Shimon Peres in South Africa, as a man whose courageous contribution to the peace process remains an inspiration.

Today, we cannot but share the anxiety of all who are concerned for peace, at the loss of momentum; at the erosion of trust; at the halting of the implementation of the accord; and at the rising level of tensions in which extremism on either side thrives.

Today, at the end of a century which has seen such a desert of devastation caused by horrific wars, a century which at last has gained much experience in the peaceful resolution of conflicts, we must ask: is this a time for war; is this a time for sending young men to their death?

As we have done before, we appeal to all those concerned to follow the path laid out in the Oslo Agreement towards its goals of peace and security for all.

We admire the efforts that are being made by Palestinian and Israeli citizens to transcend the historical divide and thereby lessen the tensions endangering the process. May their courageous message of peace and partnership be heard throughout the communities they are seeking to unite, across the Middle East and further afield, including here in our own country of South Africa. May their noble actions serve as a force of example, for us, whoever and wherever we are, to make our voices heard in support of reason, rationality and integrity in dealing with this complex situation.

For South Africa, peace, democracy and freedom brought the opportunity at last to address the basic needs of our people, and to bring the improvements to their lives without which our peace would be fragile and our freedom hollow.

The ending of apartheid has brought peace to our whole region and allowed the countries of Southern Africa to work together to realize the potential of development through cooperation. It has allowed us to join the international community of nations in striving for world peace and prosperity.

We are proud to welcome so many distinguished visitors to our country, so that you can sense for yourselves the pride of a nation that is united in working to overcome the legacy of our divided past, through reconstruction and development.

We have only just begun this task, whose difficulties we do not underestimate and which will take us years to achieve. But we face the future with confidence, knowing that those who are ready to join hands can overcome the greatest challenges.

Our welcome to you is made all the warmer by your association with an institution which has embraced a mission of international partnership for development.

We welcome you too for your links with a community which has made a unique and indispensable contribution to our nation.

The award which you bestow on me today, and through me on the people of South Africa, is treasured for the same reasons. May I thank you once more for this great honour, from the bottom of my heart.

And may we always be partners in turning deserts into gardens of peace and prosperity.

I thank you.

Well, let me speak plainly: the United States of America is and must remain a nation of openness to people of all beliefs. Our very unity has been strengthened by this pluralism. That's how we began; this is how we must always be. The ideals of our country leave no room whatsoever for intolerance, anti-Semitism, or bigotry of any kind – none. The unique thing about America is a wall in our Constitution separating church and state. It guarantees there will never be a state religion in this land, but at the same time it makes sure that every single American is free to choose and practise his or her religious beliefs or to choose no religion at all. Their rights shall not be questioned or violated by the state.

**RONALD REAGAN, REMARKS AT THE
INTERNATIONAL CONVENTION OF B'NAI B'RITH,
6 SEPTEMBER 1984**

Bill Clinton

*I*n 1995, thirty years on from the height of the Civil Rights protests, racism and social disparity were still serious issues for America. The events which led to the 1992 Los Angeles riots, and the riots themselves, the release after serving three years for rape of Mike Tyson, the O. J. Simpson trial and acquittal, and the mainstream emergence and establishment of hip-hop and gangsta rap – with their culture as significant as their music, and high-profile figures who courted controversy and in some cases violence – had all provided the media and public consciousness with powerful racial dividers. On 16 October (a scant two weeks since O. J. Simpson's acquittal had divided the nation, with black Americans believing the verdict was right and white Americans believing it was wrong) President Clinton went to Texas to address the University and a million men marched on Washington. The Million Man March was the first significant Civil Rights march since the 1960s. It was organized to protest against the economic and social woes of African Americans as well as to change prejudiced perceptions of 'the black man' and show responsible and constructive behaviour that the organizers hoped would give the mass media positive imagery.

The march was controversial at the time and has been since, for many reasons. In the immediate aftermath there was contention between the organizers and the National Park Service due to the latter estimating the crowd size as 400,000. The focus on 'Man' and the lack of female speakers (though as in contrast to the 1963 March on Washington, Rosa Parks was allowed to speak this time, along with a small handful of other female speakers) was widely criticized. Though the organizers defended themselves with the assertion that the march was designed to encourage and stimulate black men to overcome apathy and resentment and start making a difference, critics argued that the twofold message was also to remind women of their place in the home.

However, the largest controversy was over the keynote speaker, Louis Farrakhan, the Nation of Islam leader, who was publicly antisemitic and had long been a divisive figure in the African-American community, stirring up prejudice and tension against the Jewish community.

Clinton used the opportunity of his speech at the University to praise and highlight equality, family values, community cohesion and the need of Americans to pull together, not apart, to eliminate injustice and prejudices.

Address to the Liz Sutherland Carpenter Distinguished Lectureship in the Humanities and Sciences

The Erwin Centre, University of Texas at Austin, 1995

My fellow Americans, I want to begin by telling you that I am hopeful about America. When I looked at Nikole Bell up here introducing me, and I shook hands with these other young students – I looked into their eyes; I saw the AmeriCorps button on that gentleman's shirt – I was reminded, as I talk about this thorny subject of race today, I was reminded of what Winston Churchill said about the United States when President Roosevelt was trying to pass the Lend-Lease Act so that we could help Britain in their war against Nazi Germany before we, ourselves, were involved. And for a good while the issue was hanging fire. And it was unclear whether the Congress would permit us to help Britain, who at that time was the only bulwark against tyranny in Europe.

And Winston Churchill said: 'I have great confidence in the judgement and the common sense of the American people and their leaders. They invariably do the right thing after they have examined every other alternative.' So I say to you, let me begin by saying that I can see in the eyes of these students and in the spirit of this moment, we will do the right thing.

In recent weeks, every one of us has been made aware of a simple truth – white Americans and black Americans often see the same world in drastically different ways – ways that go beyond and beneath the Simpson trial and its aftermath, which brought these perceptions so starkly into the open.

The rift we see before us that is tearing at the heart of America exists in spite of the remarkable progress black Americans have made in the last generation, since Martin Luther King swept America up in his dream, and President Johnson spoke so powerfully for the dignity of man and the destiny of democracy in demanding that Congress guarantee full voting rights to blacks. The rift between blacks and whites exists still in a very special way in America, in spite of the fact that we have become much more racially and ethnically diverse, and that Hispanic Americans – themselves no strangers to discrimination – are now almost 10 per cent of our national population.

The reasons for this divide are many. Some are rooted in the awful history and stubborn persistence of racism. Some are rooted in the different ways we experience the threats of modem life to personal security, family values, and strong communities. Some are rooted in the fact that we still haven't learned to talk frankly, to listen carefully, and to work together across racial lines.

Almost thirty years ago, Dr Martin Luther King took his last march with sanitation workers in Memphis. They marched for dignity, equality and economic justice. Many carried placards that read simply: 'I am a man.' The throngs of men marching in Washington today, almost all of them, are doing so for the same stated reason. But there is a profound difference between this march today and those of thirty years ago. Thirty years ago, the marchers were demanding the dignity and opportunity they were due because in the face of terrible discrimination, they had worked hard, raised their children, paid their taxes, obeyed the laws, and fought our wars.

Well, today's march is also about pride and dignity and respect. But after a generation of deepening social problems that disproportionately impact black Americans, it is also about black men taking renewed responsibility for themselves, their families and their communities. It's about saying no to crime and drugs and violence. It's about standing up for atonement and reconciliation. It's about insisting that others do the same, and offering to help them. It's about the frank admission that unless black men shoulder their load, no one else can help them or their brothers, their sisters, and their children escape the hard, bleak lives that too many of them still face.

Of course, some of those in the march do have a history that is far from its message of atonement and reconciliation. One million men are right to be standing up for personal responsibility. But one million men do not make right one man's message of malice and division. No good house was ever built on a bad foundation. Nothing good ever came of hate. So let us pray today that all who march and all who speak will stand for atonement, for reconciliation, for responsibility.

Let us pray that those who have spoken for hatred and division in the past will turn away from that past and give voice to the true message of those ordinary Americans who march. If that happens, the men and the women who are there with them will be marching into better lives for themselves and their families. And they could be marching into a better future for America.

Today we face a choice – one way leads to further separation and bitterness and more lost futures. The other way, the path of courage and wisdom, leads to unity, to reconciliation, to a rich opportunity for all Americans to make the most of the lives God gave them. This moment in which the racial divide is so clearly out in the open need not be a setback for us. It presents us with a great opportunity, and we dare not let it pass us by.

In the past when we've had the courage to face the truth about our failure to live up to our own best ideals, we've grown stronger, moved forward and restored proud American optimism. At such turning points America moved to preserve the union and abolished slavery; to embrace women's suffrage; to guarantee basic legal rights to America without regard to race, under the leadership of President Johnson. At each of these moments, we looked in the national mirror and were brave enough to say, this is not who we are; we're better than that.

Abraham Lincoln reminded us that a house divided against itself cannot stand. When divisions have threatened to bring our house down, somehow we have always moved together to shore it up. My fellow Americans, our house is the greatest democracy in all human history. And with all its racial and ethnic diversity, it has beaten the odds of human history. But we know that divisions remain, and we still have work to do.

The two worlds we see now each contain both truth and distortion. Both black and white Americans must face this, for honesty is the only gateway to the many acts of reconciliation that will unite our worlds at last into one America.

White America must understand and acknowledge the roots of black pain. It began with unequal treatment first in law and later in fact. African Americans indeed have lived too long with a justice system that in too many cases has been and continues to be less than just. The record of abuses extends from lynchings and trumped-up charges to false arrests and police brutality. The tragedies of Emmett Till and Rodney King are bloody markers on the very same road.

Still today too many of our police officers play by the rules of the bad old days. It is beyond wrong when law-abiding black parents have to tell their law-abiding children to fear the police whose salaries are paid by their own taxes.

And blacks are right to think something is terribly wrong when African American men are many times more likely to be victims of homicide than any other group in this country; when there are more African American men in our corrections system than in our colleges; when almost one in three African American men in their twenties are either in jail, on parole, or otherwise under the supervision of the criminal justice system – nearly one in three. And that is a disproportionate percentage in comparison to the percentage of blacks who use drugs in our society. Now, I would like every white person here and in America to take a moment to think how he or she would feel if one in three white men were in similar circumstances.

And there is still unacceptable economic disparity between blacks and whites. It is so fashionable to talk today about African Americans as if they have been some sort of protected class. Many whites think blacks are getting more than their fair share in terms of jobs and promotions. That is not true. That is not true.

The truth is that African Americans still make on average about 60 per cent of what white people do; that more than half of African American children live in poverty. And at the very time our young Americans need access to college more than ever before, black college enrolment is dropping in America.

On the other hand, blacks must understand and acknowledge the roots of white fear in America. There is a legitimate fear of the violence that is too prevalent in our urban areas; and often by experience or at least what people see on the news at night, violence for those white people too often has a black face.

It isn't racist for a parent to pull his or her child close when walking through a high-crime neighbourhood, or to wish to stay away from neighbourhoods where innocent children can be shot in school or standing at bus stops by thugs driving by with assault weapons or toting handguns like old west desperados.

It isn't racist for parents to recoil in disgust when they read about a national survey of gang members saying that two-thirds of them feel justified in shooting someone simply for showing them disrespect. It isn't racist for whites to say they don't understand why people put up with gangs on the corner or in the projects, or with drugs being sold in the schools or in the open. It's not racist for whites to assert that the culture of welfare dependency, out-of-wedlock pregnancy and absent fatherhood cannot be broken by social programmes unless there is first more personal responsibility.

The great potential for this march today, beyond the black community, is that whites will come to see a larger truth – that blacks share their fears and embrace their convictions; openly assert that without changes in the black community and within individuals, real change for our society will not come.

This march could remind white people that most black people share their old-fashioned American values, for most black Americans still do work hard, care for their families, pay their taxes, and obey the law, often under circumstances which are far more difficult than those their white counterparts face.

Imagine how you would feel if you were a young parent in your twenties with a young child living in a housing project, working somewhere for $5 an hour with no health insurance, passing every day people on the street selling drugs, making 100 times what you make. Those people are the real heroes of America today, and we should recognize that.

And white people too often forget that they are not immune to the problems black Americans face – crime, drugs, domestic abuse and teen pregnancy. They are too prevalent among whites as well, and some of those problems are growing faster in our white population than in our minority population.

So we all have a stake in solving these common problems together. It is therefore wrong for white Americans to do what they have done too often, simply to move further away from the problems and support policies that will only make them worse.

Finally, both sides seem to fear deep down inside that they'll never quite be able to see each other as more than enemy faces, all of whom carry at least a sliver of bigotry in their hearts. Differences of opinion rooted in different experiences are healthy, indeed essential, for democracies. But differences so great and so rooted in race threaten to divide the house Mr Lincoln gave his life to save. As Dr King said, 'We must learn to live together as brothers, or we will perish as fools.'

Recognizing one another's real grievances is only the first step. We must all take responsibility for ourselves, our conduct and our attitudes. America, we must clean our house of racism.

To our white citizens, I say, I know most of you every day do your very best by your own lights – to live a life free of discrimination. Nevertheless, too many destructive ideas are gaining currency in our midst. The taped voice of one policeman should fill you with outrage. And so I say, we must clean the house of white America of racism. Americans who are in the white majority should be proud to stand up and be heard denouncing the sort of racist rhetoric we heard on that tape – so loudly and clearly denouncing it, that our black fellow citizens can hear us. White racism may be black people's burden, but it's white people's problem. We must clean our house.

To our black citizens, I honour the presence of hundreds of thousands of men in Washington today, committed to atonement and to personal responsibility, and the commitment of millions of other men and women who are African Americans to this cause. I call upon you to build on this effort, to share equally in the promise of America. But to do that, your house, too, must be cleaned of racism. There are too many today, white and black, on the left and the right, on the street corners and radio waves, who seek to sow division for their own purposes. To them I say, no more. We must be one.

Long before we were so diverse, our nation's motto was E Pluribus Unum – out of many, we are one. We must be one – as neighbours, as fellow citizens; not separate camps, but family – white, black, Latino, all of us, no matter how different, who share basic American values and are willing to live by them.

When a child is gunned down on a street in the Bronx, no matter what our race, he is our American child. When a woman dies from a beating, no matter what our race or hers, she is our American sister, And every time drugs course through the vein of another child, it clouds the future of all our American children.

Whether we like it or not, we are one nation, one family, indivisible. And for us, divorce or separation are not options.

Here, in 1995, on the edge of the twenty-first century, we dare not tolerate the existence of two Americas. Under my watch, I will do everything I can to see that as soon as possible there is only one – one America under the rule of law; one social contract committed not to winner take all, but to giving all Americans a chance to win together – one America.

Barack Obama

*I*n January 2007, Senator Obama had launched a campaign to be the Democratic Party's candidate for the 2008 presidential elections. By March 2008 he was in the midst of one of the most closely run primary campaigns in history against Hillary Rodham Clinton, with whoever won achieving a major equal rights first by being either the first African-American or the first woman to be the presidential nominee of a major party. Obama eventually went on to win by the narrowest of margins and in November 2008 was elected President.

In early March, at the start of what was a month-long pause between primaries, clips surfaced on YouTube, and received considerable airtime, of Reverend Jeremiah Wright, Obama's former pastor, being highly and aggressively critical of America and the government, particularly in relation to their treatment of other countries and non-white races. At first Obama attempted to distance himself from Wright's remarks with a few brief statements, whilst neither disowning the now retired Reverend or the church. But it wasn't enough to quell the growing commentary that was building and beginning to question Obama's Americanism. Rather than

leaving the initial preparation to his speech writers, Obama dictated the
speech and then worked late into the night redrafting it himself. When
the final version was sent to a campaign strategist his response to it was:
'This is why you should be president.' The speech became a milestone in the
campaign and has subsequently been credited with helping Obama win
the election.

Sadly, following the speech Reverend Wright's behaviour became even
more controversial. He gave a notably anti-white speech at the NAACP
which caused Obama to disavow him and to withdraw his membership
of the church. In 2009 White publicly blamed Jewish elements of the
government for not allowing Obama to continue their relationship and
for controlling policy regarding Darfur. He later clarified that he meant
Zionist elements rather than all Jewish-Americans, and continues to
condemn Israel.

A More Perfect Union

18 March 2008

'We the people, in order to form a more perfect union.'

Two hundred and twenty-one years ago, in a hall that still stands
across the street, a group of men gathered and, with these simple words,
launched America's improbable experiment in democracy. Farmers and
scholars; statesmen and patriots who had travelled across an ocean to
escape tyranny and persecution finally made real their declaration of
independence at a Philadelphia convention that lasted through the
spring of 1787.

The document they produced was eventually signed but ultimately
unfinished. It was stained by this nation's original sin of slavery, a question
that divided the colonies and brought the convention to a stalemate until
the founders chose to allow the slave trade to continue for at least twenty
more years, and to leave any final resolution to future generations.

Of course, the answer to the slavery question was already embedded
within our Constitution – a Constitution that had at its very core the
ideal of equal citizenship under the law; a Constitution that promised
its people liberty, and justice, and a union that could be and should be
perfected over time.

And yet words on a parchment would not be enough to deliver slaves
from bondage, or provide men and women of every colour and creed

their full rights and obligations as citizens of the United States. What would be needed were Americans in successive generations who were willing to do their part – through protests and struggle, on the streets and in the courts, through a civil war and civil disobedience and always at great risk – to narrow that gap between the promise of our ideals and the reality of their time.

This was one of the tasks we set forth at the beginning of this campaign – to continue the long march of those who came before us, a march for a more just, more equal, more free, more caring and more prosperous America. I chose to run for the presidency at this moment in history because I believe deeply that we cannot solve the challenges of our time unless we solve them together – unless we perfect our union by understanding that we may have different stories, but we hold common hopes; that we may not look the same and we may not have come from the same place, but we all want to move in the same direction – towards a better future for our children and our grandchildren.

This belief comes from my unyielding faith in the decency and generosity of the American people. But it also comes from my own American story.

I am the son of a black man from Kenya and a white woman from Kansas. I was raised with the help of a white grandfather who survived a Depression to serve in Patton's Army during World War Two and a white grandmother who worked on a bomber assembly line at Fort Leavenworth while he was overseas. I've gone to some of the best schools in America and lived in one of the world's poorest nations. I am married to a black American who carries within her the blood of slaves and slave owners – an inheritance we pass on to our two precious daughters. I have brothers, sisters, nieces, nephews, uncles and cousins, of every race and every hue, scattered across three continents, and for as long as I live, I will never forget that in no other country on Earth is my story even possible.

It's a story that hasn't made me the most conventional candidate. But it is a story that has seared into my genetic makeup the idea that this nation is more than the sum of its parts – that out of many, we are truly one.

Throughout the first year of this campaign, against all predictions to the contrary, we saw how hungry the American people were for this message of unity. Despite the temptation to view my candidacy through a purely racial lens, we won commanding victories in states with some of the whitest populations in the country. In South Carolina, where the Confederate flag still flies, we built a powerful coalition of African Americans and white Americans.

This is not to say that race has not been an issue in the campaign. At various stages in the campaign, some commentators have deemed me either 'too black' or 'not black enough'. We saw racial tensions bubble to the surface during the week before the South Carolina primary. The press has scoured every exit poll for the latest evidence of racial polarization, not just in terms of white and black, but black and brown as well.

And yet, it has only been in the last couple of weeks that the discussion of race in this campaign has taken a particularly divisive turn.

On one end of the spectrum, we've heard the implication that my candidacy is somehow an exercise in affirmative action; that it's based solely on the desire of wide-eyed liberals to purchase racial reconciliation on the cheap. On the other end, we've heard my former pastor, Reverend Jeremiah Wright, use incendiary language to express views that have the potential not only to widen the racial divide, but views that denigrate both the greatness and the goodness of our nation; that rightly offend white and black alike.

I have already condemned, in unequivocal terms, the statements of Reverend Wright that have caused such controversy. For some, nagging questions remain. Did I know him to be an occasionally fierce critic of American domestic and foreign policy? Of course. Did I ever hear him make remarks that could be considered controversial while I sat in church? Yes. Did I strongly disagree with many of his political views? Absolutely – just as I'm sure many of you have heard remarks from your pastors, priests or rabbis with which you strongly disagreed.

But the remarks that have caused this recent firestorm weren't simply controversial. They weren't simply a religious leader's effort to speak out against perceived injustice. Instead, they expressed a profoundly distorted view of this country – a view that sees white racism as endemic, and that elevates what is wrong with America above all that we know is right with America; a view that sees the conflicts in the Middle East as rooted primarily in the actions of stalwart allies like Israel, instead of emanating from the perverse and hateful ideologies of radical Islam.

As such, Reverend Wright's comments were not only wrong but divisive, divisive at a time when we need unity; racially charged at a time when we need to come together to solve a set of monumental problems – two wars, a terrorist threat, a falling economy, a chronic health-care crisis and potentially devastating climate change; problems that are neither black or white or Latino or Asian, but rather problems that confront us all.

Given my background, my politics and my professed values and ideals, there will no doubt be those for whom my statements of condemnation are not enough. Why associate myself with Reverend Wright in the first place? they may ask. Why not join another church? And I confess that if all that I knew of Reverend Wright were the snippets of those sermons that have run in an endless loop on the television and YouTube, or if Trinity United Church of Christ conformed to the caricatures being peddled by some commentators, there is no doubt that I would react in much the same way

But the truth is, that isn't all that I know of the man. The man I met more than twenty years ago is a man who helped introduce me to my Christian faith, a man who spoke to me about our obligations to love one another; to care for the sick and lift up the poor. He is a man who served his country as a US Marine; who has studied and lectured at some of the finest universities and seminaries in the country, and who for over thirty years led a church that serves the community by doing God's work here on Earth – by housing the homeless, ministering to the needy, providing day-care services and scholarships and prison ministries, and reaching out to those suffering from HIV/AIDS.

In my first book, *Dreams from My Father*, I described the experience of my first service at Trinity:

People began to shout, to rise from their seats and clap and cry out, a forceful wind carrying the reverend's voice up into the rafters ... And in that single note – hope! – I heard something else; at the foot of that cross, inside the thousands of churches across the city, I imagined the stories of ordinary black people merging with the stories of David and Goliath, Moses and Pharaoh, the Christians in the lion's den, Ezekiel's field of dry bones. Those stories – of survival, and freedom, and hope – became our story, my story; the blood that had spilled was our blood, the tears our tears; until this black church, on this bright day, seemed once more a vessel carrying the story of a people into future generations and into a larger world. Our trials and triumphs became at once unique and universal, black and more than black; in chronicling our journey, the stories and songs gave us a means to reclaim memories that we didn't need to feel shame about … memories that all people might study and cherish – and with which we could start to rebuild.

That has been my experience at Trinity. Like other predominantly black churches across the country, Trinity embodies the black community in its entirety – the doctor and the welfare mom, the model student and the former gang-banger. Like other black churches, Trinity's services are full of raucous laughter and sometimes bawdy humour. They are full of dancing, clapping, screaming and shouting that may seem jarring to the untrained ear. The church contains in full the kindness and cruelty, the fierce intelligence and the shocking ignorance, the struggles and successes, the love and yes, the bitterness and bias that make up the black experience in America.

And this helps explain, perhaps, my relationship with Reverend Wright. As imperfect as he may be, he has been like family to me. He strengthened my faith, officiated my wedding, and baptized my children. Not once in my conversations with him have I heard him talk about any ethnic group in derogatory terms, or treat whites with whom he interacted with anything but courtesy and respect. He contains within him the contradictions – the good and the bad – of the community that he has served diligently for so many years.

I can no more disown him than I can disown the black community. I can no more disown him than I can my white grandmother – a woman who helped raise me, a woman who sacrificed again and again for me, a woman who loves me as much as she loves anything in this world, but a woman who once confessed her fear of black men who passed by her on the street, and who on more than one occasion has uttered racial or ethnic stereotypes that made me cringe.

These people are a part of me. And they are a part of America, this country that I love.

Some will see this as an attempt to justify or excuse comments that are simply inexcusable. I can assure you it is not. I suppose the politically safe thing would be to move on from this episode and just hope that it fades into the woodwork. We can dismiss Reverend Wright as a crank or a demagogue, just as some have dismissed Geraldine Ferraro, in the aftermath of her recent statements, as harbouring some deep-seated racial bias.

But race is an issue that I believe this nation cannot afford to ignore right now. We would be making the same mistake that Reverend

Wright made in his offending sermons about America – to simplify and stereotype and amplify the negative to the point that it distorts reality.

The fact is that the comments that have been made and the issues that have surfaced over the last few weeks reflect the complexities of race in this country that we've never really worked through – a part of our union that we have yet to perfect. And if we walk away now, if we simply retreat into our respective corners, we will never be able to come together and solve challenges like health care, or education, or the need to find good jobs for every American.

Understanding this reality requires a reminder of how we arrived at this point. As William Faulkner once wrote, 'The past isn't dead and buried. In fact, it isn't even past.' We do not need to recite here the history of racial injustice in this country. But we do need to remind ourselves that so many of the disparities that exist in the African-American community today can be directly traced to inequalities passed on from an earlier generation that suffered under the brutal legacy of slavery and Jim Crow.

Segregated schools were, and are, inferior schools; we still haven't fixed them, fifty years after *Brown v. Board of Education*, and the inferior education they provided, then and now, helps explain the pervasive achievement gap between today's black and white students.

Legalized discrimination – where blacks were prevented, often through violence, from owning property, or loans were not granted to African-American business owners, or black homeowners could not access FHA mortgages, or blacks were excluded from unions, or the police force, or fire departments – meant that black families could not amass any meaningful wealth to bequeath to future generations. That history helps explain the wealth and income gap between black and white, and the concentrated pockets of poverty that persist in so many of today's urban and rural communities.

A lack of economic opportunity among black men, and the shame and frustration that came from not being able to provide for one's family, contributed to the erosion of black families – a problem that welfare policies for many years may have worsened. And the lack of basic services in so many urban black neighbourhoods – parks for kids to play in, police walking the beat, regular garbage pick-up and building code enforcement – all helped create a cycle of violence, blight and neglect that continue to haunt us.

This is the reality in which Reverend Wright and other African-Americans of his generation grew up. They came of age in the late Fifties and early Sixties, a time when segregation was still the law of the land and opportunity was systematically constricted. What's remarkable is not how many failed in the face of discrimination, but rather how many men and women overcame the odds; how many were able to make a way out of no way for those like me who would come after them.

But for all those who scratched and clawed their way to get a piece of the American Dream, there were many who didn't make it – those who were ultimately defeated, in one way or another, by discrimination. That legacy of defeat was passed on to future generations – those young men and increasingly young women who we see standing on street corners or languishing in our prisons, without hope or prospects for the future. Even for those blacks who did make it, questions of race, and racism, continue to define their worldview in fundamental ways. For the men and women of Reverend Wright's generation, the memories of humiliation and doubt and fear have not gone away; nor has the anger and the bitterness of those years. That anger may not get expressed in public, in front of white co-workers or white friends. But it does find voice in the barbershop or around the kitchen table. At times, that anger is exploited by politicians, to gin up votes along racial lines, or to make up for a politician's own failings.

And occasionally it finds voice in the church on Sunday morning, in the pulpit and in the pews. The fact that so many people are surprised to hear that anger in some of Reverend Wright's sermons simply reminds us of the old truism that the most segregated hour in American life occurs on Sunday morning. That anger is not always productive; indeed, all too often it distracts attention from solving real problems; it keeps us from squarely facing our own complicity in our condition, and prevents the African-American community from forging the alliances it needs to bring about real change. But the anger is real; it is powerful; and to simply wish it away, to condemn it without understanding its roots, only serves to widen the chasm of misunderstanding that exists between the races.

In fact, a similar anger exists within segments of the white community. Most working- and middle-class white Americans don't feel that they have been particularly privileged by their race. Their experience is the immigrant experience – as far as they're concerned, no one's handed them anything, they've built it from scratch. They've worked hard all their lives, many times only to see their jobs shipped overseas or their pension dumped after a lifetime of labour. They are anxious about their futures, and feel their dreams slipping away; in an era of stagnant wages and global competition, opportunity comes to be seen as a zero-sum game, in which your dreams come at my expense. So when they are told to bus their children to a school across town; when they hear that an African American is getting an advantage in landing a good job or a spot in a good college because of an injustice that they themselves never committed; when they're told that their fears about crime in urban neighbourhoods are somehow prejudiced, resentment builds over time.

Like the anger within the black community, these resentments aren't always expressed in polite company. But they have helped shape the political landscape for at least a generation. Anger over welfare and affirmative action helped forge the Reagan Coalition. Politicians routinely exploited fears of crime for their own electoral ends. Talk-show hosts and conservative commentators built entire careers unmasking bogus claims of racism while dismissing legitimate discussions of racial injustice and inequality as mere political correctness or reverse racism.

Just as black anger often proved counterproductive, so have these white resentments distracted attention from the real culprits of the middle-class squeeze – a corporate culture rife with inside dealing, questionable accounting practices, and short-term greed; a Washington dominated by lobbyists and special interests; economic policies that favour the few over the many. And yet, to wish away the resentments of white Americans, to label them as misguided or even racist, without recognizing they are grounded in legitimate concerns – this too widens the racial divide, and blocks the path to understanding.

This is where we are right now. It's a racial stalemate we've been stuck in for years. Contrary to the claims of some of my critics, black and white, I have never been so naïve as to believe that we can get beyond our racial divisions in a single election cycle, or with a single candidacy – particularly a candidacy as imperfect as my own.

But I have asserted a firm conviction – a conviction rooted in my faith in God and my faith in the American people – that working together we can move beyond some of our old racial wounds, and that in fact we have no choice if we are to continue on the path of a more perfect union.

John Mann

J ohn Mann was elected as Labour Member of Parliament for Bassetlaw in June 2001. A member of the highly influential Treasury Select Committee, he led the campaign for more transparency in the consumer credit industry. John was also Parliamentary Private Secretary to the then Minister for the Olympics Tessa Jowell, and to Richard Caborn, then Minister for Sport.

Before entering parliament he worked for the Amalgamated Engineering and Electrical Union (AEEU), the Trades Union Congress and the Trade Union and Labour Party Liaison Organization. He is a former Chair of Labour Students and prior to his election to parliament he was involved in running the family business.

Since 2005 he has been Chair of the All-Party Group Against Antisemitism and commissioned the two major All-Party Parliamentary Inquiries into Antisemitism.

Accepting Jan Karski Award

May 2009

I asked for advice on what I should say to this audience in response to your kind words and award and was told by a Jewish friend that if I was lost for words to talk about my mother …

I remember what my mother once told me. She was a feisty arguer who never suffered a fool gladly, especially her eldest son: 'I have no time for these people who only want to be someone and not to do something.'

We have too many politicians, too many leaders, who want the offices of state but who freeze at the responsibilities of power. Those who only want to be told the good news. I am sure that Jan Karski encountered such people. I am humbled and somewhat embarrassed to receive this award. All I do with my committee is our little bit and all I ask of the British Jewish Community is that they gently increase their ask of us politicians. Gently but consistently and incrementally.

I never attend any event just for the sake of so doing. I have the privilege to serve and my role is to make things happen. That is why I led the UK parliamentary inquiry into antisemitism and co-founded the ICCA with Irwin Cotler. We have cross-party support for our work, including at the heart of government. And I want to thank the AJC for all your support and advice, especially of course David Harris, who I think I can now call my friend, but also Emanuele Ottolenghi in Brussels and Ken Stern in New York for their invaluable assistance, and many others as well.

But of course there are those who decry our work.

Some in silence. Some in ridicule. Some in hatred.

And of these it is the cowards who I most despise, for their silence creates the tempest on whose winds the messages of hatred and prejudice and ignorance are carried far and wide.

And the coward fears the Jew. For to them, with minds warped by delusions of conspiracy and wealth, the confidence, the artistry, the sociability of Jewish life can only have been created by wicked means.

And the silence encourages the deepening of the prejudice. Of course other changes, threats, events spark the ferment of evil, the restrictions, the animosities and the pogroms, but the curse of silence has never once ended with the abuse of the Jews. Never once. Because every lesson from history shows us that the Jews are hit first, but then the others. We, the others.

I don't do this work for votes. I have no Jewish constituents. Not one identifiable Jewish resident. I receive and will accept no personal gain.

I do my work because fortune has given me the opportunity. That is why I am here today.

I have the honour of representing a coal-mining area in Northern England. It was decimated by the economics of the 1980s, but before then every generation had dug and hewed the coal that fired the British economy.

And in the heat of underground mining those miners took their canaries in cages to warn against the dangers of toxic gases and impending catastrophe.

The analogy of the canary in the cage is not original, nor is it mine. But I represent those elderly retired miners, with their dust-filled dying lungs and their battered and broken knees where they crawled to work and cut coal in shafts half the size of a man.

And I tell you my credence: I bow to no man. I crawl for no one.

I do not intend any member of my family will ever be forced to crawl on their knees. No constituent of mine will ever again be forced to kneel to work.

And what is good enough for me, and my family and my constituents, is good enough for you, for your families, for your friends. For all families. For all friends.

And what I observe is that when the Jewish people walk tall some people don't like it. The successful Jew is the conspirator, benefiting from secret cabals. How I sometimes wish that British Jewry could be that well organized.

The powerful Jew is the aggressor and yet the culturally brilliant Jew is an American, or a Russian, or a Briton. How our nations love to subsume and own cultural virtuosity. But in particular there are those who dislike the proud and confident Jew. These people sadly still exist across the globe. Whether they hide in their tea houses or their bars, their golf clubs or their madrasa.

And with their minds poisoned by the pollution of ignorance, prejudice, malice and lies, it is our job to free them from their mental torture. That is the *raison d'être* of my committee. That is why we do what we are doing.

And I come not to elaborate on the threats, threats that you know all too well. And there are many:

The satellite stations of Saudi Arabia

The resurgent Nazis of Eastern Europe

The new revisionists of the Baltics

The President of Iran

The British intellectuals who get nervous when I label them accurately, not as the anti-Zionists they wish to be known as, but as the racists that they have become.

The scholars including Americans, who answer every argument with a but. When there are no ifs, no buts in the fight against antisemitism.

We have our enemies. Their tortured minds warped by ignorance and loathing.

And I share the despair of all who yearn for our international organizations to act with reason and with justice. The United Nations was born out of depravities of intolerance and hatred but also out of the impotence of national political complacencies. We should therefore expect the UN to have the countering of intolerance in its organizational DNA. The abuse of its Durban and now Geneva conferences highlights its own impotence and the inevitability of its consequential irrelevance.

But should we, the democracies of the world, allow ourselves to be undermined by demagogues and dictators yet again? Whatever tactics are applied to turn around the UN – and they are of great importance – in addition there needs to be at the heart of the UN, properly resourced and suitably empowered, a UN unit charged with dealing directly with countering antisemitism. Its establishment is one small, but essential bridgehead needed in our political armoury.

I have little complacency. But I have no fear. These antisemites relish fear and indecision.

When I look to my heroes and heroines for inspiration – my role models, my teachers – I see of course see Mr Mandela – who doesn't? – and I see Rev. King. And Rosa Parkes.

Let me quote from Rosa Parkes: 'As I got up on the bus I saw that there was only one vacancy, so this was the seat that I took.'

This world and past generations are full of Rosa Parkes. People going about their everyday business quietly and with dignity. But people not prepared to be bullied and cowed and intimidated. No doubt a little scared, but those who do their bit by doing what is right.

That is why I am a little reluctant to accept your kind award, your accolades. But I do so on behalf of all my committee and all our friends and allies and all those we attempt to give confidence to.

Because every Jewish student who is empowered to stand up and says, this is not right, every youth who says no, that is not acceptable, every mother and grandmother who is proud of their child's defiance – these are my heroes and heroines.

But I also have one particular Jewish hero. Or rather heroine.

I quote these autobiographical words:

And now I have only this desire left: never to lose the feeling that it is I who am indebted for what has been given to me … I have seen my own grandchildren grow up as free Jews in a country that is their own. Let no one have any doubts about this: our children and our children's children will never settle for anything else.

Just as the AJC was being created in New York, Golda Meir[1] as a young child saw and heard the hatred of the mob; she became aware of her identity. Golda Meir is a suitable and appropriate role model.

For I seek results. I seek progress. Others can write the books, paint the pictures. I admire their talents, but my priorities include:

Building on the London declaration, agreed by forty countries in London this February, endorsed by all British political leaders and blueprint of what must spread throughout the European Union and its countries.

Let me quote just one of the elements of the London Declaration, but one which suitably sums up the content and direction of the entire declaration, which is available online: 'We today in London resolve that: parliamentarians shall expose, challenge, and isolate political actors who engage in hate against Jews and target the State of Israel as a Jewish entity.'

My priorities also include repeating this year's successful UK Internet prosecution of antisemites with a website hosted overseas.

Challenging the lack of action by civil society, including fence-sitting university leaders or the prevaricating European football leaders. You know in Łódź, Poland, football fanatics still abuse one another with the term 'Jew'. We have a lot more work to do.

What would Jan Karski now think, as a man born ninety-five years ago in the city of Łódź? We rightly honour Jan Karski, but he is an exception. Because we now know his story. We can never know the stories of most of those who stood up. Their bravery, their ingenuity. Their sacrifice.

Let me tell you a story that you have never heard. Of the white man who with his white brothers refused to allow their father to cast out their sister when she had a child with a black African and then dared to have a second such child. That man never told me his story, which I started to learn only at his funeral.

Of the woman he married whose grandfather was thrown out of work for helping form the Labour Party at the turn of the last century. Whose mother had to leave school despite winning a scholarship in order to work as a domestic cleaner to feed the family.

And of the Jewish community in that city of Leeds, the city where I was born, who stood by that family as part of the trade union movement. That little part of Jewish history is hardly recorded, or known.

But I know it. Because that is my family. My parents. Long dead. But they would be crying with pride tonight.

Because those values that stirred the Jewish workers in Leeds to stand by my family are exactly the same values that inspired my parents and through their teachings inspired me.

We know too little of who we are, of what came before and of its relevance to us, but my family will always stand by its friends.

Emile Zola in his trial stated: 'I have for me only an ideal of truth and justice. But I am quite calm. I shall conquer.'

Friends, we shall conquer.

Zola was right when he proclaimed: 'We will not allow our countries to remain the victims of lies and injustice.'

I hardly know this great country. My passions for mountains may eventually bring me back, as my daughter studies in Berkeley next academic year. But to date I have never seen the curvaceous peaks of California. Nor the snow-capped Rockies of Colorado. I have never climbed Stone Mountain in Georgia. I have not even surveyed the view from Lookout Mountain in Tennessee.

But I tell you this, in concluding, my friends. From every Jewish student rally I attend, in every Limmud debate I participate in to every global conference that we organize, to every racist that we send running:

I may still smell the intolerance of antisemitism, I may read the literature of hate,

But when I look out from the mountain, I see not a promise but a reality grounded in the self-belief and self-determination of those children, grandchildren and now even great-grandchildren.

And I also hear the bells of freedom and I say to you, my friends, be confident, be confident because the bells of freedom are ringing today and through our efforts, Jew and non-Jew, the bells of freedom will ring again tomorrow. Thank you.

PART III

ZIONISM

Zionism, the movement for the re-establishment, and now protection and development, of the Jewish state of Israel, arose in the late 1800s largely as a result of rising antisemitism in Europe from the Dreyfus affair in France to the Russian pogroms. In 1897 the First Zionist Congress was held in Basel and the World Zionist Organization – and modern Zionism – was born. Palestine was at the time a part of the Ottoman Empire and small-scale immigration of European Jews began. In 1903 the British offered some land in Uganda to form a Jewish state, but the congress rejected this, even as a temporary measure, in its desire to return the Jewish people to Israel. The First World War saw the Ottoman Empire join the Central Axis opposing the Allies and ultimately losing. This changed the landscape in the Middle East, and the British, through the Balfour Declaration, endorsed the creation of a Jewish homeland in Palestine. This was subsequently ratified by the League of Nations, with the British given a mandate for administration of the area. Immigration subsequently increased, rising still further in the early Thirties following Hitler's rise to power, but this led to violent rioting as a result of which the British established the Peel Commission and subsequently restricted immigration.

After the Second World War and the Holocaust, surviving Jews started emigrating to Palestine in defiance of British law. The British either imprisoned them in Cyprus or returned them to Germany, but such was the wave of support, particularly in America, for establishing a Jewish homeland in Israel that the British referred the situation to the UN, who recommended and subsequently voted for partition. On 14 May 1948 the State of Israel was declared by David Ben-Gurion, its first prime minister, and the Arab–Israeli war began when seven countries immediately invaded, ultimately leading to a huge exodus of Palestinians and influx of Jews from neighbouring Arab countries.

But the history and controversy of Zionism was very far from ended with the establishment of the State of Israel. The varying rights of Jews and Palestinians in the state led some to compare Israeli policy with apartheid. In 1975 the UN passed a resolution by 72 to 35 (with 32 abstentions) declaring 'that Zionism is a form of racism and racial discrimination'. In his response, quoted in full in this chapter, Chaim Herzog, the Israeli Ambassador, called the resolution 'another manifestation of the bitter anti-Semitic, anti-Jewish hatred which animates Arab society … We are being attacked by a society which is motivated by the most extreme form of racism known in the world today.'

The UN revoked the resolution in 1991, but to this day Zionism, anti-Zionism and whether either is, at heart, racist, remain hotly and bitterly contested among and between Jews and Gentiles alike.

Chaim Weizmann

*W*eizmann was born in Belarus in 1874, the third of fifteen children of a timber merchant. He studied chemistry at university in Germany and Switzerland, settling in Manchester in 1904 as a senior lecturer at the university.

The first Zionist conference was held in Switzerland in 1897 and though Weizmann wasn't there, he subsequently attended every single one. He became a prominent British Zionist after his move to Manchester and conveniently lived in the constituency of Arthur Balfour, then Prime Minister and later Foreign Secretary, who would issue the Balfour Declaration in 1917. He remained an active and influential Zionist and when the Peel Commission was convened in 1936 it was Weizmann who spoke on behalf of Jews. Speaking without a prepared text, though aware that his was a seminal task in Jewish history, Weizmann held the floor for two and a half hours. The Peel Commission eventually recommended partition, though the subsequent Woodhead Commission quashed this as unfeasible.

David Ben-Gurion described Weizmann as the most gifted envoy the Jewish people ever produced. 'There was no other Jew in whom the non-Jewish world perceived the embodiment of the Jewish people, with their ability, their will, and their longings ... He was perhaps the only truly great ambassador produced by the Jewish people throughout the generations.'

Later, in his autobiography, Weizmann wrote of his speech: 'I felt that I would be speaking for generations long since dead, for those who lay buried on Mount Scopus and those whose last resting places were scattered all over the world ... I knew that any misstep of mine, any error, however involuntary, would be not mine alone but would redound to the discredit of my people. I was aware of a crushing sense of responsibility.'

In 1949 Weizmann became the first President of Israel – a largely ceremonial post – which he held till his death in 1952. Though best remembered for his political activism, Weizmann was first and foremost a chemist and it was his pioneering of industrial fermentation, crucial to the war effort from 1915 onwards, that enabled his influence to extend so far in British politics.

'The Jews carry Palestine in their hearts'

25 November 1936

I should like to put before you the Jewish problem, as it presents itself today. It is a twofold problem; but its nature can perhaps be expressed in one word: it is the problem of the homelessness of a people. Speaking of homelessness, I should like to state that individual Jews, and individual groups of Jews, may have homes and sometimes very comfortable homes. Indeed, if one thinks of the small communities in the west of Europe beginning with England and continuing further down to the South – France, Switzerland, Italy, Belgium and Holland – these Jewish communities are, as compared to the Jews in Central, Eastern and South-eastern Europe, in a fairly comfortable position. Then again, the position of the great Jewish community further west in America is, economically, and to a certain extent politically and morally, such that Jews there are free to work and labour without let or hindrance. But if one draws a line and takes the Rhine as the geographical boundary, almost everything to the east of the Rhine is today in a position, politically and economically, which may be described – and I am not given, I think, to exaggeration – as something that is neither life nor death; and one may add that if Europe today were in the same state as it was in 1914 before the War, with the highways and byways of Europe and the world in general open, then we should have witnessed an emigration of Jews that would probably have dwarfed the pre-war emigration – and the pre-war emigration was not by any means small. I think that in the year 1914 alone there emigrated out of Russia, which then included Poland as well, something in the neighbourhood of 120,000 Jews.

They went in the majority of cases to America, where they could readily be absorbed in a highly developed industrial country. The emigrant found his livelihood almost immediately on arrival. This, as Your Lordship and the members of the Commission are well aware, cannot happen today. The world is closed; and we have recently heard it said in authoritative quarters in Geneva, in Poland, and in England, that there are one million Jews too many in Poland. This is not the place to enter into a discussion as to why exactly one million *Jews*? They are citizens of Poland; their fate and their destinies have been bound up with the fate and destinies of Poland for well-nigh a thousand years. They passed through all the vicissitudes of the Polish nation. They desire to make their contribution, good, bad or indifferent – like everybody else – to Polish development. Why should they be singled out as being a million too many?

What does it mean? Where can they go? Is there any place in the world which can rapidly absorb one million people, whoever they may be, Jews or non-Jews? The poor Polish peasant, perhaps ignorant and not very subtle, when he hears people in authority making a pronouncement like that, may possibly interpret it as meaning: here is a superfluous people standing in my way, which must be got rid of somehow.

I do not want to press the point any further. I shall not waste the time of the Commission by describing in any way what is happening in Germany. It is too well known to need elaboration. This accounts for the position of something like 3,600,000 Jews. Poland has slightly over three million; Germany had in 1932 or 1933 something like 600,000, but that number has since diminished. If one goes further afield, and takes the Jewries of Romania, Latvia, Austria, one sees practically the same picture; and it is no exaggeration on my part to say that today almost six million Jews – I am not speaking of the Jews in Persia and Morocco and such places, who are very inarticulate, and of whom one hears very little – there are in this part of the world six million people pent up in places where they are not wanted, and for whom the world is divided into places where they cannot live, and places into which they may not enter.

Now we think this is not merely a problem which concerns the Jewish community. It is in our view a world problem of considerable importance. Naturally, it is one which affects primarily the Jewish community, and secondarily the state of affairs in that particular part of the world, a part of the world which since the War has moved towards new forms of political and social life, and which is not yet very strong or very mature either politically or economically. These six million people to whom I have referred are condemned to live from hand to mouth, they do not know today what is going to happen tomorrow. I am not speaking now of organized anti-Semitism; even assuming the host-nations were quite friendly, there would still be purely objective reasons in those parts of the world which would tend to grind down the Jewish community and make it into the flotsam and jetsam of the world – grind it into economic dust, so to speak.

Since my early youth, My Lord, I have fought destructive tendencies in Jewry, but it is almost impossible to avoid destructive tendencies amongst a younger generation which lives in the state I have described, unless some hope is given to the young people that one day, some day in some distant future, one in five, one in ten, one in twenty, will find refuge somewhere where he can work, where he can live, and where he can straighten himself up and look with open eyes at the world and at his fellow men and women. It is no wonder that a certificate for Palestine is considered the highest boon in this part of the world. One in twenty, one in thirty, may get it, and for them it is redemption; it is tantamount to freedom, the opportunity to live and work, and that is why they watch with such intensity all that is going on here, and whether or not the doors of Palestine will remain open or will remain closed.

I could go on dwelling on the tense position in Jewry today, aggravated, as it naturally has been, by the effects of the Great War. This is the moral side of the problem. In all countries we try to do our best, but somehow in many countries we are not entirely accepted as an integral part of the communities to which we belong. This feeling is one of the causes which have prompted Jews throughout the ages, and particularly in the last hundred years, to try to make a contribution towards the solution of the problem and to normalize – to some, to normalize – the position of the Jews in the world. We are sufficiently strong, My Lord, to have preserved our identity, but an identity which is *sui generis* and not like the identity of other nations. When one speaks of the English or the French or the German nation, one refers to a definite State, a definite organization, a language, a literature, a history, a common destiny; but it is clear that when one speaks of the Jewish people, one speaks of a people which is a minority everywhere, a majority nowhere, which is to some extent identified with the races among which it lives, but still not quite identical. It is, if I may say so, a disembodied ghost of a race, without a body, and it therefore inspires suspicion, and suspicion breeds hatred. There should be one place in the world, in God's wide world, where we could live and express ourselves in accordance with our character, and make our contribution towards the civilized world, in our own way and through our own channels. Perhaps if we had, we would be better understood in ourselves, and our relation to other races and nations would become more normal. We would not have to be always on the defensive or, on the contrary, become too aggressive, as always happened with a minority forced to be constantly on the defensive.

What has produced this particular mentality of the Jews which makes me describe the Jewish race as a sort of disembodied ghost – an entity and yet not an entity in accordance with the usual standards which are applied to define an entity? I believe the main cause which has produced the particular state of Jewry in the world is its attachment to Palestine. We are a stiff-necked people and a people of long memory. We never forget. Whether it is our misfortune or whether it is our good fortune, we have never forgotten Palestine, and this steadfastness, which has preserved the Jew throughout the ages and throughout a career that is almost one long chain of inhuman suffering, is primarily due to some physiological or psychological attachment to Palestine. We have never forgotten it nor given it up. We have survived our Babylonian and Roman conquerors. The Jews put up a fairly severe fight, and the Roman Empire, which digested half of the civilized world, did not digest small Judaea. Whenever they once got a chance, the slightest chance, there the Jews returned, there they created their literature, their villages, towns, and communities. If the Commission would take the trouble to study the post-Roman period of the Jews and the life of the Jews in Palestine, they would find that during the nineteen centuries which have passed since the destruction of Palestine as a Jewish political entity, there was not a single century in which the Jews did not attempt to come back.

It is, I believe, a fallacy to regard those 1,900 years as, so to say, a desert of time; they were not. When the material props of the Jewish commonwealth were destroyed, the Jews carried Palestine in their hearts and in their heads wherever they went. That idea continued to express itself in their ritual and in their prayers. In the East End of London the Jew still prays for dew in the summer and for rain in the winter, and his seasons and festivals are all Palestinian seasons and Palestinian festivals. When Rome destroyed their country, the intellectual leader of the Jewish Community came to the Roman commander and said: 'You have destroyed all our material possessions; give us, I pray, some refuge for our houses of learning.' A refuge was found; the place still exists; it was then a big place, and is now any railway station by the name of Yebna – in Hebrew, *Yabneh*. There were schools there, and there the Jews continued their intellectual output, so that those schools became, so to speak, the spiritual homes, not only of Palestinian Jewry, but of Jewry at large, which was gradually filtering out of Palestine and dispersing all over the world. They replaced the material Palestine, the political Palestine, by a moral Palestine which was indestructible, which remained indestructible; and this yearning found its expression in a mass of literature, sacred and non-sacred, secular and religious.

The Balfour Declaration was issued by His Majesty's Government on 2 November 1917.

It has sometimes glibly been said: 'Here is a document, somewhat vague in its nature, issued in time of war. It was a wartime expedient.' I have a much higher opinion of British statesmen than to attribute to them an act of that kind. It was a solemn act, a promise given to a people, an ancient people, which finds itself in the position which I have described.

What did the Balfour Declaration mean? It meant something quite simple at that time, and I am saying so advisedly. It meant that Judaea was restored to the Jews or the Jews were restored to Judaea. I could submit to the Commission a series of utterances of responsible statesmen and men in every walk of life in England to show that this Declaration was at the time regarded as the Magna Carta of the Jewish people; it was in a sense comparable with another Declaration made thousands of years before, when Cyrus allowed a remnant of the Jews to return from Babylon and to rebuild the Temple. To the ordinary man at that time reading the Declaration, what it meant is broadly indicated by the various speeches at a solemn meeting at the Opera House in London, where (among others)

Lord Cecil spoke and said: 'Arabia for the Arabs, Judaea for the Jews, Armenia for the Armenians.' Much water and much blood have flowed under the various bridges of the world since that time, and not all of his predictions have been realized; but we read into the Declaration what the statesmen of Great Britain told us it meant. It meant a National Home, 'national' meaning that we should be able to live like a nation in Palestine, and 'Home' a place where we might live as free, men in contradistinction to living on sufferance everywhere else. To English people I need not explain what the word 'home' means, or what it does *not* mean, to us everywhere else.

The meaning is clear, and the Jewry of the world, in the trenches of Europe, in the pogrom-swept area of Russia, saw it like that. Tens of thousands of Jews marched before the house of the British Consul at Odessa at the time. Behind them were half-organized bands of marauders and murderers sweeping the countryside and destroying everything in their wake. But those Jews poured out their hearts in gratitude to the one accessible representative of the British Government, whom they had never seen, of whom they had never heard, whose language they could not speak, whose mentality they could not understand. They felt that here something had been done for us which, after two thousand years of hope and yearning, would at last give us a resting-place in this terrible world.

The Peel Report recommended partition into separate Arab and Jewish states, a drastic solution that was rejected by the Arabs and most Zionists (but accepted by Weizmann). It was never implemented by the British government. The six million Jews for whom Weizmann spoke were exterminated by the Nazis, Israel was established as a Jewish state in Palestine in 1948, and Weizmann was elected president.

Winston Churchill

I n the canonization of Winston Churchill it can be shocking for modern audiences to read what first appears to be a casual acceptance, even an endorsement, of antisemitism. But what this article actually sheds light on is the view in Britain at the time that support of Zionism was, in a way, a method of opposing Bolshevism. Twentieth-century history is carved out in part by the attempts of Western capitalist governments to oppress, oppose and destabilize Bolshevik and communist regimes. The Russian Revolution of 1917 had not only sent ripples of fear through Europe, it had also released the previously unknown outside of Russia 'Protocols of the Elders of Zion', the forged antisemitic tract which claimed to demonstrate a secret Jewish desire for world domination. Published for the first time in Britain in the same month this article appeared, Churchill's writing constitutes a warning by a senior member of the British government against antisemitic lies. Without doubt, Churchill's words in 1920 seem arcane and highly insensitive today, but his purpose is clear – to stifle at birth the libellous claim (which gained currency in other European countries) that Bolshevism was a function of Zionism.

By this time, Churchill was well aware of the predicament of British Jews. As First Lord of the Admiralty he was aware of Chaim Weizmann, who worked as director of the British Admiralty laboratories while also working *as head of the British Zionist Federation. His role in the Admiralty give Weizmann unprecedented access to the upper echelons of British politics. In 1944, following the assassination of Lord Moyne by Jewish terrorists in Palestine, Churchill referred in parliament to Weizmann as 'a very old friend of mine' and in this same speech expressed a little more on his views on the future of Zionism:*

> *This shameful crime has shocked the world. It has affected none more strongly than those, like myself, who, in the past, have been consistent friends of the Jews and constant architects of their future. If our dreams for Zionism are to end in the smoke of assassins' pistols and our labours for its future to produce only a new set of gangsters worthy of Nazi Germany, many like myself will have to reconsider the position we have maintained so consistently and so long in the past. If there is to be any hope of a peaceful and successful future for Zionism, these wicked activities must cease, and those responsible for them must be destroyed root and branch.*

The following article is reproduced without editing other than typographical.

A Struggle for the Soul of the Jewish People

Illustrated Sunday Herald, 8 February 1920

Some people like Jews and some do not; but no thoughtful man can doubt the fact that they are beyond all question the most formidable and the most remarkable race which has ever appeared in the world.

And it may well be that this same astounding race may at the present time be in the actual process of producing another system of morals and philosophy, as malevolent as Christianity was benevolent, which, if not arrested would shatter irretrievably all that Christianity has rendered possible. It would almost seem as if the gospel of Christ and the gospel of Antichrist were destined to originate among the same people; and that this mystic and mysterious race had been chosen for the supreme manifestations, both of the divine and the diabolical.

The National Russian Jews, in spite of the disabilities under which they have suffered, have managed to play an honourable and successful part in the national life even of Russia. As bankers and industrialists they have strenuously promoted the development of Russia's economic resources, and they were foremost in the creation of those remarkable organizations, the Russian Co-operative Societies. In politics their support has been given, for the most part, to liberal and progressive movements, and they have been among the staunchest upholders of friendship with France and Great Britain.

International Jews

In violent opposition to all this sphere of Jewish effort rise the schemes of the International Jews. The adherents of this sinister confederacy are mostly men reared up among the unhappy populations of countries where Jews are persecuted on account of their race. Most, if not all, of them have forsaken the faith of their forefathers, and divorced from their minds all spiritual hopes of the next world. This movement among the Jews is not new. From the days of Spartacus Weishaupt to those of Karl Marx, and down to Trotsky (Russia), Bela Kun (Hungary), Rosa Luxemburg (Germany), and Emma Goldman (United States),[1] this worldwide conspiracy for the overthrow of civilization and for the reconstitution of society on the basis of arrested development, of envious malevolence, and impossible equality, has been steadily growing. It played, as a modern writer, Mrs Webster,[2] has so ably shown, a definitely recognizable part in the tragedy of the French Revolution. It has been the mainspring of every subversive movement during the nineteenth century; and now at last this band of extraordinary personalities from the underworld of the great cities of Europe and America have gripped the Russian people by the hair of their heads and have become practically the undisputed masters of that enormous empire.

Terrorist Jews

There is no need to exaggerate the part played in the creation of Bolshevism and the actual bringing about of the Russian Revolution by these international and for the most part atheistic Jews. It is certainly a very great one; it probably outweighs all others. With the notable exception of Lenin, the majority of the leading figures are Jews. Moreover, the principal inspiration and driving power comes from the Jewish leaders. Thus Tchitcherin, a pure Russian, is eclipsed by his nominal subordinate

Litvinoff, and the influence of Russians like Bukharin or Lunacharski cannot be compared with the power of Trotsky, or of Zinovieff, the Dictator of the Red Citadel (Petrograd), or of Krassin or Radek[3] – all Jews. In the Soviet institutions the predominance of Jews is even more astonishing. And the prominent, if not indeed the principal, part in the system of terrorism applied by the Extraordinary Commissions for Combating Counter-Revolution has been taken by Jews, and in some notable cases by Jewesses.

The same evil prominence was obtained by Jews in the brief period of terror during which Bela Kun ruled in Hungary. The same phenomenon has been presented in Germany (especially in Bavaria), so far as this madness has been allowed to prey upon the temporary prostration of the German people. Although in all these countries there are many non-Jews every whit as bad as the worst of the Jewish revolutionaries, the part played by the latter in proportion to their numbers in the population is astonishing.

'Protector of the Jews'

Needless to say, the most intense passions of revenge have been excited in the breasts of the Russian people. Wherever General Denikin's[4] authority could reach, protection was always accorded to the Jewish population, and strenuous efforts were made by his officers to prevent reprisals and to punish those guilty of them. So much was this the case that the Petlurist propaganda against General Denikin denounced him as the Protector of the Jews. The Misses Healy, nieces of Mr Tim Healy, relating their personal experiences in Kieff, have declared that to their knowledge on more than one occasion officers who committed offences against Jews were reduced to the ranks and sent out of the city to the front. But the hordes of brigands by whom the whole vast expanse of the Russian Empire is becoming infested do not hesitate to gratify their lust for blood and for revenge at the expense of the innocent Jewish population whenever an opportunity occurs. The brigand Makhno, the hordes of Petlura and of Gregorieff,[5] who signalized their every success by the most brutal massacres, everywhere found among the half-stupefied, half-infuriated population an eager response to anti-Semitism in its worst and foulest forms. The fact that in many cases Jewish interests and Jewish places of worship are excepted by the Bolsheviks from their universal hostility has tended more and more to associate the Jewish race in Russia with the villainies which are now being perpetrated.

A Home for the Jews

Zionism offers the third sphere to the political conceptions of the Jewish race. In violent contrast to international communism.

Zionism has already become a factor in the political convulsions of Russia, as a powerful competing influence in Bolshevik circles with the international communistic system. Nothing could be more significant than the fury with which Trotsky has attacked the Zionists generally, and Dr Weissmann in particular. The cruel penetration of his mind leaves him in no doubt that his schemes of a worldwide communistic State under Jewish domination are directly thwarted and hindered by this new ideal, which directs the energies and the hopes of Jews in every land towards a simpler, a truer, and a far more attainable goal. The struggle which is now beginning between the Zionist and Bolshevik Jews is little less than a struggle for the soul of the Jewish people.

Maurice Rosette

*T*hroughout the twentieth century the British Labour Party worked hard to win the support of the country's Jewish population. Critical to this were various organizations including Poale Zion, a movement of Marxist-Zionist Jewish workers founded in the Russian Empire at the beginning of the century after the Bund (the Jewish Socialist Party) rejected Zionism. Contrary to Churchill's views that the struggle for the Jewish soul was between either Marxism or Zionism, Poale Zion believed in the Marxist view of history with the additional role of nationalism and saw a future in the land of Israel where a Jewish proletariat would then take part in the class struggle.

Although Poale Zion had played an important role in promoting the cause of Zionism within the Labour Party between the two world wars, membership had fallen from 3,000 in 1920 to a mere 450 in the late 1930s; by the end of the war membership had risen back up into the thousands. Maurice Rosette was an activist in the Poale Zion movement. Having previously worked in the Information Department of the Jewish Agency, the Palestine Labour Political Committee and Zionist Organization,[1] he had been secretary of Poale Zion for some years when he came to give his most important speech at the Labour Conference in May 1943. Five years later Rosette was once more speaking at the Labour Conference, just five days after the formation of Israel. On that occasion he began: 'I have waited for two thousand years to make this speech.'

Ultimately, the 1943 Conference offered a powerful endorsement of the establishing of a Jewish national state, though the Second World War would continue for another two long years. Rosette would later become Secretary General to the Israeli Knesset, a post in which he would serve for some twenty years[2].

Sympathy is not Enough

Printed in *Labour and the Jewish People*[3]

'This Conference gives renewed expression to the horror and indignation with which all civilized mankind witnesses Hitler's bestial campaign of extermination of European Jewry and declares that the work of salvation must be on a scale proportionate to this unparalleled crime. It urges the Governments of those of the United Nations which are in a position to admit victims of this terror to do so, and to encourage neutral States to similar action by example and, where necessary, financial and other guarantees.

'The Conference declares that victory must ensure for the Jews full civil, political and economic equality and their national rights. It reaffirms the traditional policy of the British Labour Party in favour of building Palestine as the Jewish National Home. It asks that the Jewish Agency be given authority to make the fullest use of the economic capacity of the country to absorb immigrants and to develop the country, including the development of unoccupied and undeveloped lands. It demands for the Jewish people an equal status among the free nations of the world. It urges the National Executive Committee to take all possible steps to combat the growth of anti-Semitism, and, as a factor, the development of which is vitally connected with the Nazi and Fascist outlook.'

Delegates may recall that I have spoken from this rostrum on this subject before, but never with a heavier heart. This Conference and all humanity is now painfully familiar with the stark horror of the policy which is being carried out in the slaughterhouse of Europe today. Never in the history of mankind, not even within the recollection of my own people, whose past has never been free from the nightmare of persecution, has there been anything to equal this ghastly tragedy, so fearful that the human mind can barely grasp it.

The Jewish people today is a sad people; but it is also a fighting people. Human memory is short, and the suffering which we are witnessing today may be forgotten. But as long as freedom will endure, men will speak with pride of the incomparable courage of the Jews in the ghetto of Warsaw. A bare remnant of 40,000, unarmed except for a few arms supplied by the underground movement, fought desperately for weeks. Without hope of victory, they fought a tenacious battle and held up Nazi troops, who subdued them finally with tanks and aeroplanes, but only after they had accounted for 300 killed and 1,000 wounded. These men and women will be cited for all time as a testimony of the will to live of the Jewish people and the unquenchable flame of human liberty.

But is our sympathy and our action comparable to their courage? Recently the House of Commons debated the question of plans for rescue of some of these tortured men and women. Those who feel deeply on this subject registered their bitter disappointment at the meagre steps which have been taken. Excuses and pleas for inaction were advanced, and we cannot believe that those who did so spoke in the name of the British People.

There are some who say, Why this emphasis on the Jews? They are not the only ones who suffer. My answer is, They are the only people who are being totally destroyed, men, women, and children. Millions of Jews have been brutally murdered in Poland alone. Has any other people suffered like this? Has any other people been singled out as a people for total destruction? There are 5½ million Jews in occupied territory. Two million of them have already been exterminated. This Conference has struck a note of optimism lit up by the sunbeams of impending victory. But for the Jewish people in Europe this victory may be Dead Sea fruit, for unless something is speedily done there may not be a single Jew left in Europe to enjoy the benefits of victory. Therefore, when this resolution asks for speedy action and asks Great Britain to set an example, I know that it voices the feelings of this Conference.

This problem is not a new one. We were singled out in 1933 as the first victims of Nazi aggression. Would that the nations of the world had realized in 1933 where this was leading. What bloodshed might have been saved the world? As I say, this problem is not a new one. It is our proud boast that the Labour Party was the first in this country to understand the age-long Jewish problem, and to associate itself with the great work of revival in Palestine, which envisaged its solution.

The Jewish Homeland

Today in Palestine the foundation of a civilization has been laid, a civilization which has become a bastion of liberty and an arsenal of democracy in the present conflict. British, Dominion and Allied soldiers in Palestine have been inspired by our work, especially in the Jewish villages and communal settlements. The young men and women of these settlements have gone forth to take their places side by side with all free men and women. Thirty thousand Palestine Jews are serving in the British armies alone and were privileged to take part in the glorious North African campaign. The new and up-to-date Jewish factories are teeming with war production. The fields are helping to feed the Allied Forces.

The resolution asks you to reaffirm the traditional policy of sympathy which this Labour Party has shown for the Jewish National Home. The European Jewish tragedy has shocked mankind; but its most melancholy feature has been the short-sighted policy which has condemned the Jews of Palestine to stand frustrated behind closed doors when there is so much that their land can and would do to receive the hunted and the oppressed from Europe. After this war the Jewish people must be given the chance to develop and bring to fruition this great human experiment. The Jewish people have, by their sufferings and by their efforts, earned the right to a place amongst the free nations of the world. The achievements of the Jewish Labour Movement in Palestine are a guarantee that this privilege will be used wisely and on progressive lines.

I come finally to the last point in the resolution to which Mr James Walker made reference – namely, the section which deals with anti-Semitism in this country. At the beginning of this war, men and women were terrified by stories of a ghastly plan by which disease would be scattered by aeroplane upon unsuspecting countries. We have hardly realized that this has in a sense actually begun. The disease which the enemy has dropped is the disease of anti-Semitism. A disease foul and virulent, which rotted the bodies and encompassed the defeat of countries now under the Nazi yoke. It is the bounden duty of the Labour Movement to fight this foul and virulent thing with every weapon. Its victims will not only be the Jews against whom it is directed, but those who have been contaminated by touching it. By speech or action, by word or deed, anyone who allows himself to be duped by this campaign of lies and calumny is serving the forces of darkness as assuredly as if he were fighting on the enemy's side. We ask this Conference to take the lead in action to root out the evil thing before it roars to ugly head in this country.

Thus this resolution deals with three points which the Conference is asked to accept as being in line with the traditions and spirit of our Movement. The news of its acceptance will reverberate far beyond the confines of this hall. It will be a message of hope to men and women – aye, and children languishing in the concentration camps of Europe – a message which says: 'Hold on, our fellow-workers, we are with you. Victory is near. Justice will be done.'

Chaim Herzog

*I*n 1975 the UN passed a resolution by 72 to 35 (with 32 abstentions) declaring 'that Zionism is a form of racism and racial discrimination'.

Resolution 3379 was sponsored by 25 nations including the majority of Arab nations and Cuba. A further 47 nations voted in favour of it, including China, India, the Soviet Bloc, Brazil and Portugal. The 35 against were in the main the Western democracies of North America, Europe and Australasia as well as a small number of Latin American and African nations.

Born in Belfast in 1918, the son of a Rabbi, Herzog studied law and spent some time in Palestine before the war. He served in the British Army, primarily in Germany, and was involved in the liberation of concentration camps as well as the capture of Himmler. After the war he returned to Palestine and became involved in the military, intelligence and politics as well as continuing to practise law after the formation of the State of Israel. He was Israel's ambassador to the UN from 1975 to 1978 and subsequently was elected to the Knesset, becoming President of Israel in 1983 and serving two terms before retiring in 1993. He died in 1997.

The resolution was revoked in 1991. This time the revocation was sponsored by 90 nations and supported by a total of 111 with 25 against (for the most part the original sponsoring nations).

The full text of the resolution is:

3379. Elimination of all forms of racial discrimination
The General Assembly,
Recalling its resolution 1904 (XVIII) of 20 November 1963, proclaiming the United Nations Declaration on the Elimination of All Forms of Racial Discrimination, and in particular its affirmation that 'any doctrine of racial differentiation or superiority is scientifically false, morally condemnable, socially unjust and dangerous' and its expression of alarm at 'the manifestations of racial discrimination still in evidence in some areas in the world, some of which are imposed by certain Governments by means of legislative, administrative or other measures',

Recalling also that, in its resolution 3151 G (XXVIII) of 14 December 1973, the General Assembly condemned, inter alia, the unholy alliance between South African racism and Zionism,

Taking note of the Declaration of Mexico on the Equality of Women and Their Contribution to Development and Peace 1975, proclaimed by the World Conference of the International Women's Year, held at Mexico City from 19 June to 2 July 1975, which promulgated the principle that 'international co-operation and peace require the achievement of national liberation and independence, the elimination of colonialism and neo-colonialism, foreign occupation, Zionism, apartheid and racial discrimination in all its forms, as well as the recognition of the dignity of peoples and their right to self-determination',

Taking note also of resolution 77 (XII) adopted by the Assembly of Heads of State and Government of the Organization of African Unity at its twelfth ordinary session, held at Kampala from 28 July to 1 August 1975, which considered 'that the racist regime in occupied Palestine and the racist regime in Zimbabwe and South Africa have *a common imperialist origin, forming a whole and having the same racist structure and being organically linked in their policy aimed at repression of the dignity and integrity of the human being',*

Taking note also of the Political Declaration and Strategy to Strengthen International Peace and Security and to Intensify Solidarity and Mutual Assistance among Non-Aligned Countries, adopted at the Conference of Ministers for Foreign Affairs of Non-Aligned Countries held at Lima from 25 to 30 August 1975, which most severely condemned Zionism as a threat to world peace and security and called upon all countries to oppose this racist and imperialist ideology,

Determines that Zionism is a form of racism and racial discrimination.

Response to Zionism is Racism Resolution

10 November 1975

Mr President,

It is symbolic that this debate, which may well prove to be a turning point in the fortunes of the United Nations and a decisive factor in the possible continued existence of this organization, should take place on 10 November.

Tonight, thirty-seven years ago, has gone down in history as Kristallnacht, the Night of the Crystals. This was the night in 1938 when Hitler's Nazi storm-troopers launched a coordinated attack on the Jewish community in Germany, burned the synagogues in all its cities and made bonfires in the streets of the Holy Books and the Scrolls of the Holy Law and Bible.

It was the night when Jewish homes were attacked and heads of families taken away, many of them never to return. It was the night when the windows of all Jewish businesses and stores were smashed, covering the streets in the cities of Germany with a film of broken glass which dissolved into the millions of crystals which gave that night its name. It was the night which led eventually to the crematoria and the gas chambers, Auschwitz, Birkenau, Dachau, Buchenwald, Theresienstadt and others. It was the night which led to the most terrifying Holocaust in the history of man.

It is indeed befitting, Mr President, that this debate, conceived in the desire to deflect the Middle East from its moves towards peace and born of a deep pervading feeling of anti-Semitism, should take place on the anniversary of this day. It is indeed befitting, Mr President, that the United Nations, which began its life as an anti-Nazi alliance, should thirty years later find itself on its way to becoming the world centre of anti-Semitism. Hitler would have felt at home on a number of occasions during the past year, listening to the proceedings in this forum, and above all to the proceedings during the debate on Zionism.

It is sobering to consider to what level this body has been dragged down if we are obliged today to contemplate an attack on Zionism. For this attack constitutes not only an anti-Israeli attack of the foulest type, but also an assault in the United Nations on Judaism – one of the oldest established religions in the world, a religion which has given the world the human values of the Bible, and from which two other great religions, Christianity and Islam, sprang.

Is it not tragic to consider that we here at this meeting in the year 1975 are contemplating what is a scurrilous attack on a great and established religion which has given to the world the Bible with its Ten Commandments, the great prophets of old, Moses, Isaiah, Amos; the great thinkers of history, Maimonides, Spinoza, Marx, Einstein, many of the masters of the arts and as high a percentage of the Nobel Prize-winners in the world, in the sciences, in the arts and in the humanities as has been achieved by any people on earth? …

The resolution against Zionism was originally one condemning racism and colonialism, a subject on which we could have achieved consensus, a consensus which is of great importance to all of us and to our African colleagues in particular. However, instead of permitting this to happen, a group of countries, drunk with the feeling of power inherent in the automatic majority and without regard to the importance of achieving a consensus on this issue, railroaded the UN in a contemptuous manoeuvre by the use of the automatic majority into bracketing Zionism with the subject under discussion.

I do not come to this rostrum to defend the moral and historical values of the Jewish people. They do not need to be defended. They speak for themselves. They have given to mankind much of what is great and eternal. They have done for the spirit of man more than can readily be appreciated by a forum such as this one.

I come here to denounce the two great evils which menace society in general and a society of nations in particular. These two evils are hatred and ignorance. These two evils are the motivating force behind the proponents of this resolution and their supporters. These two evils characterize those who would drag this world organization, the ideals of which were first conceived by the prophets of Israel, to the depths to which it has been dragged today.

The key to understanding Zionism is in its name. The easternmost of the two hills of ancient Jerusalem during the tenth century BCE was called Zion. In fact, the name Zion, referring to Jerusalem, appears 152 times in the Old Testament. The name is overwhelmingly a poetic and prophetic designation. The religious and emotional qualities of the name arise from the importance of Jerusalem as the Royal City and the City of the Temple. 'Mount Zion' is the place where God dwells. Jerusalem, or Zion, is a place where the Lord is King, and where He has installed His king, David.

King David made Jerusalem the capital of Israel almost three thousand years ago, and Jerusalem has remained the capital ever since. During the centuries the term 'Zion' grew and expanded to mean the whole of Israel. The Israelites in exile could not forget Zion. The Hebrew Psalmist sat by the waters of Babylon and swore: 'If I forget three, O Jerusalem, let my right hand forget her cunning.' This oath has been repeated for thousands of years by Jews throughout the world. It is an oath which was made over seven hundred years before the advent of Christianity and over twelve hundred years before the advent of Islam, and Zion came to mean the Jewish homeland, symbolic of Judaism, of Jewish national aspirations.

While praying to his God every Jew, wherever he is in the world, faces towards Jerusalem. For over two thousand years of exile these prayers have expressed the yearning of the Jewish people to return to their ancient homeland, Israel. In fact, a continuous Jewish presence, in larger or smaller numbers, has been maintained in the country over the centuries.

Zionism is the name of the national movement of the Jewish people and is the modern expression of the ancient Jewish heritage. The Zionist ideal, as set out in the Bible, has been, and is, an integral part of the Jewish religion.

Zionism is to the Jewish people what the liberation movements of Africa and Asia have been to their own people.

Zionism is one of the most dynamic and vibrant national movements in human history. Historically it is based on a unique and unbroken connection, extending some four thousand years, between the People of the Book and the Land of the Bible.

In modern times, in the late nineteenth century, spurred by the twin forces of anti-Semitic persecution and of nationalism, the Jewish people organized the Zionist movement in order to transform their dream into reality. Zionism as a political movement was the revolt of an oppressed nation against the depredation and wicked discrimination and oppression of the countries in which anti-Semitism flourished. It is no coincidence that the co-sponsors and supporters of this resolution include countries who are guilty of the horrible crimes of anti-Semitism and discrimination to this very day.

Support for the aim of Zionism was written into the League of Nations Mandate for Palestine and was again endorsed by the United Nations in 1947, when the General Assembly voted by overwhelming majority for the restoration of Jewish independence in our ancient land.

The re-establishment of Jewish independence in Israel, after centuries of struggle to overcome foreign conquest and exile, is a vindication of the fundamental concepts of the equality of nations and of self-determination. To question the Jewish people's right to national existence and freedom is not only to deny to the Jewish people the right accorded to every other people on this globe, but it is also to deny the central precepts of the United Nations.

As a former Foreign Minister of Israel, Abba Eban, has written:

Zionism is nothing more – but also nothing less – than the Jewish people's sense of origin and destination in the land linked eternally with its name. It is also the instrument whereby the Jewish nation seeks an authentic fulfilment of itself. And the drama is enacted in twenty states comprising a hundred million people in 4½ million square miles, with vast resources. The issue therefore is not whether the world will come to terms with Arab nationalism. The question is at what point Arab nationalism, with its prodigious glut of advantage, wealth and opportunity, will come to terms with the modest but equal rights of another Middle Eastern nation to pursue its life in security and peace.

The vicious diatribes on Zionism voiced here by Arab delegates may give this Assembly the wrong impression that while the rest of the world supported the Jewish national liberation movement the Arab world was always hostile to Zionism. This is not the case. Arab leaders, cognizant of the rights of the Jewish people, fully endorsed the virtues of Zionism. Sherif Hussein, the leader of the Arab world during World War I, welcomed the return of the Jews to Palestine. His son, Emir Feisal, who represented the Arab world in the Paris Peace Conference, had this to say about Zionism:

> We Arabs, especially the educated among us, look with deepest sympathy on the Zionist movement ... We will wish the Jews a hearty welcome home ... We are working together for a reformed and revised Near East, and our two movements complement one another. The movement is national and not imperialistic. There is room in Syria for us both. Indeed, I think that neither can be a success without the other.

It is perhaps pertinent at this point to recall that when the question of Palestine was being debated in the United Nations in 1947, the Soviet Union strongly supported the Jewish independence struggle. It is particularly relevant to recall some of Andrei Gromyko's remarks:

> As we know, the aspirations of a considerable part of the Jewish people are linked with the problem of Palestine and of its future administration. This fact scarcely requires proof ... During the last war, the Jewish people underwent exceptional sorrow and suffering. Without any exaggeration, this sorrow and suffering are indescribable. It is difficult to express them in dry statistics on the Jewish victims of the fascist aggressors. The Jews in the territories where the Hitlerites held sway were subjected to almost complete physical annihilation. The total number of Jews who perished at the hands of the Nazi executioners is estimated at approximately six million ...
>
> The United Nations cannot and must not regard this situation with indifference, since this would be incompatible with the high principles proclaimed in its Charter, which provides for the defence of human rights, irrespective of race, religion or sex ...
>
> The fact that no Western European State has been able to ensure the defence of the elementary rights of the Jewish people and to safeguard it against the violence of the fascist executioners explains

the aspirations of the Jews to establish their own State. It would be unjust not to take this into consideration and to deny the right of the Jewish people to realize this aspiration.

How sad it is to see here a group of nations, many of whom have but recently freed themselves of colonial rule, deriding one of the most noble liberation movements of this century, a movement which not only gave an example of encouragement and determination to the peoples struggling for independence but also actively aided many of them either during the period of preparation for their independence or immediately thereafter.

Here you have a movement which is the embodiment of a unique pioneering spirit, of the dignity of labour, and of enduring human values, a movement which has presented to the world an example of social equality and open democracy being associated in this resolution with abhorrent political concepts.

We in Israel have endeavoured to create a society which strives to implement the highest ideals of society – political, social and cultural – for all the inhabitants of Israel, irrespective of religious belief, race or sex.

Show me another pluralistic society in this world in which despite all the difficult problems, Jew and Arab live together with such a degree of harmony, in which the dignity and rights of man are observed before the law, in which no death sentence is applied, in which freedom of speech, of movement, of thought, of expression are guaranteed, in which even movements which are opposed to our national aims are represented in our Parliament.

The Arab delegates talk of racism. What has happened to the 800,000 Jews who lived for over two thousand years in the Arab lands, who formed some of the most ancient communities long before the advent of Islam. Where are they now?

The Jews were once one of the important communities in the countries of the Middle East, the leaders of thought, of commerce, of medical science. Where are they in Arab society today? You dare talk of racism when I can point with pride to the Arab ministers who have served in my government; to the Arab deputy speaker of my Parliament; to Arab officers and men serving of their own volition in our border and police defence forces, frequently commanding Jewish troops; to the hundreds of thousands of Arabs from all over the Middle East crowding the cities of Israel every year; to the thousands of Arabs from all over the Middle East coming for medical treatment to Israel; to the peaceful coexistence which has developed; to the fact that Arabic is an official language in Israel on a par with Hebrew; to the fact that it is as natural for an Arab to serve in public office in Israel as it is incongruous to think of a Jew serving in any public office in an Arab country, indeed being admitted to many of them. Is that racism? It is not! That, Mr President, is Zionism.

Zionism is our attempt to build a society, imperfect though it may be, in which the visions of the prophets of Israel will be realized. I know that we have problems. I know that many disagree with our government's policies. Many in Israel too disagree from time to time with the government's policies ... and are free to do so because Zionism has created the first and only real democratic state in a part of the world that never really knew democracy and freedom of speech.

This malicious resolution, designed to divert us from its true purpose, is part of a dangerous anti-Semitic idiom which is being insinuated into every public debate by those who have sworn to block the current move towards accommodation and ultimately towards peace in the Middle East. This, together with similar moves, is designed to sabotage the efforts of the Geneva Conference for peace in the Middle East and to deflect those who are moving along the road towards peace from their purpose. But they will not succeed, for I can but reiterate my government's policy to make every move in the direction towards peace, based on compromise.

We are seeing here today but another manifestation of the bitter anti-Semitic, anti-Jewish hatred which animates Arab society. Who would have believed that in this year, 1975, the malicious falsehoods of the 'elders of Zion' would be distributed officially by Arab governments? Who would have believed that we would today contemplate an Arab society which teaches the vilest anti-Jewish hate in the kindergartens? ... We are being attacked by a society which is motivated by the most extreme form of racism known in the world today. This is the racism which was expressed so succinctly in the words of the leader of the PLO, Yassir Arafat, in his opening address at a symposium in Tripoli, Libya: 'There will be no presence in the region other than the Arab presence ...' In other words, in the Middle East from the Atlantic Ocean to the Persian Gulf only one presence is allowed, and that is Arab presence. No other people, regardless of how deep are its roots in the region, is to be permitted to enjoy its right to self-determination.

Look at the tragic fate of the Kurds of Iraq. Look what happened to the black population in southern Sudan. Look at the dire peril in which an entire community of Christians finds itself in Lebanon. Look at the avowed policy of the PLO, which calls in its Palestine Covenant of 1964 for the destruction of the State of Israel, which denies any form of compromise on the Palestine issue and which, in the words of its representative only the other day in this building, considers Tel Aviv to be occupied territory. Look at all this, and you see before you the root cause of the twin evils of this world at work, the blind hatred of the Arab proponents of this resolution, and the abysmal ignorance and wickedness of those who support them.

The issue before this Assembly is neither Israel nor Zionism. The issue is the fate of this organization. Conceived in the spirit of the prophets of Israel, born out of an anti-Nazi alliance after the tragedy of World War Two, it has degenerated into a forum which was this last week described by one of the leading writers in a foremost organ of social and liberal thought in the West [Paul Johnson] as 'rapidly becoming one of the most corrupt and corrupting creations in the whole history of human institutions ... almost without exception those in the majority came from states notable for racist oppression of every conceivable hue'. He goes on to explain the phenomenon of this debate:

Israel is a social democracy, the nearest approach to a free socialist state in the world; its people and government have a profound respect for human life, so passionate indeed that, despite every conceivable provocation, they have refused for a quarter of a century to execute a single captured terrorist. They also have an ancient but vigorous culture, and a flourishing technology. The combination of national qualities they have assembled in their brief existence as a state is a perpetual and embittering reproach to most of the new countries whose representatives swagger about the UN building. So Israel is envied and hated; and efforts are made to destroy her. The extermination of the Israelis has long been the prime objective of the Terrorist International; they calculate that if they can break Israel, then all the rest of civilization is vulnerable to their assaults ...

The melancholy truth, I fear, is that the candles of civilization are burning low. The world is increasingly governed not so much by capitalism, or communism, or social democracy, or even tribal barbarism, as by a false lexicon of political clichés, accumulated over half a century and now assuming a kind of degenerate sacerdotal authority ... We all know what they are ...

Over the centuries it has fallen to the lot of my people to be the testing agent of human decency, the touchstone of civilization, the crucible in which enduring human values are to be tested. A nation's level of humanity could invariably be judged by its behaviour towards its Jewish population. Persecution and oppression have often enough begun with the Jews, but it has never ended with them. The anti-Jewish pogroms in Czarist Russia were but the tip of the iceberg which revealed the inherent rottenness of a regime that was soon to disappear in the storm of revolution. The anti-Semitic excesses of the Nazis merely foreshadowed the catastrophe which was to befall mankind in Europe ...

On the issue before us, the world has divided itself into good and bad, decent and evil, human and debased. We, the Jewish people, will recall in history our gratitude to those nations who stood up and were counted and who refused to support this wicked proposition. I know that this episode will have strengthened the forces of freedom and decency in this world and will have fortified the free world in their resolve to strengthen the ideals they so cherish. I know that this episode will have strengthened Zionism as it has weakened the United Nations.

As I stand on this rostrum, the long and proud history of my people unravels itself before my inward eye. I see the oppressors of our people over the ages as they pass one another in evil procession into oblivion. I stand here before you as the representative of a strong and flourishing people which has survived them all and which will survive this shameful exhibition and the proponents of this resolution.

The great moments of Jewish history come to mind as I face you, once again outnumbered and the would-be victim of hate, ignorance and evil. I look back on those great moments. I recall the greatness of a nation which I have the honour to represent in this forum. I am mindful at this moment of the Jewish people throughout the world wherever they may be, be it in freedom or in slavery, whose prayers and thoughts are with me at this moment.

I stand here not as a supplicant. Vote as your moral conscience dictates to you. For the issue is neither Israel nor Zionism. The issue is the continued existence of this organization, which has been dragged to its lowest point of discredit by a coalition of despots and racists.

The vote of each delegation will record in history its country's stand on anti-Semitic racism and anti-Judaism. You yourselves bear the responsibility for your stand before history, for as such will you be viewed in history. We, the Jewish people, will not forget.

For us, the Jewish people, this is but a passing episode in a rich and event-filled history. We put our trust in our Providence, in our faith and beliefs, in our time-hallowed tradition, in our striving for social advance and human values, and in our people wherever they may be. For us, the Jewish people, this resolution based on hatred, falsehood and arrogance, is devoid of any moral or legal value.

Anwar Sadat

A nwar Sadat was the third President of Egypt, serving from 1970 till his assassination by fundamentalist army officers in 1981. He had been a senior member of the Free Officers who overthrew King Farouk and a close confidant of President Nasser, whom he succeeded.

He oversaw one of the most progressive periods in Egypt's history, considerably changing its trajectory and policies. In 1973 he liberated Egypt's Sinai peninsula, which Israel had occupied since 1967, and became a hero at home and throughout the Arab world. The subsequent negotiations for peace led in 1978 to Sadat and Israeli Prime Minister Menachem Begin being jointly awarded the Nobel Peace Prize and ultimately to Sadat's assassination in 1981 by extremists opposed to Egypt's relationship with Israel. In 1977 he became the first Arab leader to visit the Knesset and laid out his views for a comprehensive Arab–Israeli peace.

Address to the Knesset

20 November 1977

In the name of God, the Gracious and Merciful.

Mr Speaker, Ladies and Gentlemen:

Peace and the mercy of God Almighty be upon you and may peace be for us all, God willing. Peace for us all on the Arab land, and in Israel as well, as in every part of this big world, which is so complexed by its sanguinary conflicts, disturbed by its sharp contradictions, menaced now and then by destructive wars launched by man to annihilate his fellow man. Finally, amidst the ruins of what man has built and the remains of the victims of Mankind, there emerges neither victor nor vanquished. The only vanquished remains man, God's most sublime creation, man whom God has created – as Gandhi the apostle of peace puts it: to forge ahead to mould the way of life and worship God Almighty.

I come to you today on solid ground, to shape a new life, to establish peace. We all, on this land, the land of God; we all, Muslims, Christians and Jews, worship God and no one but God. God's teachings and commandments are love, sincerity, purity and peace.

I do not blame all those who received my decision – when I announced it to the entire world before the Egyptian People's Assembly – with surprise and amazement. Some, gripped by violent surprise, believed that my decision was no more than verbal juggling to cater for world public opinion. Others, still, interpreted it as political tactics to camouflage my intention of launching a new war. I would go as far as to tell you that one of my aides at the Presidential Office contacted me at a late hour following my return home from the People's Assembly and sounded worried as he asked me: 'Mister President, what would be our reaction if Israel should actually extend an invitation to you?' I replied calmly, I will accept it immediately. I have declared that I will go to the end of the world; I will go to Israel, for I want to put before the People of Israel all the facts.

I can see the point of all those who were astounded by my decision or those who had any doubts as to the sincerity of the intentions behind the declaration of my decision. No one would have ever conceived that the President of the biggest Arab State, which bears the heaviest burden and the top responsibility pertaining to the cause of war and peace in the Middle East, could declare his readiness to go to the land of the adversary while we were still in a state of war. Rather, we all are still bearing the consequences of four fierce wars waged within thirty years. The families of the 1973 October War are still moaning under the cruel pains of widowhood and bereavement of sons, fathers and brothers.

As I have already declared, I have not consulted, as far as this decision is concerned, with any of my colleagues and brothers, the Arab Heads of State or the confrontation States. Those of them who contacted me, following the declaration of this decision, expressed their objection, because the feeling of utter suspicion and absolute lack of confidence between the Arab States and the Palestinian People on the one hand, and Israel on the other, still surges in us all. It is sufficient to say that many months in which peace could have been brought about had been wasted over differences and fruitless discussions on the procedure for the convocation of the Geneva Conference, all showing utter suspicion and absolute lack of confidence.

But, to be absolutely frank with you, I took this decision after long thinking, knowing that it constitutes a grave risk for, if God Almighty has made it my fate to assume the responsibility on behalf of the Egyptian People and to share in the fate-determining responsibility of the Arab Nation and the Palestinian People, the main duty dictated by this responsibility is to exhaust all and every means in a bid to save my Egyptian Arab People and the entire Arab Nation the horrors of new, shocking and destructive wars, the dimensions of which are foreseen by no other than God himself.

After long thinking, I was convinced that the obligation of responsibility before God, and before the people, make it incumbent on me that I should go to the farthest corner of the world, even to Jerusalem, to address Members of the Knesset, the representatives of the People of Israel, and acquaint them with all the facts surging in me. Then, I would leave you to decide for yourselves. Following this, may God Almighty determine our fate.

Ladies and Gentlemen, there are moments in the life of nations and peoples when it is incumbent on those known for their wisdom and clarity of vision to overlook the past, with all its complexities and weighing memories, in a bold drive towards new horizons. Those who, like us, are shouldering the same responsibility entrusted to us, are the first who should have the courage to take fate-determining decisions which are in consonance with the circumstances. We must all rise above all forms of fanaticism, self-deception and obsolete theories of superiority. The most important thing is never to forget that infallibility is the prerogative of God alone.

If I said that I wanted to save all the Arab People the horrors of shocking and destructive wars, I most sincerely declare before you that I have the same feelings and bear the same responsibility towards all and every man on earth, and certainly towards the Israeli People.

Any life lost in war is a human life, irrespective of its being that of an Israeli or an Arab. A wife who becomes a widow is a human being entitled to a happy family life, whether she be an Arab or an Israeli. Innocent children who are deprived of the care and compassion of their parents are ours, be they living on Arab or Israeli land. They command our top responsibility to afford them a comfortable life today and tomorrow.

For the sake of them all, for the safeguard of the lives of all our sons and brothers, for affording our communities the opportunity to work for the progress and happiness of man and his right to a dignified life, for our responsibilities before the generations to come, for a smile on the face of every child born on our land – for all that, I have taken my decision to come to you, despite all hazards, to deliver my address.

I have shouldered the prerequisites of the historical responsibility and, therefore, I declared – on 4 February 1971, to be precise – that I was willing to sign a peace agreement with Israel. This was the first declaration made by a responsible Arab official since the outbreak of the Arab–Israeli conflict.

Motivated by all these factors dictated by the responsibilities of leadership, I called, on 16 October 1973, before the Egyptian People's Assembly, for an international conference to establish permanent peace based on justice. I was not in the position of he who was pleading for peace or asking for a ceasefire.

Motivated by all these factors dictated by duties of history and leadership, we signed the first disengagement agreement, followed by the second disengagement agreement in Sinai. Then we proceeded trying both open and closed doors in a bid to find a certain path leading to a durable and just peace. We opened our hearts to the peoples of the entire world to make them understand our motivations and objectives, and to leave them actually convinced of the fact that we are advocates of justice and peace-makers.

Motivated by all these factors, I decided to come to you with an open mind and an open heart, and with a conscious determination, so that we might establish permanent peace based on justice.

It is so fated that my trip to you, the trip of peace, should coincide with the Islamic feast, the holy Feast of Courban Bairam, the Feast of Sacrifice when Abraham – peace be upon him – great-grandfather of the Arabs and Jews, submitted to God; I say when God Almighty ordered him, and to Him Abraham went, with dedicated sentiments, not out of weakness, but through a giant spiritual force and by a free will, to sacrifice his very own son, prompted by a firm and unshakable belief in ideals that lend life a profound significance.

This coincidence may carry a new meaning to us all, which may become a genuine aspiration heralding security and peace.

Ladies and Gentlemen, let us be frank with each other, using straightforward words and a clear conception, with no ambiguity. Let us be frank with each other today while the entire world, both East and West, follows these unparalleled moments which could prove to be a radical turning point in the history of this part of the world, if not in the history of the world as a whole. Let us be frank with each other as we answer this important question: how can we achieve permanent peace based on justice?

I have come to you carrying my clear and frank answer to this big question, so that the people in Israel as well as the whole world might hear it, and so that all those whose devoted prayers ring in my ears, pleading to God Almighty that this historic meeting may eventually lead to the results aspired to by millions, might also hear it.

Before I proclaim my answer, I wish to assure you that, in my clear and frank answer, I am basing myself on a number of facts which no one can deny.

The first fact: no one can build his happiness at the expense of the misery of others.

The second fact: never have I spoken or will ever speak in two languages. Never have I adopted or will adopt two policies. I never deal with anyone except in one language, one policy, and with one face.

The third fact: direct confrontation and a straight line are the nearest and most successful methods to reach a clear objective.

The fourth fact: the call for permanent and just peace, based on respect for the United Nations resolutions, has now become the call of the whole world. It has become a clear expression of the will of the international community, whether in official capitals, where policies are made and decisions taken, or at the level of world public opinion which influences policy-making and decision-taking.

The fifth fact: and this is probably the clearest and most prominent, is that the Arab Nation, in its drive for permanent peace based on justice, does not proceed from a position of weakness or hesitation, but it has the potential of power and stability which tells of a sincere will for peace.

The Arab-declared intention stems from an awareness prompted by a heritage of civilization that, to avoid an inevitable disaster that will befall us, you and the entire world, there is no alternative to the establishment of permanent peace based on justice – peace that is not shaken by storms, swayed by suspicion, or jeopardized by ill intentions.

In the light of these facts which I meant to place before you the way I see them, I would also wish to warn you in all sincerity; I warn you against some thoughts that could cross your minds; frankness makes it incumbent upon me to tell you the following:

First: I have not come here for a separate agreement between Egypt and Israel. This is not part of the policy of Egypt. The problem is not that of Egypt and Israel. Any separate peace between Egypt and Israel, or between any Arab confrontation State and Israel, will not bring permanent peace based on justice in the entire region. Rather, even if peace between all the confrontation States and Israel were achieved, in the absence of a just solution to the Palestinian problem, never will there be that durable and just peace upon which the entire world insists today.

Second: I have not come to you to seek a partial peace, namely to terminate the state of belligerency at this stage, and put off the entire problem to a subsequent stage. This is not the radical solution that would steer us to permanent peace.

Equally, I have not come to you for a third disengagement agreement in Sinai, or in the Golan and the West Bank. For this would mean that we are merely delaying the ignition of the fuse; it would mean that we are lacking the courage to confront peace, that we are too weak to shoulder the burdens and responsibilities of a durable peace based on justice.

I have come to you so that together we might build a durable peace based on justice, to avoid the shedding of one single drop of blood from an Arab or an Israeli. It is for this reason that I have proclaimed my readiness to go to the farthest corner of the world.

Here, I would go back to the answer to the big question: how can we achieve a durable peace based on justice?

In my opinion, and I declare it to the whole world from this forum, the answer is neither difficult nor impossible, despite long years of feud, blood vengeance, spite and hatred, and breeding generations on concepts of total rift and deep-rooted animosity. The answer is not difficult, nor is it impossible, if we sincerely and faithfully follow a straight line.

You want to live with us in this part of the world. In all sincerity, I tell you, we welcome you among us, with full security and safety. This, in itself, is a tremendous turning point; one of the landmarks of a decisive historical change.

We used to reject you. We had our reasons and our claims, yes. We used to brand you as 'so-called' Israel, yes. We were together in international conferences and organizations and our representatives did not, and still do not, exchange greetings, yes. This has happened and is still happening.

It is also true that we used to set, as a precondition for any negotiations with you, a mediator who would meet separately with each party. Through this procedure, the talks of the first and second disengagement agreements took place.

Our delegates met in the first Geneva Conference without exchanging a direct word. Yes, this has happened.

Yet today I tell you, and declare it to the whole world, that we accept to live with you in permanent peace based on justice. We do not want to encircle you or be encircled ourselves by destructive missiles ready for launching, nor by the shells of grudges and hatred. I have announced on more than one occasion that Israel has become a fait accompli, recognized by the world, and that the two superpowers have undertaken the responsibility of its security and the defence of its existence.

As we really and truly seek peace, we really and truly welcome you to live among us in peace and security.

There was a huge wall between us which you tried to build up over a quarter of a century, but it was destroyed in 1973. It was a wall of a continuously inflammable and escalating psychological warfare. It was a wall of fear of the force that could sweep the entire Arab Nation. It was a wall of propaganda, that we were a Nation reduced to a motionless corpse. Rather, some of you had gone as far as to say that, even after fifty years, the Arabs would not regain any strength. It was a wall that threatened always with the long arm that could reach and strike anywhere. It was a wall that warned us against extermination and annihilation if we tried to use our legitimate right to liberate the occupied territories. Together we have to admit that that wall fell and collapsed in 1973.

Yet, there remained another wall. This wall constitutes a psychological barrier between us. A barrier of suspicion. A barrier of rejection. A barrier of fear of deception. A barrier of hallucinations around any action, deed or decision. A barrier of cautious and erroneous interpretations of all and every event or statement. It is this psychological barrier which I described in official statements as representing 70 per cent of the whole problem.

Today, through my visit to you, I ask you: why don't we stretch our hands with faith and sincerity so that, together, we might destroy this barrier? Why shouldn't ours and your will meet with faith and sincerity, so that together we might remove all suspicion of fear, betrayal and ill intentions? Why don't we stand together with the bravery of men and the boldness of heroes who dedicate themselves to a sublime objective? Why don't we stand together with the same courage and boldness to erect a huge edifice of peace that builds and does not destroy? An edifice that is a beacon for generations to come – the human message for construction, development and the dignity of man? Why should we bequeath to the coming generations the plight of bloodshed, death, orphans, widowhood, family disintegration, and the wailing of victims?

Why don't we believe in the wisdom of God conveyed to us by the Proverbs of Solomon:

'Deceit is in the heart of them that imagine evil; but to the counsellors of peace is joy. Better is a dry morsel, and quietness therewith, than a house full of sacrifices with strife.'

Why don't we repeat together from the Psalms of David:

'Hear the voice of my supplications, when I cry unto thee, when I lift up my hands toward thy holy oracle. Draw me not away with the wicked, and with the workers of iniquity, which speak peace to their neighbours, but mischief is in their hearts. Give them according to their deeds, and according to the wickedness of their endeavours.'

To tell you the truth, peace cannot be worth its name unless it is based on justice, and not on the occupation of the land of others. It would not be appropriate for you to demand for yourselves what you deny others. With all frankness, and with the spirit that has prompted me to come to you today, I tell you: you have to give up, once and for all, the dreams of conquest, and give up the belief that force is the best method for dealing with the Arabs. You should clearly understand and assimilate the lesson of confrontation between you and us.

Expansion does not pay. To speak frankly, our land does not yield itself to bargaining. It is not even open to argument. To us, the national soil is equal to the holy valley where God Almighty spoke to Moses – peace be upon him. None of us can, or accept to, cede one inch of it, or accept the principle of debating or bargaining over it.

I sincerely tell you that before us today lies the appropriate chance for peace, if we are really serious in our endeavours for peace. It is a chance that time cannot afford once again. It is a chance that, if lost or wasted, the plotter against it will bear the curse of humanity and the curse of history.

What is peace for Israel? It means that Israel lives in the region with her Arab neighbours, in security and safety. To such logic, I say yes. It means that Israel lives within her borders, secure against any aggression. To such logic, I say yes. It means that Israel obtains all kinds of guarantees that ensure those two factors. To this demand, I say yes. More than that: we declare that we accept all the international guarantees you envisage and accept. We declare that we accept all the guarantees you want from the two superpowers or from either of them, or from the Big Five, or some of them.

Once again, I declare clearly and unequivocally that we agree to any guarantees you accept because, in return, we shall obtain the same guarantees.

In short, then, when we ask: What is peace for Israel, the answer would be: It is that Israel live within her borders with her Arab neighbours, in safety and security within the framework of all the guarantees she accepts and which are offered to the other party. But how can this be achieved? How can we reach this conclusion which would lead us to permanent peace based on justice?

There are facts that should be faced with all courage and clarity. There are Arab territories which Israel has occupied by armed force. We insist on complete withdrawal from these territories, including Arab Jerusalem.

I have come to Jerusalem, as the City of Peace, which will always remain as a living embodiment of coexistence among believers of the three religions. It is inadmissible that anyone should conceive the special status of the City of Jerusalem within the framework of annexation or expansionism, but it should be a free and open city for all believers.

Above all, the city should not be severed from those who have made it their abode for centuries. Instead of awakening the prejudices of the Crusaders, we should revive the spirit of Omar ibn el-Khattab and Saladin, namely the spirit of tolerance and respect for rights. The holy shrines of Islam and Christianity are not only places of worship, but a living testimony of our uninterrupted presence here politically, spiritually and intellectually. Let us make no mistake about the importance and reverence we Christians and Muslims attach to Jerusalem.

Let me tell you, without the slightest hesitation, that I did not come to you under this dome to make a request that your troops evacuate the occupied territories. Complete withdrawal from the Arab territories occupied in 1967 is a logical and undisputed fact. Nobody should plead for that. Any talk about permanent peace based on justice, and any move to ensure our coexistence in peace and security in this part of the world, would become meaningless, while you occupy Arab territories by force of arms. For there is no peace that could be in consonance with, or be built on, the occupation of the land of others. Otherwise, it would not be a serious peace.

Yes, this is a foregone conclusion which is not open to discussion or debate – if intentions are sincere and if endeavours to establish a just and durable peace for ours and the generations to come are genuine.

As for the Palestinians' cause, nobody could deny that it is the crux of the entire problem. Nobody in the world could accept, today, slogans propagated here in Israel, ignoring the existence of the Palestinian People, and questioning their whereabouts. The cause of the Palestinian People and their legitimate rights are no longer ignored or denied today by anybody. Rather, nobody who has the ability of judgement can deny or ignore it.

It is an acknowledged fact received by the world community, both in the East and in the West, with support and recognition in international documents and official statements. It is of no use to anybody to turn deaf ears to its resounding voice which is being heard day and night, or to overlook its historical reality. Even the United States, your first ally which is absolutely committed to safeguard Israel's security and existence, and which offered and still offers Israel every moral, material and military support – I say, even the United States has opted to face up to reality and facts, and admit that the Palestinian People are entitled to legitimate rights and that the Palestinian problem is the core and essence of the conflict and that, so long as it continues to be unresolved, the conflict will continue to aggravate, reaching new dimensions. In all sincerity, I tell you that there can be no peace without the Palestinians. It is a grave error of unpredictable consequences to overlook or brush aside this cause.

I shall not indulge in past events since the Balfour Declaration sixty years ago. You are well acquainted with the relevant facts. If you have found the legal and moral justification to set up a national home on a land that did not all belong to you, it is incumbent upon you to show understanding of the insistence of the People of Palestine on establishing, once again (*sic*), a state on their land. When some extremists ask the

Palestinians to give up this sublime objective, this, in fact, means asking them to renounce their identity and every hope for the future.

I hail the Israeli voices that called for the recognition of the Palestinian People's rights to achieve and safeguard peace. Here I tell you, ladies and gentlemen, that it is no use to refrain from recognizing the Palestinian People and their rights to statehood and rights of return.

We, the Arabs, have faced this experience before, with you and with the reality of Israeli existence. The struggle took us from war to war, from victims to more victims, until you and we have today reached the edge of a horrifying abyss and a terrifying disaster, unless, together, we seize the opportunity, today, of a durable peace based on justice.

You have to face reality bravely as I have done. There can never be any solution to a problem by evading it or turning a deaf ear to it. Peace cannot last if attempts are made to impose fantasy concepts on which the world has turned its back and announced its unanimous call for the respect of rights and facts. There is no need to enter a vicious circle as to Palestinian rights. It is useless to create obstacles. Otherwise the march of peace will be impeded or peace will be blown up.

As I have told you, there is no happiness to the detriment of others. Direct confrontation and straightforwardness are the short-cut and the most successful way to reach a clear objective. Direct confrontation concerning the Palestinian problem, and tackling it in one single language with a view to achieving a durable and just peace, lie in the establishment of their state. With all the guarantees you demand, there should be no fear of a newly-born state that needs the assistance of all countries of the world. When the bells of peace ring, there will be no hands to beat the drums of war. Even if they existed, they would be soundless.

Conceive with me a peace agreement in Geneva that we would herald to a world thirsty for peace, a peace agreement based on the following points:

First: ending the Israeli occupation of the Arab territories occupied in 1967.

Second: achievement of the fundamental rights of the Palestinian People and their right to self-determination, including their right to establish their own state.

Third: the right of all states in the area to live in peace within their boundaries, which will be secure and guaranteed through procedures to be agreed upon, which provide appropriate security to international boundaries, in addition to appropriate international guarantees.

Fourth: commitment of all states in the region to administer the relations among them in accordance with the objectives and principles of the United Nations Charter, particularly the principles concerning the non-resort to force and the solution of differences among them by peaceful means.

Fifth: ending the state of belligerency in the region.

Ladies and Gentlemen, peace is not the mere endorsement of written lines; rather, it is a rewriting of history. Peace is not a game of calling for peace to defend certain whims or hide certain ambitions. Peace is a giant struggle against all and every ambition and whim. Perhaps the examples taken from ancient and modern history teach us all that missiles, warships and nuclear weapons cannot establish security. Rather, they destroy what peace and security build. For the sake of our peoples, and for the sake of the civilizations made by man, we have to defend man everywhere against the rule of the force of arms, so that we may endow the rule of humanity with all the power of the values and principles that promote the sublime position of Mankind.

Allow me to address my call from this rostrum to the People of Israel. I address myself with true and sincere words to every man, woman and child in Israel.

From the Egyptian People who bless this sacred mission of peace, I convey to you the message of peace, the message of the Egyptian People who do not know fanaticism, and whose sons, Muslims, Christians, and Jews, live together in a spirit of cordiality, love and tolerance. This is Egypt whose people have entrusted me with that sacred message, the message of security, safety and peace. To every man, woman and child in Israel, I say: encourage your leadership to struggle for peace. Let all endeavours be channelled towards building a huge edifice for peace, instead of strongholds and hideouts defended by destructive rockets. Introduce to the entire world the image of the new man in this area, so that he might set an example to the man of our age, the man of peace everywhere.

Be the heralds to your sons. Tell them that past wars were the last of wars and the end of sorrows. Tell them that we are in for a new beginning to a new life – the life of love, prosperity, freedom and peace.

You, bewailing mother; you, widowed wife; you, the son who lost a brother or a father; you, all victims of wars – fill the earth and space with recitals of peace. Fill bosoms and hearts with the aspirations of peace. Turn the song into a reality that blossoms and lives. Make hope a code of conduct and endeavour. The will of peoples is part of the will of God.

Ladies and Gentlemen, before I came to this place, with every beat of my heart and with every sentiment, I prayed to God Almighty, while performing the Curban Bairarn prayers, and while visiting the Holy Sepulchre, to give me strength and to confirm my belief that this visit may achieve the objectives I look forward to, for a happy present and a happier future.

I have chosen to set aside all precedents and traditions known by warring countries, in spite of the fact that occupation of the Arab territories is still there. Rather, the declaration of my readiness to proceed to Israel came as a great surprise that stirred many feelings and astounded many minds. Some opinions even doubted its intent. Despite that, the decision was inspired by all the clarity and purity of belief, and with all the true expression of my People's will and intentions.

And I have chosen this difficult road which is considered, in the opinion of many, the most difficult road. I have chosen to come to you with an open heart and an open mind. I have chosen to give this great impetus to all international efforts exerted for peace. I have chosen to present to you, and in your own home, the realities devoid of any schemes or whims, not to manoeuvre or to win a round, but for us to win together, the most dangerous of rounds and battles in modern history – the battle of permanent peace based on justice.

It is not my battle alone, nor is it the battle of the leadership in Israel alone. It is the battle of all and every citizen in all our territories whose right it is to live in peace. It is the commitment of conscience and responsibility in the hearts of millions.

When I put forward this initiative, many asked what is it that I conceived as possible to achieve during this visit, and what my expectations were. And, as I answered the questioners, I announce before you that I have not thought of carrying out this initiative from the concept of what could be achieved during this visit, but I have come here to deliver a message. I have delivered the message, and may God be my witness.

I repeat with Zechariah, 'Love right and justice.'

I quote the following verses from the holy Koran:

We believe in God and in what has been revealed to us and what was revealed to Abraham, Ismail, Isaac, Jacob, and the tribes and in the books given to Moses, Jesus, and the prophets from their lord. We make no distinction between one and another among them and to God we submit.

If a phantom has at some time travelled this earth, it is racism.
I understand this as a phenomenon that is supported by the belief
of superiority in the face of difference, in the belief that one's
own culture possesses values superior to those of other cultures.
It has not been stated often enough that racism has historically
been a banner to justify the enterprises of expansion, conquest,
colonization and domination and has walked hand in hand with
intolerance, injustice and violence.

RIGOBERTA MENCHÚ TUM, 'THE PROBLEM OF RACISM ON
THE THRESHOLD OF THE TWENTY-FIRST CENTURY',
SPEECH IN GUATEMALA, C.A. 21 MAY 1996

Nicole Fontaine

*N*icole Fontaine is a French politician and Member of the European
Parliament. She was President of the European Parliament
between 1999 and 2002 and visited Israel in February 2000. Her
speech to the Knesset followed the speech four days previously by Johannes
Rau, the first German President to visit Israel. Rau's speech, the first ever
delivered to the Knesset in German, opened with an apology on behalf of
Germany for the Shoah.

> *I know what it means for some among you to hear the German language*
> *spoken in this High House. Your decision to invite me here fills me with*
> *gratitude. It testifies, I believe, to your determination never to suppress*
> *the past and to your courage in seeking, despite that past, to overcome*
> *the paralysis induced by its horrors.*
>
> *Before the people of Israel I pay humble tribute to those who were*
> *murdered, who have no graves at which I could ask their forgiveness.*
> *I ask forgiveness for what Germans have done – for myself and my*
> *generation, for the sake of our children and children's children, whose*
> *future I would like to see at the side of the children of Israel.*
>
> *I do this before you, the representatives of the State of Israel, which*
> *was reborn after two thousand years and has given refuge to Jews around*
> *the world, but above all to the survivors of the Shoah.*

Both speeches were made in the immediate aftermath of a new coalition government in Austria being formed which included the far-right Freedom Party whose roots could be traced directly to Nazism and who were actively xenophobic.

Israeli Knesset Speech

21 February 2000

Mr President,

Honourable Members of the Knesset,

It is a great honour for me as President of the European Parliament to be invited to give this speech today to your Assembly.

This visit comes at a doubly important moment, particularly in the light of unexpected events in Europe.

The current state of the peace process

The European Parliament is keeping an extremely watchful eye on the process which your Prime Minister, with your support, has bravely relaunched with a view to achieving a fair and lasting peace between Israel and all its neighbours, despite difficulties which no one underestimates. I am here to give you a message of support intended to bolster that determination to achieve peace.

Current events in Austria

The establishment in Austria – that is to say within the European Union itself – of a coalition government which includes a party with xenophobic tendencies is quite rightly giving you cause for concern. Let me take this opportunity, at the very start of my speech, to tell you just how much we share your concerns and to make clear that we in the European Union will do everything to ensure that they are allayed.

The European Union's firm and vigilant approach

As you know, as soon as the negotiations with a view to the formation of this government were launched I expressed my serious personal misgivings. At the part-session which followed, our Assembly adopted by an overwhelming majority a resolution which took a very firm approach to the events in Austria. The fourteen other EU governments likewise adopted a categorical and vigilant stance and decided to keep bilateral relations with Austria to a minimum in order to show that no drift towards xenophobic attitudes or policies would be tolerated by its partners.

This firm, united stance is in no way surprising. As long ago as 1984, the European Parliament issued a major report on the rise of xenophobia, racism and anti-Semitism. This gave rise, subsequently, to the first joint inter-institutional declaration by the European Parliament, the European Commission and the Council of Ministers of the Union. Since then, the European Parliament has never deviated from this firm line and I can assure you that it will never do so in the future.

Europe and its duty to see justice done and memory preserved

The duty to see justice done

Only a few days ago, you played host to the President of the Federal Republic of Germany, Mr Johannes Rau. He came to this same platform to make, on behalf of his country, the gesture you had been waiting for in memory of all the victims of the Holocaust who are lost for good.

Recently, other countries and various religious authorities have taken similar steps towards an acknowledgement of our collective responsibility for the most heinous crime ever committed against humanity. That responsibility often took the form of cowardice as much as hatred. The outcome, however, was no less serious.

Virtually the whole of Europe, with its two thousand years of history, bears the burden of the moral debt towards the Jewish people whose eradication was planned during a dark period of the century which is now coming to an end.

Admittedly, during the two millennia which have followed the destruction of the Temple, many, both humble and powerful, have been honoured as 'righteous persons'. However, throughout that period in which the Christian religion had such a profound influence on the development of European societies, the collective curse borne by the Jewish people contributed greatly to its tragic destiny, that of a people cast out of the land of Abraham and then continually rejected or humiliated almost everywhere else.

Anti-Semitism, which fifty years ago produced the horrors we have heard and read so much about, has its roots in this long historical development which is common to Europe as a whole.

If we wish to see justice done, it is our duty to acknowledge it, and I do so now.

Justice also requires, however much time has elapsed, the return of property stolen from the families of those who were sent to their death in such unspeakable circumstances and I support the campaign you have launched in all the various countries, where some would hide or forget a shameful past.

The duty to remember

Keeping alive the memory of the process that led to the Holocaust is our second duty, second only to the commitment to see justice done. Not in a spirit of vengeance, not to go on blaming children or grandchildren for crimes that their fathers or grandfathers may have committed, but to ensure that it never happens again. Those who forget their history are doomed to relive it.

The Jewish community has made great efforts to remain alert to the risk of the resurgence of old demons and to find different ways and means of keeping alive our collective memory, through the cinema, television, historical works and commemorative ceremonies, and keeping intact places steeped in memories. The European Parliament intends actively to support these efforts; it has, for instance, set up the European Observatory to combat the resurgence of racism, xenophobia and anti-Semitism.

I am convinced that European integration itself has played and will continue to play an important role in support of these efforts.

In the European Parliament, where the political families reflect the groupings and opinions in European society and where I have served for sixteen years, all the resolutions that we have adopted against racism in general, and anti-Semitism in particular, have always secured an overwhelming majority rejecting everything that could cause these phenomena to emerge again in Europe or further afield.

This is because the European Union is not only an economic area – it is first and foremost a community of values, and the recent crisis in Austria has given us a painful reminder of how vulnerable the ideal of democracy is, even in the territory of the countries making up the Union.

This realization has been even more pronounced because the Union is preparing for its enlargement over the coming decade to include a dozen applicant countries in Central and Eastern Europe, which, although undoubtedly freed from Communist oppression, are in some cases still unstable democracies. We have just opened the intergovernmental conference, which will make this enlargement possible by reforming the European institutions. The new Treaty, which will be the outcome of the conference, will incorporate a Charter of Fundamental Citizens' Rights, which will consolidate the moral values on which the Union is founded. You may be sure that the fight against all forms of racism and xenophobia will be one of its main planks.

The refusal to compromise

The threat we face and always will face is that we become accustomed to things, that we accept as commonplace a process which at the outset did not involve acts that were really reprehensible but which led to them little by little. Once irreparable damage has been done, it is too late to take action, and when we finally resolve to intervene, as in Bosnia or Kosovo, the price paid is much higher than if a resolute approach had been adopted from the outset.

Allow me, if I may, to quote these very fine words from a Protestant pastor,[1] who was taken to the camps having realized too late the force of this imperceptible process:

> When they came for the Jews, I did not speak up because I was not a Jew.
> When they came for Communists, I did not speak up because I was not a Communist.
> When they came for the trade unionists, I did not speak up because I was not a trade unionist.
> Then they came for me – and by that time there was nobody left to speak up.

The time and the duty to seek peace

I would now like to say something about this peace to which the people of Israel, its neighbours, and as you know, the whole world aspire.

The world's holiest land

This land, where the people of Israel have finally been able to return, is undoubtedly the world's holiest land, since it is the land that remains deeply marked by the three great monotheistic religions which have shaped, and continue to shape, most of the world's societies with the exception of the Far East. As a result, it is also the land that has been the most fought over. It will remain one of the powder kegs that can destabilize the world until peace has been finally secured.

Israel has rightly taken the view that peace cannot be secured without direct negotiation with its neighbours. Europe understands this, while insisting on the need for the agreements to be guaranteed by the support of all the major powers meeting within the Security Council. Furthermore, the European Union is now able to be an active and constructive partner in foreign policy matters, and the appointment of a European Union High Representative for the Middle East demonstrates its determination to lend you effective support. Our visit, which will continue to Beirut, Amman and Ramallah, and possibly to Damascus at a later stage, does not seek to interfere in this process of direct relations. We merely want to tell you of the high priority that Europe gives to peace and to send you and your interlocutors the clear message of the European Parliament's support and the hope that each of the parties will have the determination and courage to make the mutual concessions that are necessary for any lasting agreement.

The courage needed for peace

It is time to make peace. Following the courageous peace agreements already concluded with Egypt and Jordan, peace is now within reach. This historic opportunity must not be missed, for Israel, for its neighbours, for the Palestinians, for peace in the world.

In the past Europe too was caught in the same dilemma, caught between war and peace, hatred and reconciliation. When Nazism collapsed fifty-five years ago, a catalogue of horrors of which most people had no knowledge was revealed to the world at large. The death of fifty million people had fuelled hatreds which appeared impossible to overcome. However, even as those responsible for such horrors were being judged at Nuremberg, visionaries from both sides, some of whom had themselves suffered greatly, came together to decide not to draw a veil over what had happened but to seek new ways of bringing about peace, principally through reconciliation.

This vision, which led to the formation of the European Community in 1957, has remained undimmed since then, bringing peace to nations that had been at war for centuries, consolidating and developing democracy in each of them and bringing progress for all despite the challenges thrown up by economic globalization.

Israel and its neighbours are now facing the same challenge. It is a challenge which calls for sometimes painful efforts to be made to overcome psychological barriers – efforts which we Europeans were obliged to make in order to come together, to understand each other despite the stifling burden of our history, and to make peace with one another and seek a common future for our children. Our reward has been to enjoy the fruits of peace.

An awareness of the problems that lie ahead

The European Parliament is well aware of the problems that lie ahead, the most delicate of which are: the safety of borders, with particular reference to the Golan Heights and the border with Lebanon; the hard-line extremists and their support bases in other countries; what is to happen to the settlements in areas that are to come under Palestinian authority; the establishment of a Palestinian State, which, as everyone here and elsewhere in the world knows, must perforce come into being one day; and the fair distribution of water resources.

In its resolutions on such problems, the European Parliament has consistently emphasized the basic precepts which continue to underpin the Oslo process as a whole. It has repeatedly stressed the need to find solutions to which all of the parties concerned can agree and stated its opposition to unilateral acts which are in breach of the formal undertakings which those parties have given. It has repeatedly called on the negotiators in the peace talks to ensure that all the parties recognize the existence of the State of Israel and its right to security, which will also require them to ensure the viability of any future Palestinian State.

The European Parliament and the other EU institutions are convinced that the current Israeli Government, which represents a broad range of political opinion in the Knesset, is capable of settling the crucial issues in the peace process, with particular regard to relations between Israelis and Palestinians, in good time and in compliance with the undertakings entered into.

In this connection, we are of course extremely concerned at the recent events in Lebanon. No external or internal events must be allowed to hamper the progress of the peace negotiations.

The dangers of extremism

We must never forget how much it costs not to have peace, not to dare to be visionary, to allow old fears to prevent the making of decisions which are essential to the establishment of a climate of mutual trust, without which no progress in relations between individuals and between peoples can be possible.

There are moments in the history of all countries when national unity must take precedence over political affiliations. Your parliament, which represents all the political movements and schools of thought in your country – religious and secular, conservative and progressive, Jewish and Muslim – is the ideal forum in which to build a national consensus on a subject of such overriding importance to the future of Israel's children.

To conclude, therefore, I should like to take a look at what a stable peace will mean for Israel and for the region as a whole.

The possibility of closer cooperation with the European Union

It is vital for Europe to look to the south, to the Mediterranean and the Middle East, where the progress and stability of the nations and peoples of the region have such profound repercussions on its own. As you know, the European Union is already making a major financial contribution to the development programmes which must form an integral part of the peace process. I can assure you that you can continue to count on its support.

Through its standing delegations for relations with Israel and the Palestinian Legislative Council, and with the Mashreq countries, the European Parliament has maintained valuable contacts with all the parties which have a shared interest in securing a long-term, peaceful settlement to the Middle East question. It wishes to pursue and build on these relations in a spirit of mutual interest and good will and to foster regional cooperation and a culture of peace between all the countries of the region, on the basis of arrangements which will need to be invented from scratch, since they must necessarily be specific to each individual situation. The talks which we will be holding as part of this official visit will give us an opportunity to go over the various aspects of such action, such as the establishment of a regional water authority.

It is my hope that one day relations between Israel and the European Union will be based on even closer cooperation than is at present the case; if, of course, Israel wishes this to be so. I myself certainly do.

Through centuries of struggle, Jews across the world have been witnesses not only against the crimes of men, but for faith in God, and God alone. Theirs is a story of defiance in oppression and patience in tribulation – reaching back to the exodus and their exile into the diaspora. That story continued in the founding of the State of Israel. The story continues in the defence of the State of Israel.

GEORGE W. BUSH, ADDRESS ON OBSERVANCE OF THE NATIONAL DAYS OF REMEMBRANCE, 19 APRIL 2001

Tarek Fatah

*T*arek Fatah is a Canadian writer and secular Muslim. He was born in Pakistan in 1949, when the country was in its infancy, grew up and worked in Karachi before moving first to Saudi Arabia and finally to Canada. His first book challenged the idea of an Islamic state being necessary to entering the state of Islam. His second book, The Jew Is Not My Enemy: Unveiling the Myths That Fuel Muslim Anti-Semitism, was published in 2010. Though a staunch activist against Muslim antisemitism, he has been critical of the State of Israel and its treatment of Palestinians.

Towards a New Jerusalem

From *The Jew Is Not My Enemy: Unveiling the Myths That Fuel Muslim Anti-Semitism*

If there is a place on earth today where identifying oneself as a Jew means inviting serious danger to life and liberty, then the historic Pakistani city of Peshawar would easily win that honour.

The city that has its roots in Hindu Vedic mythology and the epic Ramayana and that was a major centre of Buddhist learning until the tenth century has undergone many transformations in its two-thousand-year history. From Alexander the Great to Babur the Mughal, from the Sikh emperor Ranjit Singh to Rudyard Kipling, Peshawar has witnessed the rise and fall of many empires. In modern times, it is also, the city Nikita Khrushchev threatened to obliterate after the Soviets shot down, in 1960, an American spy plane that had taken off from a nearby secret CIA airbase. Decades later, CIA would return to Peshawar, from where it would wage its jihad against the Soviet Union in Afghanistan, just across the nearby border. By the time the Red Army was defeated, Peshawar had lost much of its accommodating character, indigenous to Pashtun culture. The city was transformed into a hotbed of Islamic jihadism introduced in the area by Osama bin Laden and the thousands of 'Arab Afghans' who arrived to fight a jihad for the CIA. Today, it is a place where men are willing to slit the throat of a kuffar and confess to the crime with pride. Lately these jihadis have extended their killing spree to target Muslims who promote secular democracy as an antidote to Islam.

It is in this environment that Simcha Jacobovici, a Jewish-Canadian film producer, shot his documentary *The Lost Tribes* in 2004. He told me of anxiety he felt while filming. 'The fear was palpable. I had been advised to not disclose my Jewishness under any circumstances; the murder of Daniel Pearl still resonated in my mind.' The Jew, after all, was ultimate enemy in the minds of the jihadis, the epitome of evil that needed to be crushed.

Yet this was not always the case. Until the early 1950s, Peshawar was home to a prosperous and thriving Jewish community with a synagogue that was open to the city's Muslim majority. Col. Anwar Ahmed of Toronto, a former officer in the Pakistan army who hails from Peshawar, remembers as a boy seeing the arrival of Jews in the city ... 'Times have changed. Today the deluge of petrodollars and the so-called jihad by bin Laden has destroyed the inherent decency and hospitality of the people of Peshawar and filled it with hate and suspicion of all non-Muslims.'

The Jews of Peshawar numbered no more than a few hundred in the 1940s. They were prominent in the textile trade and dominated the cloth market of the city. Interaction between Muslim and Jew was remarkably pleasant. 'They bought a huge house in one of the nicer districts of the city and converted it into a synagogue,' says Colonel Anwar. 'No one objected, not even the mullahs, and trust me, they were aplenty. This was also my first visit to a Jewish temple and I visited it frequently, always welcomed by the rabbi ... There was not even a hint that Muslims would have an issue with Jews. Today, people deny that Jews ever lived in Peshawar,' he adds.

Ten years later, Israel emerged as a Jewish state after the partition of British Palestine. The same year, Pakistan came into being as an Islamic state after the partition of British India. One partition was mourned by Muslims, the other celebrated. How could Muslims, enjoying their new state, then tell Jews they could not have one of their own?

In the early 1950s, Peshawar's Jews and those domiciled in the capital, Karachi, started leaving for their new home in the Middle East, never to return. Pakistan lost a thread from its fabric that would be missed by no more than a handful. I asked Colonel Anwar if there was ever a backlash against the Jews considering the troubled events that were unfolding in British Palestine with the wars of 1936–9 and 1948. 'None whatsoever,' he said. 'Of course, we were on the side of the Arabs, but it did not cross our minds to target the Jews of Peshawar.'

Colonel Anwar reminds me that the chief instructor at the Pakistan Army Infantry School in Quetta in 1948 was a Jewish lieutenant-colonel. Being Jewish in Pakistan, officially called the world's first Islamic republic, was not then an issue. 'In 1966, my first son was born in Rawalpindi, and guess who was the gynaecologist? A Jewish physician from Poland who had been seconded as an officer in the Pakistan army.'

Even the actions of founder of Pakistan, Mohammed Ali Jinnah, showed there was no anti-Semitism among the Muslims of Pakistan or even India. After the creation of Pakistan in August 1947, Jinnah invited a leading Jewish artist in Bombay to move to Pakistan and awarded him citizenship of the Islamic Republic of Pakistan. His name was Samuel Fyzee-Rahamin, and he became one of the country's leading figures in the arts. Even though an art gallery bearing his name still thrives in Karachi, the tolerance of Jews in the Pakistan of 1947 is a far cry from the visceral hatred directed towards them sixty years later.

Today, with the last Jewish Pakistanis having fled to Israel, where their children and grandchildren play cricket for the Israeli team, their Karachi cemetery remains, abandoned in one of the older neighbourhoods, on the banks of the Lyari River. A nondescript steel door bearing the Star of David marks the entrance to the last resting place of Jews who once lived in this city of my birth among Muslims, Catholics, Hindus, and Zoroastrians.

It is not only in Pakistan where today's Muslims believe their ill will towards Jews is deeply rooted and centuries old. Compared with the Arab world, the people of Pakistan could be considered moderate. A 2010 report by the Pew Research Center on attitudes in the Muslim world makes for some disturbing reading.

The report is based on a survey carried out by the Washington-based think tank in 2009. Among other issues, the survey gauged the attitude of Muslims towards other religious groups, including Jews. The results confirm the anecdotal evidence. Ninety-five per cent of Egyptians, 97 per cent of Jordanians, 98 per cent of Lebanese, and 97 per cent of Palestinians had an unfavourable view of Jews. Among non-Arab Muslims, the rates were only slightly lower. The report said, 'Negative views of Jews are also widespread in the predominantly Muslim countries surveyed in Asia: more than seven in ten in Pakistan (78 per cent) and Indonesia (74 per cent) express unfavourable opinions. A majority in Turkey (73 per cent) also hold a critical view.'

However, lost in the gloomy statistics was a single ray of hope. Bucking the trend of the entire Muslim world were the Muslims who know the Jews best; whose lives are intertwined with those of Jews on a daily basis; who work with and travel with and at times serve in the same armed forces as Jews: Muslim Israelis. If the Jews were the monsters they have been made out to be in Muslim narrative, then conventional wisdom would dictate that Muslim Israelis, living under the banner of the Star of David in cities like Nazareth, Haifa, Beersheba, and Tel Aviv, would have the most negative opinion about the Jews. Instead, the Pew survey found that the majority of Muslims living in Israel hold a favourable view of Jews. The report says, 'Only 55 percent of Israeli Arabs express a negative opinion of Jews, while 56 percent voice a favourable opinion.'

How could Muslims who have no interaction with Jews – those living across the border in the West Bank, Jordan, Lebanon, or Egypt – hate them while Muslims who live among Jews have a favourable view? I asked the same question myself when I met with Israel's Arab community during my visit there in 2008.

While dining in an Arab restaurant in Haifa, I asked the former Arab deputy mayor of the city, Elias Mtanes, the question I had asked every Arab Israeli I met on the trip: 'Do you believe Israel is an apartheid state?' Mtanes shook his head in bewilderment. 'What sort of a question is that!'

he said. 'Do you think I could be deputy mayor of Haifa if Israel was an apartheid state? I am not saying relations between Arabs and Jews inside Israel are perfect or even cordial, but our lives are intertwined by destiny and there is no escape … so we make the best of what we have.' He then talked about the 2006 Hezbollah–Israel conflict, during which Hezbollah fired missiles that killed Arab and Jew without discrimination. 'Nasrallah gave fiery speeches asking the Arabs of Haifa and other towns in the Galilee to vacate the cities because his missiles were on the way … My father reminded me of similar calls by Arab leaders in the 1948 war who asked us to leave our homes because the Arab armies were coming. Look what happened. We Israeli Arabs are Israelis, not the fifth column of some Arab leader who knows little about us nor cares for his own Arab population.'

Similar sentiments were expressed by a waiter at a wayside restaurant in Tel Aviv. I asked Muhammad if he would like his village to become part of a future Palestinian state. '*Ya Khee* [brother], I am Arab – that does not make me stupid,' he joked. 'If my village is given over to the Palestinians, all of us will protest. I do not wish to live under the dictatorship of Hamas or Fatah.' Muhammad found it curious that a Pakistani Canadian was probing him so. He threw back a question at me. 'Would you want to give up your Canadian citizenship and live under your General Musharraf in Pakistan?' There. He stumped me.

Back in Canada, I discussed my conversations with fellow Muslims, only to be told that the men I met must have been Mossad agents or that I had been set up and given a false image about an oppressive regime that kills and starves Arabs. 'Ask Jews like Naomi Klein and Judy Rebick and they will tell you how Israel oppresses its Arab population,' I was chided. When I explained that the people I met were people on the street whom I chose at random, they doubted me. When I showed them pictures of the sign reading '*Allahu Akbar*' at the gateway of a northern Israeli town, or the Circassian Muslim wedding in the Israeli city of Kfar Kama, or the imam in Haifa, I was met with a unanimous dismissal of the facts, I had been brainwashed by the Jews, they said.

To the same friends, I sent the Pew report showing the contrasting attitude towards Jews held by, say, Egyptians on one hand and Arab Israelis on the other. Some said bluntly that the Israelis most have manipulated the survey, while others confided that they were shocked by the variance. One Muslim couple admitted that they had visited Jerusalem and had found Arab–Jewish relations far more amiable than they had been conditioned to believe by media reports. 'Why hide the fact you visited Israel?' I asked. 'You know why,' said the wife. 'We have to live in our community and cannot be seen as not being anti-Israel.'

Many pundits argue that dislike of Jews was triggered by the creation of the state of Israel. However, fifteen years later, in 1963, Jew-hatred had not yet entered the collective consciousness of Pakistan's hundred million Muslims. That was the year cinemas across the country were showing the film *Yahudi ki Larki*, or 'The Jew's Daughter', to packed houses.

Cynics may scoff at the relevance of this movie's popularity. Such melodramatic entertainment, they would argue, should not be seen as a reflection of people's political or religious attitudes. To them I say, try showing *Yahudi ki Larki* in the Pakistan of today. Cinemas would be burned to the ground, such is the animosity towards Jews, fuelled by thirty years of anti-Semitism and financed by petrodollars. The fact that original run of 'The Jew's Daughter' ended without incident, and that the Jew in the film was the victim, not the villain, is significant. It shows that irrespective of how Muslims in India and Pakistan felt about the Israel–Arab dispute, hatred towards the Jew had not yet entered the consciousness of the man on the street, who still viewed the Jew in positive terms.

Today, Muslims need to educate their clerics and inform them that the days of caliphates and kingdoms are long gone. Never again will any Jew be willing to live as 'dhimmis' under Muslim protection. In medieval times, this arrangement may have worked and was much more progressive than the harsh treatment the Jews received in Christendom, but the world has evolved into a place where neither race nor religion, gender nor sexual orientation, can be invoked to legislate a hierarchy of citizenship rights, be it in Saudi Arabia today or South Africa under apartheid.

We Muslims need to reflect on our predicament. We need to understand that our hatred of the Jew or the West is an admission of our own sense of failure. We need to recognize that blaming the other for our dismal contribution to contemporary civilization is a sedative, not the cure for the disease that afflicts us all. To join the nations and peoples of this world, as brothers and sisters of a common humanity, we need to wean ourselves from our addiction to victimhood and hate. Without rejecting our heritage, we need to recognize that in the modern nation state as it exists in the United States, Europe, and the West, in countries like India, Brazil, and South Africa, the doctrines of jihad and sharia law cannot apply, will not be accepted, and should not be preached. We need to stand up to members of our community who spread hate against the Jew, the atheist, apostate, the Hindu, and the Christian and then hide behind the Quran. We should not hesitate to say they are hate-mongers and cowards.

Muslim history and heritage allow us to enter the modern era without the baggage of anti-Semitism. Many Muslims and Jews in the past have worked together and befriended each other. If Averroes and Maimonides could do it in the twelfth century, surely we can do it in the twenty-first. Together, we can build a New Jerusalem. But to arrive there, we Muslims will have to remember that the Jew is not the enemy. It is us.

Wolfgang Benz

Wolfgang Benz is a German historian and director of the Centre for Research on Anti-Semitism (ZfA) of the Technische Universität Berlin. Born in 1941, he studied history, political science and arts history and worked at the Institute for Contemporary History in Munich from 1969 until he joined the ZfA in 1990.

In the twenty-first century, antisemitism has developed a new face in Germany, as well as across much of Europe, as lines between antisemitism and anti-Zionism have blurred. Liberalism has made mainstream discussion more acceptable and the threat of Islamic terrorism and broader vilification of Islam has further confused already morally troubling issues. Benz has been both praised and criticized for his comparisons between the contemporary Islamophobia and historical (and contemporary) antisemitism, particularly as, in the wake of conflict escalations and heightened tensions across the Middle East, both crimes and oppression are increasing.

Anti-Semites and Enemies of Islam: Agitators with Parallel Strategies

21 March 2012

Anti-Semites of the nineteenth century and some 'critics of Islam' of the twenty-first century employ similar means in portraying their enemies.

The enemy portrayal of 'The West' throughout the Arabic culture is reciprocated by populists in the West with an enemy portrayal of 'Islam'. Both stereotypes follow the same basic principles.

Enemy stereotypes stem from the widespread longing for a simplified explanation of the world, one based on the rigorous distinction between good (which always represents oneself) and evil (which always embodies the outsider) and the ensuing actions of blame and exclusion that follow this logic. Enemy stereotypes that evoke such a world serve to alleviate political and social frustrations and to raise self-esteem.

Enemy stereotypes are a product of hysteria. They construct and exploit distorted images of others.

If we define hysteria as a widespread behavioural disorder characterized, among other things, by the impairment of perception, by emotional instability, by theatrical gestures and egocentric habits, then we may explain phobias of other cultures or of different minorities within our own society as a defensive reflex.

Reduced to a Negative

The building blocks for creating an enemy stereotype are generalizations and the reduction of real or supposed facts into something negative. Rumours, subliminal messages, hearsay and literary and popular narratives are exalted as 'facts' and are sustained only by believers' faith in them.

A classic example is given by the construction of the most widely used anti-Semitic text: *The Protocols of the Elders of Zion*. Originating at the end of the nineteenth century, this text emerged as an anti-Semitic pamphlet which supposedly proved a Jewish world conspiracy. Although the details of the *Protocols* were subsequently wholly exposed, the text nonetheless served the purposes of the Russian Czar as well as the Nazis; today they are commonly exploited in the Islamic world. They serve as a powerful weapon of propaganda against Israel. There are millions who believe in the idea of the Jew as the incarnation of evil in the world, as the *Protocols* suggest.

Whoever is outraged, and rightly so, over the narrow-mindedness of such a portrayal of the Jews must also critically consider the counter-portrayal of Islam as the enemy (which occasionally also serves as an aggressive, superimposed Philo-Semitism, or Judeophilia). It is a law of science, the exploitation and reverse application of the insights extracted from an analysis of anti-Semitic resentment.

The defamation of Muslims as a group is undertaken by so-called 'critics of Islam', who use both subtle and crude methods for their task. These methods have historical parallels. At present, Islam is conceptually linked to ideas of extremism and terrorism, in which the enemy stereotype is imposed upon all members of the Islamic religion and culture, thereby subjecting them to discrimination.

Incitement and Defamation

Were you to define the Catholic Church only by its history of suffering, by its papal crusades against 'infidels' in the Middle Ages, by the Inquisition and witch trials and litany of countless innocent victims up until modern times (and nowadays by priests who abuse minorities), it would be a slanderous defamation. The generalization and reduction of the Church to these deplorable acts is incitement with intent to discriminate. However, 'critics of Islam' use precisely the same method, and to increasing approval, when they invoke the dangers of Islam.

In his fear of foreign infiltration, the renowned German historian and popular journalist Heinrich von Treitschke (1834–96) once imagined Germany surrounded by enemies and threatened internally by the unwillingness of the Jewish minority to assimilate. He used his authority and rhetoric to add momentum and respectability to the anti-Semitic movement. This was in 1879, as he sparked the Berlin debate on anti-Semitism. 'From the inexhaustible Polish cradle,' the scholar declared, 'is rising a flock of aspiring, trouser-selling young men whose children and children's children will one day come to dominate the German economy and media.'

The parallel to today is unmistakable, when an image of post-partum Muslim women is tactically summoned as a weapon in the suspicious battle for the 'Islamization of Europe'. Attacks on the German Jews marked the end of a hard-won liberal consensus on integration. The

Berlin debate on anti-Semitism was largely a debate about identity. Following the emancipation of the Jews, it was a dispute about what it should mean to be German and to be a German Jew.

Intolerance and Self-Affirmation

Today a similar debate is ongoing. It is no longer about the emancipation of the Jews, but about the integration of the Muslims. The rage is palpable – with its barricades and defences – and the intonation of the debates frightening, when the refusal to tolerate the Muslim minority is taken as self-evident.

On Internet forums, where the portrayal of Islam as an enemy is particularly shameless, a recent murder of an Egyptian in a courtroom in Dresden circulated jubilation among commentators. The act was condemned, yet one commentator wrote: 'That at least makes one less Islam birthing-machine.'

Another claimed that the Koran calls on 'the murder of believers of other faiths, especially of Jews and of Christians, in over sixty of its Suras'. And against all evidence as to the actual content of the Koran, he defended this conviction with as much vigour as would an anti-Semite who cannot let go of his belief in the evil content of the Talmud, in Jewish ritual murders and in other such delusional phantasies. A third commentator was convinced that an urgent conspiracy was taking place, namely, 'the destruction of Germany through immigration and Islamization'.

The Challenge to Democracy

It is with this type of distinctive language that the discourse on headscarves and minarets, as symbols of a fundamentally rejected and threatening culture, is carried out on the Internet's public arena. But this has been a long time coming. It is a successful method – that of equating German citizens who practise the Islamic religion with fanatical terrorists – and appeals to popular sentiment as well as underlining the self-affirmation of the majority group.

In reality, the symbolic discourse about minarets is actually a campaign to discriminate against people who are members of a group. It is a challenge to tolerance and democracy.

Translated by Becky L. Crook

Jan Karski

*I*n 1982 Jan Karski had been recognized as one of the Righteous Among the Nations for his efforts to save Jews by spreading word of the Shoah.

In May 1994 he was made an honorary citizen of the State of Israel in further recognition of his unique efforts. Though Jan Karski died in 2000, in 2012 he was also awarded the Presidential Medal of Freedom in his adopted homeland, America. This second contribution is a mark of Karski's significant voice in the fight against antisemitism.

Acceptance of the State of Israel's Honorary Citizenship

12 May 1994

Mr Ambassador, Mr Chargé d'Affaires of the Embassy of the Republic of Poland, Senator Levin, Representative Lantos, Mr Lehrman, Father O'Connor, Distinguished Friends,

This is the proudest and the most meaningful day in my life. Through the honorary citizenship of the State of Israel, I have reached the spiritual source of my Christian faith. In a way, I also became a part of the Jewish community.

For some nineteen centuries, the Jews lived in the diaspora. In whatever country they established themselves and whatever their fate had been – they preserved their biblical identity. Thus, in a Christian Europe, they were always 'alien' – different ones.

Their fate was marked more often than not by pain; enslavement; expulsions; forced conversions; Inquisition; persecutions.

Not everywhere though. In Poland, where since the fourteenth century almost half of them sought refuge, they found a religious, cultural and judiciary autonomy.

There was no Inquisition in Catholic Poland.

Whatever the conditions of their lives, the Jews have been enriching humanity with lasting contributions in every field of creativity and labour; in philosophy and medicine; economy and music; poetry and law; physics and the performing arts; astronomy and the visual arts. Also, in modern dance.

Then came the nineteenth and twentieth centuries with their triumphant totalitarian ideologies: fascism, communism, nazism. Their poisonous influences spread all over Europe and affected every nation. Intolerance, fanaticism, racism, hatred, bigotry and, most of all, anti-Semitism triumphed – resulting in the Second World War, more destructive than any other war. Some fifty million people perished; in Poland alone, over three million ethnic Poles lost their lives.

For the Jews, the war meant the Holocaust. Elie Wiesel put it well: 'All nations under the Nazi domination had victims – but all Jews were victims.'

I saw it all.

The Jews were helpless and abandoned. As in the long past, they had no country of their own, no national army, no representation in the inter-allied war councils.

Abandoned by governments, by Church hierarchies, by societal structures, the Jews were not abandoned by all humanity. Thousands upon thousands of *individuals*: priests and nuns; workers and peasants; educated ones and simpletons extended their helping hands in Poland, Holland, Belgium, France, Greece, Denmark and Norway. Six million Jews perished … half a million survived.

What happened to the Jews shook the Christian world and changed the attitude of the Christian churches. The Second Vatican Council decreed anti-Semitism a sin. Pope John Paul II visited a Roman synagogue – an unprecedented act in the history of the Catholic Church – for a joint prayer. There, addressing the Hebrew congregation, he said:

You are our elder brothers.
We are all children of Abraham,
other Christian churches followed.

Then, the State of Israel rose from the ashes and armed struggle of the bravest ones. The Jews recovered their Promised Land – no longer homeless or helpless.

Since the early years of my high school in Łódź, I have been getting understanding, friendship or help from the Jews. And now, they took me in. And now, I, Jan Karski – by birth Kozielewski – a Pole, an American, a Catholic, have also become an Israelite!

Gloria, Gloria in excelsis Deo.

Our Lord revealed Himself to many nations in His own ways, but always with the same Commandment – Love thy neighbour, always The Same, The Only One. He endowed us with a free will. We have infinite capacity to do good. And an infinite capacity to be evil. We are all schizophrenic.

May our Lord, Whom we love and Whom we try to obey, give us moral courage and spiritual strength to prevail over fanaticism, hatred, racism, anti-Semitism, religious intolerance and bigotry.

And may He be with us all – always.

Amen and thank you.

NOTES

Albert Einstein

1   An old term used to refer to Islam. A Mohammedan was used as a term for a follower of Mohammed. It was used up until the 1960s but is now considered obsolete.

R. L. Sheil

1   Henry St John, 1st Viscount Bolingbroke (16 September 1678–12 December 1751), was an English politician, philosopher and sometime leader of the Tory party who opposed theology.

Emile Zola

1   France had signed a treaty with Russia in 1892 (lasting till 1917) that ended France's diplomatic isolation following their defeat by Germany in the Franco-Prussian War. Its success was still much celebrated in 1898.

2   The idea of World Fairs had originated with the Great Exhibition of 1851 in London, for which Crystal Palace had been built (originally constructed in Hyde Park, it was moved to South London after the exhibition). Paris had hosted a World Fair in 1889 for which the Eiffel Tower had been built, and was preparing for another World Fair in 1900.

3   The *bordereau* was a letter addressed to the German military attaché in France, recovered from the German embassy and taken to the French authorities. It stated that confidential French military documents were to be directed to a foreign power.

4   The Marquis de Morès (1858–1896) trained as a cavalry officer but moved to America, settling in the Dakota Badlands as a rancher, where he befriended Theodore Roosevelt, who had temporarily retired from politics there. When his business failed de Morès returned to France, where his antisemitism became overt and he joined Drumont's *Ligue antisémitique de France*. He eventually went to Algeria in a wild scheme to incite the Muslim population in a Holy War against the Jews and British. His caravan was infiltrated by Touareg tribesmen (who may or may not have been in the pay of his enemies in the French government) and he was assassinated.

5   Another officer involved in the investigation and miscarriage of justice.

6   Two prominent antisemitic newspapers.

Maxim Gorky

1   In traditional Russian, muzhik simply means 'man', but has also been used to mean 'peasant'.

2   Shekinah is a Hebrew term which simply means dwelling or settling place and is used to denote the dwelling or settling of the divine presence of God, particularly regarding the Temple in Jerusalem. The phrase is actually attributed to St John Chrysostom, an early Church father from the fourth century, who was Archbishop of Constantinople.

3   The Holy of Holies is a term in the Hebrew Bible used to refer to the inner sanctuary of the Tabernacle and later the Temple in Jerusalem where the Ark of the Covenant was kept. As with 'The true Shekinah – is man', it expresses the sentiment that man is the centre of religion and the fount of all belief.

4   Historical forms of oppression of the ordinary Russian people. The Tartars were an ethnic group; the Boyars were members of the aristocracy.

M. Bernatzky

1   'The Pale of Settlement' was the term given to a region of Imperial Russia in which permanent residency by Jews was allowed and beyond which Jewish residency was generally prohibited. The Pale comprised of around a fifth of European Russia, and included much of present-day Lithuania, Belarus, Poland, Moldova, Ukraine and parts of western Russia.

2   *Adscripti glebae* (persons attached to the soil) was a term applied to Roman slaves attached in perpetuity to and transferred with the land they cultivated.

3   Elizabeth of Russia (1709–62) was crowned as Empress in 1741 after a bloodless coup which deposed her infant cousin Ivan VI. She was the daughter of Peter the Great by his second wife and presided over two wars and one of the most sumptuous courts in Russian history. She was briefly succeeded by her adopted son Peter II, who was assassinated six months later, enabling his wife, Catherine the Great, to accede. She is perhaps most famous for vowing never to sign a death warrant if she became Empress, and sticking to it.

Edouard Herriot

1   Published in 1763, the *Treatise on Tolerance* calls for religious freedom and tolerance, particularly between Protestants and Catholics, and follows the trial of Jean Calas, a Protestant accused of murdering his son to prevent his conversion to Catholicism and executed on 10 March 1762.

2   Grégoire was a priest and French revolutionary leader who was a significant supporter of human rights and freedoms, fighting for and writing in favour of universal suffrage and abolitionism and against antisemitism.

Jean Pierre-Bloch

1   Here Pierre-Bloch counterposes ideological brethren Brossolette, Péri and Médéric with Nazi collaborators Xavier Vallat and Henri Béraud.

2   *Der Stürmer* was a weekly tabloid-format Nazi newspaper and *Gringoire* a political and literary weekly newspaper in France.

3   Alexandre Stavisky was involved in a financial scandal in 1934 and labelled as a Jew. This was refuted by the French weekly *Je Suis Partout*.

4   *Ephemerides Theologicae Lovanienses* (ETL), founded in 1924, is a quarterly publication by professors of Theology and Canon Law at the KU Leuven and the Université catholique de Louvain (Louvain-la-Neuve).

Jesse Jackson

1   Fannie Lou Hamer (1917–77) was an American voting rights activist and civil rights leader.

2   Jackson refers to Malcolm X, Martin Luther King, Medgar Evers, Bobby Kennedy, John F. Kennedy and Viola Liuzzo. Martin Luther King, Medgar Evers and Viola Liuzzo are three of the forty Civil Rights Martyrs commemorated on the Civil Rights Memorial in Montgomery, Alabama.

3   Three civil rights workers shot by the Ku Klux Klan in 1965. James Cheney was an African-American from Mississippi, but Andrew Goodman and Michael Schwerner were New Yorkers of Jewish descent. Their murders sparked national outrage and their bodies lay undiscovered for forty-four days.

4   The Immigration Reform and Control Act (IRCA) enacted in November 1986 made it much harder for immigrants to get legal work or rights.

Albie Sachs

1   United States Holocaust Memorial Museum podcast series.

John Mann

1   Golda Meir (1898–1978) was an Israeli teacher and politician who became
     the fourth Prime Minister of Israel and only the third woman in the world
     to hold such an office.Winston Churchill

Winston Churchill

1   Johann Adam Weishaupt (1748–1830) was a German philosopher and
     founder of the Illuminati who took the name 'Brother Spartacus' among
     them. He was born to Jewish parents but grew up a strict Catholic instilled
     by his Jesuit education.
          Béla Kun (1886–1938) was a Hungarian revolutionary who led the
     Hungarian Soviet Republic before its fall. He was tried and executed in
     Stalin's purges. His parents were Jewish but he was raised with a Calvinist
     education.
          Rosa Luxemburg (1871–1919) was a Marxist theorist and revolutionary
     socialist in Germany. Born in Poland to Jewish parents, she turned her back
     on her religion. She was murdered under orders of Friedrich Ebert, the first
     President of Germany.
          Emma Goldman (1869–1940) was born into an Orthodox Jewish
     family in the Russian Empire but became a prominent American
     anarchist whose violent beliefs spanned many issues including the
     support of atheism, freedom of speech, capitalism, free love and
     homosexuality.

2   Nesta Helen Webster (1876–1960) was a controversial writer. She wrote
     The French Revolution: a Study in Democracy, in which she argued that
     a secret conspiracy of the Freemasons and Illuminati had been behind
     the French Revolution. She was stridently antisemitic, and though she
     believed the Protocols of Zion were fake she still believed they describe
     how Jews behaved. In *The Origin and Progress of the World Revolution*,
     published in 1921, she wrote: 'What mysteries of iniquity would be
     revealed if the Jew, like the mole, did not make a point of working in the
     dark! Jews have never been more Jews than when we tried to make them
     men and citizens.'

3   All are prominent high-ranking Soviets of the era.

4   Anton Ivanovich Denikin (1872–1947) was one of the leaders of the
     White movement in the Russian Civil War. There is much debate

about whether he protected the Jews or actually ordered the murder of thousands of them.

5   All Ukrainian revolutionary leaders with responsibility for the pogroms which killed 100,000 Jews.

Maurice Rosette

1   S.E.C. Wendehorst, *British Jewry, Zionism and the Jewish State, 1936–1956*, Oxford: Oxford University Press, 2012, pp. 3-6, 140–1.

2   Association of Secretaries General of Parliaments, *Constitutional and Parliamentary Information*, 1993, 3rd Series, No. 165, First half-year 1993, available at: http://www.asgp.co/sites/default/files/documents//MMOGZIBPNBRSDQCZMNDFMEKQVKXRJM.pdf

3   London: Poale Zion/Jewish Socialist Labour Party (1943)

Nicole Fontaine

1   Martin Niemöller (1892–1984) was a German Lutheran Pastor. Though originally supportive of Nazism he opposed the extension of the 'Aryan paragraph' which restricted the rights of Jews as he considered it unchristian, but still expressed antisemitic thoughts in his sermons and other public statements. He was imprisoned in 1938 for 'activities against the state' and held from then till 1945 in Sachsenhausen and Dachau concentration camps. After the war and his release, he freely admitted to his culpability and guilt under the Nazi regime. His famous lines were a regular trope in his speeches albeit he adapted the groups he referred to for different audiences, sometimes including the Jews, sometimes leaving them out.

FURTHER READING LIST

Shmuel Almog (ed.), *Antisemitism through the Ages* (Oxford: Pergamon Press, 1988)

Hannah Arendt, *The Origins of Totalitarianism* (London: George Allen and Unwin, 1958)

Yehuda Bauer, *Rethinking the Holocaust* (New Haven: Yale University Press, 2001)

David Berger, *History and Hate: The Dimensions of Antisemitism* (Philadelphia: Jewish Publication Society, 1997)

Francisco Bethencourt, *Racisms: From the Crusades to the Twentieth Century* (Princeton: Princeton University Press, 2013)

William Brustein, *Roots of Hate: Antisemitism in Europe Before the Holocaust* (Cambridge: Cambridge University Press, 2003)

Martin Bulmer and John Solomos (ed.), *Racism* (Oxford: Oxford University Press, 1999)

Matti Bunzl, *Antisemitism and Islamophobia: Hatreds Old and New in Europe* (Chicago: Prickly Paradigm Press, 2007)

Robert Chazan (ed.), *Church, State and Jew in the Middle Ages* (New York: Behrman House, 1980)

Norman Cohn, *Warrant for Genocide: The Myth of the Jewish World Conspiracy and the Protocols of the Elders of Zion* (London: Serif, 1996 edition)

John Edwards, *The Jews in Christian Europe, 1400–1700* (London: Routledge, 1988)

Jonathan Frankel, *The Damascus Affair: 'Ritual Murder', Politics and the Jews in 1840* (Cambridge: Cambridge University Press, 1997)

Saul Friedlander, *Nazi Germany and the Jews*, 2 volumes (New York: HarperCollins, 1997–2007)

Jeffrey Herf (ed.), *Antisemitism and Anti-Zionism in Historical Perspective: Convergence and Divergence* (London: Routledge, 2007)

Jacob Katz, *From Prejudice to Destruction: Anti-Semitism 1700–1933* (Cambridge, Mass.: Harvard University Press, 1980)

John Klier, *Russians, Jews and the Pogroms of 1881–2* (Cambridge: Cambridge University Press, 2011)

Gavin Langmuir, *Toward a Definition of Antisemitism* (Berkeley: University of California Press, 1990)

Bernard Lewis, *The Jews of Islam* (Princeton; Princeton University Press, 1984)

Heinz-Dietrich Loewe, *The Tsar and the Jews: Reform, Reaction and Antisemitism in Imperial Russia* (New York: Harwood Academic Publishers, 1993)

Robert Moore, *The Formation of a Persecuting Society: Power and Deviance in Western Europe, 950–1250* (Oxford: Basil Blackwell, 1987)

George Mosse, *Towards the Final Solution: A History of European Racism* (London: Dent, 1978)

Derek Penslar, *Shylock's Children: Economics and Jewish Identity in Modern Europe* (Berkeley: University of California Press, 2001)

Peter Schafer, *Judeophobia: Attitudes towards Jews in the Ancient World* (Cambridge MA, Harvard University Press)

Shulamit Volkov, *Germans, Jews, and Antisemites: Trials in Emancipation* (Cambridge: Cambridge University Press, 2006)

Robert Wistrich, *Antisemitism: The Longest Hatred* (New York: Pantheon Books, 1991)

PERMISSIONS

Albert Einstein: © The Hebrew University of Jerusalem

Albie Sachs: Albie Sachs, Voices on Antisemitism, Courtesy of the US Holocaust Memorial Museum, Washington, DC.

Bill Clinton: Courtesy of William J. Clinton Presidential Library.

Chaim Herzog: Credit to Zionism and Israel Information Center.

Charlie Chaplin: THE GREAT DICTATOR Copyright © Roy Export S.A.S. All rights reserved.

Chaim Weizmann: Courtesy of Yad Chaim Weizmann, The Weizmann Archives, Rehovot, Israel.

George Bush: Category: Budget and Presidential Materials, Collection: Compilation of Presidential Documents, Publication Title: Weekly Compilation of Presidential Documents Volume 37, Issue 16 (23 April 2001), SuDoc Class Number: AE 2.109, Publisher: Office of the Federal Register, National Archives and Records Administration, Page Number Range: 631-2, Document Category: Addresses and Remarks, President: George W. Bush, Event Date: 19 April 2001.

George Washington Letter to the Hebrew Congregation: Picture courtesy of the Morris Morgenstern Foundation.

Jean-Paul Sartre: Excerpt(s) from ANTI-SEMITE & JEW by Jean-Paul Sartre, copyright © 1948 and renewed 1976 by Schocken Books, a division of Random House, Inc. Preface copyright © 1995 by Michael Walzer. Used by permission of Schocken Books, an imprint of the Knopf Doubleday Publishing Group, a division of Penguin Random House LLC. All rights reserved. Any third party use of this matenal, outside of this publication, is prohibited interested parties must apply directly, to penguin Random House LLC for permission.

Jean-Paul Sartre: (Digital/Electronic Rights): Jean-Paul Sartre, 'Réflexions sur la question juive' © Gallimard, 1954.

Ronald Reagan: Courtesy of Ronald Reagan Presidential Foundation and Library.

Martin Luther King: © 1967 Dr Martin Luther King Jr © Renewed 1995 Coretta Scott King.

Winston Churchill: Reproduced with permission of Curtis Brown, London on behalf of the Beneficiaries of the Estate of Winston S. Churchill. Copyright © The Beneficiaries of the Estate of Winston S. Churchill.

INDEX